In addition to being a political thinker, Gandhi was also a political activist leading the largest anti-colonial movement in history and fighting against racial injustices in South Africa and the social, economic and political injustices in India. He drew upon the Indian and Western, Hindu and Christian philosophical and religious traditions, and developed a uniquely bicultural political philosophy. It was designed to illuminate the nature of oppression and violence, and explore both new ways of fighting against them and the basis of a non-violent social order.

The book is a critical and comprehensive account of Gandhi's moral and political philosophy. It locates him in a historical context and examines his central philosophical assumptions. Unlike most other books on the same subject, it relies on his original Gujarati works and is based on discussions with his associates and followers. The book shows that Western moral and political philosophy can learn much from a sympathetic dialogue with him.

By the same author

HANNAH ARENDT AND THE SEARCH FOR A NEW
POLITICAL PHILOSOPHY
KARL MARX'S THEORY OF IDEOLOGY
CONTEMPORARY POLITICAL THINKERS
POLITICS AND EXPERIENCE (*editor*)
BENTHAM'S POLITICAL THOUGHT (*editor*)
JEREMY BENTHAM: TEN CRITICAL ESSAYS (*editor*)
COLOUR, CULTURE AND CONSCIOUSNESS (*editor*)
THE CONCEPT OF SOCIALISM (*editor*)
THE MORALITY OF POLITICS (*editor*)
KNOWLEDGE AND BELIEF IN POLITICS (*editor*)
POLITICAL DISCOURSE (*editor*)

GANDHI'S POLITICAL PHILOSOPHY

Gandhi's Political Philosophy

A Critical Examination

BHIKHU PAREKH

UNIVERSITY OF NOTRE DAME PRESS
NOTRE DAME, INDIANA

First published 1989

Published by
THE MACMILLAN PRESS LTD
Houndmills, Basingstoke, Hampshire RG21 2XS
and London
Companies and representatives
throughout the world

American edition 1989 by
University of Notre Dame Press
Notre Dame, Indiana 46556

Printed in Hong Kong

Library of Congress Cataloging-in-Publication Data

Parekh, Bhikhu C.
Gandhi's political philosophy : a critical examination / Bhikhu Parekh
    p.   cm.
Bibliography: p
Includes index.
ISBN 0–268–01016–1
1. Gandhi, Mahatma, 1869–1948—Political and social views.
I. Title.
DS481.G3P347   1989
954.03′5′0924—dc19   88–11122
                                                        CIP

To Raojibhai Patel

Contents

Acknowledgements   ix

Introduction   1

1 Critique of Modern Civilisation   11

2 Indian Civilisation and National Regeneration   36

3 Philosophy of Religion   65

4 Spirituality, Politics and the Reinterpretation of Hinduism   85

5 Theory of the State   110

6 *Satyāgraha* and a Non-rationalist Theory of Rationality   142

7 Partition and the Non-nationalist Discourse   171

8 Critical Appreciation   195

   Notes   226

   Glossary   237

   Bibliography   239

   Index   242

Acknowledgements

In the composition of this book I have incurred many debts. Ashis Nandy, Bashir Ahmed, Gopal Krishna, Jayshree Mehta, Suresh Sharma, Thomas Pantham, Sudipta Kaviraj, Vinod Kothari, J. D. Sethi and Subrata Mitra were all kind enough to read and comment on several chapters. Dhirubhai Sheth read the first draft in its entirety and made most useful and searching comments. I have also greatly benefitted from several long discussions with Ramchandra Gandhi and B. R. Nanda. Umashankarbhai Joshi kindly clarified many of Gandhi's complex ideas and made detailed and perceptive comments on the sixth chapter. Even though I have not always agreed with them, I should like to express my debt also to Joan Bondurant, Raghavan Iyer, B. R. Nanda and Lloyd and Susanne Rudolph, whose works on Gandhi remain some of the best in the field. I thank Pramila for preparing the index.

I wrote a large part of the book during the two summer vacations I spent as a Senior Visiting Fellow at the Centre for the Study of Developing Societies in Delhi. No author could have hoped for a more stimulating environment and a more friendly staff. Above all I am deeply grateful to Raojibhai Patel for his penetrating comments on the first draft and many long discussions on Gandhi during the three decades of our friendship. An acute critic of Gandhi, he offered me vital glimpses into the kind of magic the Mahatma must have exercised over his close associates.

BHIKHU PAREKH

Introduction

During the past two centuries Western political philosophy has exercised massive intellectual influence over the rest of the world. Its influence derives from several interrelated sources of which three are most important.[1] First, since Western political philosophy had the unique advantage of having been practised more or less continuously for over two and a half millennia by some of the most talented men, it has developed unparalleled analytical rigour, been constantly fertilised by new experiences, has addressed itself to an unusually large variety of questions and fostered acute methodological self-consciousness not to be found in any other tradition of political philosophy. Second, for the past two centuries the West has politically and economically dominated the rest of the world and used its economic and political power to spread its ways of life and thought. Its ideas travelled with its goods, were sometimes supported by its bayonets and acquired enormous prestige and respectability. Almost every non-Western country was and with a few exceptions still is a supplicant at the Western court, and its spokesmen could hardly expect to be understood, let alone taken seriously, unless they spoke its standard language in an approved accent. As the West economically and politically united the world under its hegemony, its vision of man and society became the only universally acceptable currency of political discourse.

Third, since the West substantially recreated the non-Western world in its own image and fashioned the shapes and forms of its political life, its political philosophy was not wholly irrelevant to the latter. The relevance was, of course, considerably limited for, while the imported institutions and ways of thought changed the traditional social order and culture, they also underwent a profound mutation. However, the fact that its categories and modes of thought informed and helped explain at least some aspects of their political life rendered the Western political philosophy intelligible and acceptable to the non-Western countries.

All three factors were important. No amount of political and economic power would have given it such influence if the Western political philosophy had not possessed considerable intellectual strength and vitality. During the colonial struggle for independence it was subjected to a searching critique by some of the ablest minds in the non-Western world, and would have been rejected or at least vigorously resisted if it had been found superficial, flimsy and incapable of defending itself. Ideas, however, do not exist in a social and political vacuum and derive their appeal and power from the prevailing cultural climate in shaping which political and economic factors play a vital role. This is particularly true of social and political ideas which, unlike the mathematical, are necessarily imprecise, essentially contested, capable of conflicting interpretations and defined and related in terms of assumptions and beliefs derived from outside. Neither the intellectual strength of its political philosophy nor its enormous political and economic power would have given the West this degree of influence if its conceptual framework had been wholly irrelevant to the experiences of the non-Western world. Indeed it would then have been totally unintelligible.

Although the familiarity with Western political philosophy gave the non-Western world access to a highly sophisticated tradition of discourse and taught it to look at itself with unaccustomed rigour, it had two unfortunate consequences. First, many a writer in the non-Western world either imported the ready-made Western conceptual packages without examining their relevance, or 'indigenised' them without bothering to ask how the ideas conceived and systematised in one context could be 'adapted' to another quite different. Like the trade in goods, the terms of intellectual exchange till today remain one-sided. The non-Western world exports the raw material of its experiences and imports the finished theoretical products from the West. As a result its unique political reality lacks adequate philosophical articulation. It remains at the mercy of every new Western fashion and lurches from crisis to crisis without comprehending their nature. Its indigenous traditions of thought remain unexplored and unfertilised by its novel political experiences. And its past and present either remain disconnected or are misconnected by the mediation of a relatively alien mode of thought, leading in one case to historical amnesia and in the other to political schizophrenia.

Second, even as an individual fails to develop fully without constant interaction with an equal, a tradition of thought loses vitality and lacks the capacity for rigorous self-criticism without the probing presence of an authentic 'other'. In the absence of a constant and critical dialogue with other traditions, Western political philosophy has remained parochial, complacent and narrow, Western not only in its provenance but also its orientation, concerns and assumptions about man and society. Since it has long enjoyed the almost divine privilege of shaping the world in its own image and universalising its forms of thought without ever being seriously challenged, it remains unable and unwilling to allow unfamiliar experiences to speak to it in their native tongues, to enrich its sensibility and deepen its insight into the range and variety of human potentialities. The Marxists, feminists, champions of animal rights and others have highlighted the economic, sexist, anthropocentric and other biases of much of Western political philosophy. It is about time we recognised its deep-seated ethnocentric and cultural biases as well.

It is in this context that Gandhi becomes extremely important, and this is how I propose to discuss him. He was one of the first non-Western thinkers of the modern age to develop a political theory grounded in the unique experiences and articulated in terms of the indigenous philosophical vocabulary of his country. He conceptualised political life in an original and stimulating manner, placing new questions on the political agenda and offering new ways of tackling the old. From a distinctly community-based Indian perspective, he highlighted some of the disturbing features of the modern state, detected its internal contradictions, and explored an alternative to it. He more or less completely bypassed the dominant nationalist vocabulary and showed that it was possible to articulate and defend the case for independence in a very different language. He showed that not every movement for independence is national, not every national struggle is nationalist and that not every nationalist movement need articulate itself in the language of European rather than home-grown theories of nationalism.[2] He drew upon the long and rich Indian tradition of non-violence and explored both the sources of and alternative to the dominant forms of violence in modern society. Reflecting the traditional Hindu understanding of moral life, he asked if morality could ever be adequately conceptualised in the language of rights and obligations, and wondered whether the dominant individualist theory of man could ever avoid reducing it to enlightened self-interest and thereby undermining its autonomy. Following the Indian philosophical anthropology he developed a fascinating theory of man which avoided the dubious concept of human nature, gave a wholly new meaning to the familiar idea of human unity and integrated the apparently contradictory demands of human sociality and uniqueness.

Although deeply rooted in the Indian ways of life and thought, Gandhi was also intimately familiar with the West. Indeed as a colonial subject he could hardly avoid being politically bilingual and bicultural. He observed the West at close quarters during his three years in England and over twenty in South Africa and drank deep at its intellectual fountains. He was trained as a lawyer in London and practised as one in South Africa, enjoyed close intellectual contacts with his Christian and Jewish friends, some of whom lived with him on his communal farm, studied more work on Christianity and Islam than do most of their adherents and extensively read European writers, including Plato (whose *Apology* he translated into his native Gujarati), Bacon, Blackstone, Bentham, J. S. Mill, Carlyle, Ruskin, Tolstoy, Thoreau, Henry Maine, and Marx. He was therefore able to draw upon both the Indian and Western traditions of thought and interpret each in the light of the other. He worked out an unusually broad-based moral and political theory that offered him a unique vantage point from which to identify the strengths and limitations of the two traditions and speak in a language at once uniquely Indian and intelligible to the Western audience. His biculturally grounded and bilingually articulated political theory shows one way in which a global political theory required by the increasingly interdependent world might be constructed.

Gandhi also had several unusual advantages for a political thinker. He was a man of both thought and action. Although not a philosopher he was a systematic and careful thinker in the habit of reflecting on and theorising his experiences. As a man of action he led many anti-racist campaigns in South Africa and later became the unquestioned leader of the Indian independence movement. He was the first anti-imperialist leader of the modern age, the first man to mobilise millions for a political cause and fashion the necessary organisational and communicational tools, the first man to invent an unusual method of political struggle and one of the few in history to fight simultaneously on moral, religious, political, social, economic and cultural fronts.

As an Indian he belonged to the oppressed race in South Africa and suffered racial insults and indignities.[3] He was thrown out of a train in the middle of a cold night for daring to travel first class, dragged down from a coach by a swearing conductor and only just saved by his fellow passengers, and kicked into the gutter by a sentry for daring to walk past Paul Kruger's house in Pretoria. In Transvaal he was arrested for protesting against the Registration Act of 1900 and kept in a cell with common criminals who made homosexual overtures to him and carried on indecent activities in his presence. And he was stoned and kicked by a racist white mob in Durban and escaped lynching only because of the sanctuary of a near-by police station which he was later able to leave disguised as a policeman. As an Indian he also belonged to a subject people in his own country and knew how much the colonial government humiliated and violated the basic dignity of his countrymen, of which the floggings and 'crawling orders' by General Dyer were the most notorious examples. He saw too that his fellow Hindus had for centuries put a large number of them beyond the pale of not only social but physical contact and consigned them to most degrading conditions. When in England he had noticed the pitiable conditions in which the working classes lived and the way they were systematically brutalised. In South Africa he observed the inhuman treatment of the blacks and was deeply pained by the way the Zulu warriors and prisoners were hunted and tortured.

Thanks to these and other experiences Gandhi became intensely sensitive to all forms of oppression and exploitation and saw himself as the spokesman and champion of the poor and the oppressed everywhere. He reflected on the nature, causes, consequences and complex relations between different forms of oppression and developed a political theory from the perspective of the victims of the established social order. Unlike Marx, whose political philosophy had a similar orientation, Gandhi refused to think in terms of antagonistic class interests. He argued that no man could degrade or brutalise another without also degrading and brutalising himself, that racism, economic exploitation and colonialism took their moral and psychological toll on *both* the masters and their victims and that no man could be human at the expense of another. He argued further that no system of oppression could come into being let alone last without the co-operation of its victims who were therefore never wholly innocent. As he repeatedly remarked, those who behaved like worms invited others to trample upon them and it was the coward who created the bully. Gandhi therefore preferred to concentrate his energies on building up the courage and organised strength of the victims in the firm belief that once they saw through the hidden mechanism of their oppression and gained a sense of power, the prevailing system of oppression based on and continuing only because of their ignorance and illusion of powerlessness would not last a day. He also thought that much of the violence and oppression of the modern age sprang from the dominant 'materialist' view of man and could only be ended by creating a civilisation based on the spiritual conception of man. As we shall see later Gandhi's moral and political philosophy had severe limitations, but it also contained most valuable and original insights.

Since Gandhi was not a political philosopher, many of his insights remained undeveloped and unsystematised. He had hoped to write a new *smriti* and even a new *śāstra* for the modern age, but lacked the time and the temperament to do so. Like the ancient *rishis* he deeply reflected on his experiences and teased out what he took to be the central and abiding truths of moral and political life, leaving it to the future *achāryas* to systematise them into coherent texts. This book is an attempt to expound and evaluate Gandhi's oppression-centred, victim-orientated, spiritually grounded and uniquely Indian political philosophy.[4]

Like the earlier generations of Indian leaders, Gandhi was deeply puzzled by the British rule in India. He wondered why the British had been able to conquer India with relative ease, how their rule differed from the earlier ones and what it had done and was doing to it. In the first chapter I outline Gandhi's answers to these and other related questions. He was convinced that India had fallen prey to the centuries of foreign rule because it had become degenerate and 'diseased', and that it had no hope of becoming or remaining a self-governing polity unless it radically revitalised itself. In the second chapter I outline his programme of national regeneration. Since the themes of the two chapters are closely connected, there is a slight repetition of material. The next four chapters deal with wider themes and outline his moral and political theory relevant in his view both to India and the world at large. The third chapter sketches his metaphysics and philosophy of religion, and the fourth draws out their moral and political implications. The fifth chapter examines his critique of and alternative to the modern state, and the sixth explores the nature and philosophical basis of his novel method of political action. The next chapter analyses the logical structure of the debate between

Gandhi and Jinnah about the partition of India and explains why his moral and political theory prevented him from adequately conceptualising and coping with the Hindu-Muslim conflict, the resolution of which he had made one of his life's greatest missions. In the last chapter I critically examine both his moral and political philosophy and his impact on India. Since Gandhi's thought has been much misunderstood I have concentrated on its exposition and separated it from its critical examination as much as possible. And since respect for the integrity of his ideas requires that they be understood in their own terms, I have systematically avoided facile and misleading comparisons between him and other Indian and Western thinkers.

Although much work has been done on Gandhi, many important gaps still remain. And until they are filled a definitive work on him cannot be written and this book makes no such claims. First, even nearly 40 years after his death we lack not only a definitive edition of his *Collected Works* but also reliable translations of his books, most of which he wrote as a matter of principle in his native Gujarati. As I have shown at length elsewhere, some of the available translations are grossly inadequate and the recently completed 90 volumes of his *Collected Works* leave a good deal to be desired.[5]

Second, Gandhi's 20 years in South Africa during the politically formative years of his life constituted his political *brahmacharyāshram* and shaped his life and thought. He acquired there intense sensitivity to racism, an acute sense of racial self-respect and a strong sense of Indian identity. He also acquired an insight into the nature and mechanism of oppression, an inaccurate view of the nature of Hindu-Muslim conflict for which he was later to pay heavily, a limited understanding of the nature of *satyāgraha* which it took him years to correct, and a close understanding of Christianity. By providing him with an emotional and physical distance from India and an unique intellectual stimulus of a few close Jewish and Christian friends, South Africa offered him an ideal environment for a detached and critical examination of the Indian and modern Western civilisation. As he put it later it was in that 'God-forsaken continent' that he 'found' his God. I therefore frequently refer to his years there to explore the genesis of his ideas, and hope that someone some day will undertake a detailed study of this sadly neglected period of his life.[6]

Thirdly, since Gandhi's ideas, our main concern, grew out of his reflections on his experiences, they cannot be fully understood without some understanding of him as a man. Surprising as it may seem in the case of someone who lived an open life and wrote an autobiography, we really know very little about him. His *Autobiography* does not go beyond 1926 and, notwithstanding the impression to the contrary, is too didactic and detached to give much insight into his volatile and restless personality. Apart from his sexual obsessions in the first few years of an early marriage and some tantalising remarks about odd events and individuals, he says little about his innermost anxieties and aspirations or his feelings about important political events and some of his mercurial colleagues and vicious opponents. It throws no light on why he was all his life worried about whether or not he would attain or was progressing towards *moksha*, the kinds of *siddhis* he hoped to obtain by his spiritual pursuits, his relations with his wife and children, his long-term strategy of cultivating one political constituency after another and the way he outmanoeuvred senior Congress leaders, took over families, distanced parents and children, husbands and wives and brothers and sisters and then reunited them on his terms, and both stimulated and sublimated the sexuality of his female colleagues, some of whom were passionately attracted to him. None of his close associates has provided an intimate portrait of him either. Mahadev Desai's *Diary* is largely a hagiographical record of his activities and conversations, and Manu Gandhi's and Pyarelal's accounts are little different. Apart from Nehru none of his close colleagues has written about him, and Nehru's portrait almost completely leaves out the man. Although some are better than others, none of Gandhi's biographies has probed his complex personality and thrown much light on some of the questions mentioned earlier.

Fourthly, like any other individual, Gandhi's world of thought was structured in terms of images and assumptions, some too deep for self-consciousness. He picked up the highly complex absolute-relative distinction from Indian philosophy and applied it to his theories of knowledge, morality and action. Since he was apparently unaware of the very different ways in which it was drawn by different Indian philosophical systems, his thought pointed in different directions and contained deep ambiguities. Again, he was unhappy with the image of the pyramid which, in his view, underlay much of modern thought and practice, and replaced it with that of concentric circles. Although he used it on several occasions he never subjected it to a careful analysis and his meaning remains unclear. Gandhi's thought was also suffused with medical images. He thought that the Indian 'body politic' had become 'weak' and 'diseased' and unable to 'resist' the attacks of 'foreign bodies'. All his life he wondered what 'medicine' and 'exercises' would restore it to 'health'. In an important sense his dietary experiments were closely connected with the political and part of a common search. Dr Gandhi was also convinced that rational discussion had only a limited value unless the parties involved were well-disposed towards one another. Accordingly he explored ways of 'melting' or 'winning over' the opponent's heart. He conducted 'researches' in the 'science of the soul' and claimed to have discovered several sophisticated 'instruments' and 'techniques' of 'spiritual surgery'. Gandhi, who had intended to train as a doctor but was put off by dissection, fancied himself all his life as both the principal political physician and the surgeon-general of India. Although I explore Gandhi's hidden assumptions and images to the extent that they are relevant to my inquiry, a good deal of work still needs to be done on his view of the human body and the theosophical influence on it, his conception of the nature of science, his reasons for using the language of research and experiments and the influence on his thought of the *Tantras* and the Hindu mysticism of number and geometrical forms.

1

Critique of Modern Civilisation

British rule in India was a relationship of economic and political domination between an imperial power and its colony. It was based on conquest, consolidated after several wars and followed economic policies designed to serve British interests. Both the parties knew it was unequal, exploitative and based on force. As such it raised moral questions and needed justification. Their self-respect, sense of morality and morale required the British to convince themselves that they were right to rule over India. In order to ensure its orderly and continued existence and secure the co-operation and support of the Indians without whom they simply could not run the country, they also needed to convince their subjects that British rule was in their 'real' interest. It was, of course, possible for them to justify it to themselves in one way and to their subjects in another. However, they knew that such a strategy was open to the charge of inconsistency, even hypocrisy, and inherently precarious.

In order to achieve the dual objective of justifying their rule to themselves and their subjects in a single and consistent language, the British needed to show that they had something to *give* to the Indians which the latter badly *needed*, were unable to acquire *unaided* and was so *precious* as to compensate for whatever economic and political price they were required to pay. The logic of justification required a perfect match between British gifts and Indian needs, the British strength and the Indian deficiency. Following the fashion of the time the British wrapped their gifts in the language of civilisation, which had latterly replaced Christianity as the unifying principle in Europe, taken over its universalist and proselytising mission and built up an ambiguous and uneasy relationship with it. Although modern civilisation was a co-operative European product, the British role in its creation and

11

dissemination was considerable. They were one of the first to industrialise themselves, more or less to recast their religion, ways of life and thought and major political, economic and other institutions in the light of the dominant liberal culture and to roam all over the world as if possessed by its inherently restless and universal spirit. They claimed to 'represent' or 'embody' it to a greater degree than any other country and saw themselves as its transcendentally or historically accredited 'vehicle'.[1]

Since their civilisation had in their view attained the highest possible level of human existence and cultivated capacities which all men *qua* men ought to develop, they had no doubt that it was universally desirable. All societies had a common destiny and destination, namely to become civilised in the British way and were to achieve this destiny by the same route. Hence the more 'advanced' among them, that is, those whose journey had brought them closer to the universal destination, provided the models for and had the moral duty to guide those who had not yet started, became stuck, were proceeding in a wrong direction or at an extremely slow pace. The British could not show that they represented the highest level of civilisation without so defining it that it broadly corresponded to their own ways of life and thought. Like all ideological systems they abstracted, reified and absolutised the distinctive features of their ways of life and thought and presented them as a universal norm for evaluating all societies, including their own. Their facts became values for others, an illicit logical move lying at the heart of every ideology. Other societies were therefore *always* deficient whereas the British was *necessarily* more or less perfect.

The British argued that they had brought to India the unique and most precious gift of civilisation.[2] Since this civilisation was deemed to be universally desirable, India obviously needed it. All they had to do was show that India lacked it and was unable to acquire it unaided. Unlike some of the other British colonies India had a well-developed *literati* tradition, a long history of civic life and considerable philosophical, artistic, scientific and other achievements. Since these were supposed to be some of the indices of civilisation, obviously it could not be contemptuously dismissed as uncivilised. Some British writers and leaders did so dismiss it; most, however, acknowledged its great achievements, but contended that they were all in the past and did not redeem its contemporary degeneration. Its social structure and practices were oppressive, unjust and sometimes inhuman; its religions were incomprehensible, replete with meaningless rituals, polytheist, lacking a single authoritative text, and not really religions in the 'proper' sense of the term; its modes of thought were 'mystical and mythological' and largely irrational; and its people were emotional, excitable, undisciplined, unambitious, lacking in self-control, unreliable and very like women and children. The British view of India did, of course, change over time, largely as a result of their increased knowledge of its past and the changes in their conceptions of themselves and the yardsticks they employed. Throughout their rule, however, they continued to think of it as neither wholly uncivilised nor fully civilised but 'semi-civilised' or 'only half-civilised', and of the Indians as a moderately talented people who needed to be disciplined, guided and trained in the ways of civilisation.

A civilisation consists of ways of life and thought, and initiating people into it is necessarily an educational enterprise. Following the logic of the language of civilisation, the British justified their rule in educational terms and used pedagogical and tutorial metaphors with great regularity in their descriptions of what they thought they were doing. They were not masters but headmasters; the Indians were their pupils; the whole of India was one big public school, almost an Eton writ large; they had carefully fashioned a comprehensive moral and political curriculum; and their stern rule was designed to create the necessary pedagogical climate and only meant to last until such time as their pupils had graduated into political manhood as judged by the periodic assessment of their performance. Accordingly the British introduced a new language and taught their pupils how to speak to each other and their rulers in a 'civilised' tongue. They taught them new subjects and introduced them to the writings of Hume, Locke, Berkeley, Bentham, J. S. Mill and Spencer more or less in that order and later to those of the European scientists. They set up schools, colleges and universities to train them how to 'think' and develop 'good character'. Over time they created a large university-trained, English-speaking and British-orientated middle class, and predictably looked upon it as one of their greatest achievements. At the economic level they established new industries, taught the 'lazy' Indians the virtues of hard work, enterprise, self-discipline, thrift and efficiency, and laid the foundations of a modern industrial society tied to and subserving British interests. At the political level they introduced the modern state standing outside and above Indian society, and established quasi-representative institutions at the local, provincial and national levels with a view to 'training' their subjects in how to run their collective affairs in a 'civilised' manner. In these and other ways the British set about recreating India in their own image, not always with the impatience and arrogance of the French but nevertheless just as effectively and comprehensively. Although honest enough to admit that their economic interests were never out of their mind, they insisted that at least since 1857 when they acquired direct control over India, the economic relations between the two countries were mutually beneficial and that their primary concern was to execute their 'great historical task' of bringing to India the 'benefits of civilisation'.

Although the basic theme of civilising the semi-civilised Indians remained at the centre of the colonial ideology, the latter was a highly complex structure of ideas articulated at different levels and in different idioms at different periods. Since we cannot here discuss it in detail, we shall highlight its four internal tensions and contradictions. First, the British ways of life and thought in which the colonial ideology was grounded were not monolithic. Since they encouraged the spirit of rational criticism, they threw up a large body of internal critics whose writings were often used by the Indians to deflate the moral pretensions of the colonial ideology. Even as the dominant British way of life never overwhelmed all Britons, its colonial extension did not overwhelm all its subjects either. Second, like all ideologies the colonial ideology was necessarily articulated in terms of such general principles as liberty, justice, the rule of law, equality and individual rights, and provided the Indians with the intellectual and moral weapons with which to criticise and counter its claims. Third, the civilisation of which the British saw themselves as missionaries contained a tension at yet another level. It was essentially secular, yet Christianity was an integral part of it. The British did not see themselves as civilisational missionaries until around the first two decades of the 19th century. It is striking and hardly a coincidence that they did not lift the earlier restrictions on the Christian missionaries until around that period. The secular and religious missions had different, at times conflicting, messages. Although both justified colonialism and claimed the divine privilege of narcissistically moulding the rest of mankind in their own image, their languages differed and their relations remained as uneasy as those between

Christianity and modern civilisation in Europe. The muted but unmistakable tensions between the two enabled the Indians to use one to embarrass the other and to retain a critical perspective.[3] Finally, the British justification of their rule paradoxically entailed its eventual dissolution. Once the Indians were inducted into British civilisation, the British had on their own admission no right to rule over them. What was more, the British had to prove their *bona fides* by accelerating the education of their pupils and thus their own eventual departure. From time to time they and the Indians bitterly disagreed about the pace of constitutional development, but they were agreed on the nature of the disagreement and the ultimate goal.

British rule in India was Gandhi's inescapable starting point and a constant frame of reference. Like the generations of leaders from Rammohun Roy onwards, he was deeply puzzled and troubled by it. He wondered why the British had come to India in the first instance, had been able to consolidate their rule and render it acceptable to their subjects with apparent ease, what it had done to them and how they should respond to it. These and related questions worried him even as a young boy and continued to exercise his mind during his years in England and especially in South Africa. His reflections led him to conclude that the answers to them were to be found in the character of modern civilisation. The British had come to India because of the inner compulsions of modern civilisation; they had been able to consolidate their rule because of their ability to legitimise it in the ideological language of civilisation; their rule was not merely political but also moral and cultural in nature; and India had to respond to it not only at the political but primarily at the moral and cultural levels.[4]

For Gandhi the British came to India not by accident, nor in the adventurous spirit of a political buccaneer, but in search of new markets for their goods. 'Many problems can be solved by remembering that money is their God.' They needed to trade because their economic life was geared to unlimited production and could not survive without turning the whole world into a vast market. 'Europeans pounce upon new territories like crows upon a piece of meat. I am inclined to think that this is due to their mass-production factories.'[5] As to why their economic life was so geared, he gave two different answers. Sometimes he pointed to its capitalist character and attributed over-production to its search for profits. More often he argued that capitalism was itself a product of the 'materialist' view of man. It was because man was defined as a creature of infinite desires that the constant satisfaction of his apparently endless wants and the accumulation of wealth acquired moral legitimacy and capitalism as a distinct economic system struck roots. For Gandhi moral tranformation always preceded the economic, and it was man's conception of himself that ultimately underpinned and sustained the economic system. Once capitalism came into existence, it had an obvious vested interest in propagating the underlying view of man and perpetuating a materialist civilisation. Gandhi was convinced that imperialism in one form or another was inherent in materialist civilisation and that Britain would have looked for colonies even if it had had a non-capitalist economy.[6] He did not explain when and why the materialist view of man emerged and why it was able to replace the older 'spiritual' view with such ease.

As to why the British had been able to consolidate their rule Gandhi's answer was more complex. He rejected the widely held view that they had a superior army, for when they first came to India they not only had none worth talking about but also no intention of conquering it. He also rejected the view that the innocent and absent-minded Indians, ill-tutored in the ways of the world, had been outwitted by the wily foreigners for, while this might explain their conquest, it did not explain why the Indians had not only acquiesced in it but also extended their co-operation to their rulers, who were too few to run a vast country on their own. In Gandhi's view the explanation was two-fold. First, the Indians had long been in the habit of fighting among themselves, and some of them turned to the newly arrived East India Company for financial and military help. The Company began to play an increasingly important role in Indian political life and its interference came to be accepted as ligitimate and necessary.[7] Over time it played off one group against another, broadened and consolidated its support and, before the Indians realised what had happened, established its rule. 'The English have not taken India; we have given it to them', Gandhi argued. 'To blame them . . . is to perpetuate their rule.'[8]

Gandhi's second explanation went deeper and centred on the ideological role of the concept of civilisation. The British were able to consolidate their rule because the Indians had 'developed *moha* for their civilisation'. *Moha*, an old and important concept Krishna had used to describe Arjuna's state of mind during the *Mahabharata* war, means being enamoured of, bewitched by or infatuated with something inherently illusory.[9] By British civilisation Gandhi meant both its industrial products and moral and political values, practices and institutions. The two were inseparable and were informed by the 'materialist' spirit. Industrial goods were not neutral material products but embodiments of the spirit of British civilisation. To want them was to want its constitutive values and institutions. Since the Indians had become enamoured of British civilisation, they traded in its products, thereby making it profitable and worthwhile for the British to rule over their country. If they had shown no interest in trade such a commercially-minded people as the British would not have conquered, let alone stayed on in, India. Since the Indians had also been bewitched by British moral and political values, they obviously needed the British to teach these to them. And rather than find their rule morally insulting and outrageous, they thought it highly desirable and in their long-term interest.

The Indians, of course, had their own civilisation and distinct views on what constituted a civilised man and society. These had to be discredited and their self-confidence undermined if British civilisation was to strike roots. Accordingly the British embarked upon a programme of systematic 'scientific indoctrination' devised and enforced by the intellectuals all too ready to place their knowledge at the service of the empire.[10] British historians either denied that India had its own civilisation or dismissed it as degenerate and the chief cause of its decline. They argued that pre-British India was a disorderly and chaotic society that had never known peace and stability and that they alone stood as a shield against chaos in India. British anthropologists produced biased accounts of Indian customs and practices and contended that they were all primitive and needed to be changed. Gandhi observed, 'The English . . . have a habit of writing history; they pretend to know the customs and practices of every society . . . They beat their own drums, and hypnotise us into believing them. In our gullibility we believe all that.'[11] British social scientists argued that material progress was the necessary precondition of moral prgress, that India's moral decline was a result of its low economic development and that its moral regeneration could only be effected by the British pattern of industrialisation. British philosophers and psychologists went further and argued that by his very nature man was a restless and desiring being and that the multiplication of wants was the only driving force of history. In these and other ways the Indians were 'brainwashed' into doubting the value of their ancestral civilisation and brought to the verge of 'civil suicide'. Once the moral conquest of the Indian mind was complete, the way was cleared for its economic and political exploitation.

For Gandhi British imperialism dominated India at three related but different levels. At the political level the arrogant colonial government oppressed the Indian people and denied their right to run their affairs themselves. At the economic level it exploited and impoverished them, destroyed their indigenous industries and subordinated their interests to those of the British economy. In Gandhi's view this was far more disturbing than political oppression and could continue even if India became independent. At the most disturbing moral and cultural level, British imperialism destroyed the identity and integrity of Indian civilisation and turned the Indians into brown Englishmen. Gandhi was convinced that the 'rule' of British *civilisation* could continue even if the British *government* were to stop ruling over India and British *capital* to cease exploiting it. British imperialism was unacceptable not only because of its political and even economic but moral and cultural consequences. The struggle against it had therefore to be mounted and independence obtained at all three levels, especially the last. At the cultural level the anti-imperialist struggle had to be fought on two fronts simultaneously. First, British civilisation, which so infatuated and blinded the Indians to the moral enormity of foreign rule and legitimised their economic and political domination must be subjected to a thorough-going critique. Second, the basic structure of Indian civilisation, which they largely saw through the biased British perspective, must be sensitively teased out and defended.

In interpreting British imperialism in this way, Gandhi integrated and went beyond the three different types of critique advanced by his predecessors. Broadly speaking Dadabhai Naoroji, Surendra Nath Banerjee, Gokhale and the so-called liberals had welcomed the political and cultural advantages of British rule but attacked it on the grounds that it had drained India's wealth, ruined its industries, imposed unfair trading arrangements and subordinated its economic development to British colonial interests. Although mindful of its economic and cultural consequences, the leaders of the terrorist movements in Bengal and Maharashtra attacked it on political grounds and were the first to develop a distinctive theory of political as distinct from cultural nationalism. They argued that the Indians had as much right to run their affairs as the British had to run theirs, that colonialism was a form of slavery and an outrage to Indian dignity and self-respect, and that the 'honour' of 'mother India' demanded that she should be freed of the 'foreign yoke'. In a culture which conceptualises energy in feminine terms and associates activity and restlessness with woman and passivity and detachment with man, it was not at all surprising that the votaries of violence should have idealised 'mother' India and drawn inspiration from the Goddess *Kali*. Finally Vivekananda, B. C. Pal, Tilak and the so-called conservative leaders concentrated on the need to preserve the integrity of traditional ways of life and thought. They introduced the concept of Indian civilisation to match the one championed by the British, sharply distinguished the two and attacked foreign rule not so much because it involved economic exploitation and violated Indian pride as because it imposed an alien materialist civilisation on India's essentially spiritual one.

Gandhi's critique of British rule encompassed all three. He was acutely aware of its economic motivation and highlighted the grave economic damage it had done and was doing to the country. He used the language of national honour, pride and dignity as freely as the terrorists and felt just as protective and reverential about 'mother' India. He was even more sensitive to the integrity of Indian civilisation than were the conservative leaders. Indeed he argued that most of them were more interested in the 'synthesis' of the two civilisations than in the integrity of their own, had unwittingly reinterpreted and anglicised it far more than they realised or cared to admit, and that their critque of British imperialism was half-hearted and lacked moral depth. Gandhi's critique not only included but also related and integrated the three earlier critiques into a comprehensive theoretical framework. He argued that political independence was important not only as an expression of India's pride and a necessary means to stop its economic exploitation but also to preserve its civilisation, without which political independence remained fragile. The economic exploitation had to be ended not only to sustain Indian independence and improve the living conditions of its people but also to preserve the social and economic basis of its civilisation. Thanks to its range and depth

Gandhi's critique of British imperialism was able to provide a coherent theoretical platform on which Indians of different ideological persuasions could unite.

The extent to which Gandhi went beyond his predecessors, especially the so-called conservatives, was evident in the way he defined the nature of the cultural encounter between Britain and India. While they had argued that the conflict was between the Indian and European or between the Eastern and Western civilisations, Gandhi insisted that it was really between the ancient and modern. As he put it, there is 'no such thing as Western or European civilisation, but there is a modern civilisation'.[12] His apparently trivial redefinition was in fact intended to alter the terms of the debate in his favour and achieve several ideological and political advantages.[13] First, he was able to reject the currently fashionable view among many British and Indian writers that the East and the West were radically different and shared nothing in common. For Gandhi such a doctrine had no basis in facts, denied the fundamental unity of mankind and bred cultural parochialism. Second, he was able to attack modern civilisation without attacking the West. He greatly admired Socrates and Christianity, such modern writers as Tolstoy, Ruskin and Thoreau and several Western values and practices, and wished to exclude them from his criticism. Third, the distinction enabled Gandhi to argue that modern civilisation was of relatively recent origin in the West and that its pre-modern counterpart was very different and more like the Indian. He hoped thereby to remind the West of its earlier traditions and values, evoke its temporarily suppressed historical memories and elicit its support for his fight against modern civilisation. He was able to argue that since Indian civilisation stood for values to which the West had itself for centuries subscribed and was only trying to preserve their common heritage, by attacking and undermining it the West not only betrayed its own great past but also damaged its chances of future redemption. Fourth, by arguing that industrial civilisation was modern and 'still very young', Gandhi intended to suggest that it lacked the wisdom and maturity conferred by age, an important argument in a country that revered age. Finally, Gandhi hoped to convince his countrymen that in fighting modern civilisation they were not being reactionary. They were only combating the arrogance and impetuosity of an historical upstart and helping to preserve the permanent values of the whole of mankind, including the West.

The idea of saving the soul of their misguided masters tickled Indian pride and made Gandhi's harsh message more acceptable.

For Gandhi, then, India was a great battlefield, the modern *kurukshetra* on which modern and ancient civilisations, the past and the present, were locked in a momentous battle for the future. The British were the best representatives of modern civilisation and the Indians of the ancient. The former had fancied themselves as the missionaries of modern civilisation; Gandhi turned the Indians into missionaries of a universal civilisation based on the great ancient values enriched by some of the valid insights of the modern. The hold of the colonial ideology was such that even its shrewdest critic did not transcend but largely reinterpreted its terms of debate.

Gandhi's critique of modern civilisation was far more complex than is generally imagined and quite different from that of such other writers as Rousseau, Carlyle, Ruskin, Tolstoy and Thoreau, by the last three of whom he was deeply influenced. In his view modern civilisation was grounded in a fatally flawed theory of man. Unlike ancient civilisation which was soul- or spirit-centred, the modern was body-centred and in that sense 'materialistic'. For Gandhi the body had two basic characteristics. First, it was distinct, self-enclosed and separated from and only capable of preserving its integrity by maintaining its separateness from other bodies. As such it was the ontological basis of the human sense of particularity, and the source of the illusion that each individual was an independent and self-centred ego only externally and contingently related to others and constantly concerned to preserve his identity by keeping the invasive others at a safe distance. Second, the body was the seat of the senses, and thus of wants and desires. By their very nature desires recurred with rhythmic regularity and were never satiated. They were also interrelated and one desire always gave rise to others. *Qua* sensual and desiring being, man was necessarily propelled by his inherently limitless desires and was always restless and dissatisfied.

A body-centred or materialist view of man thus attributed two basic properties to him and regarded them as natural and legitimate, namely 'selfishness' and an 'infinite multiplicity of wants'.[14] A civilisation based on such a flawed view necessarily suffered from several basic and interrelated limitations. First, it lacked moral and spiritual depth. Second, since it had no guiding principles to decide what desires deserved to be satisfied and within what limits, it led to a way of life devoid of meaning and purpose. Third, it de-humanised man and had a profound anti-human bias. Fourth, it perverted the human psyche and was suffused with the spirit of violence. Finally, it reduced wisdom to knowledge and the latter to a form of power only useful as an instrument of control over nature and other men. It thereby not only perverted the pursuit of truth but also lacked a system of knowledge capable of critically evaluating its basic assumptions and objectives.

For Gandhi modern civilisation was propelled by the two inter-related principles of greed and want. It was controlled by 'a few capitalist owners' who had only one aim, to make profit, and only one means to do so, to produce goods that satisfied people's wants. They had a vital vested interest in constantly whetting jaded appetites, planting new wants and creating a moral climate in which not to want the goods daily pumped into the market and to keep pace with the latest fashions was to be abnormal and archaic. Indeed, since self-discipline or restriction of desires, the very emblem of human dignity, threatened to cause mass unemployment, throw the economic system out of gear and cause human suffering, it was seen as anti-social and immoral. Not surprisingly men saw themselves not as self-determining moral subjects but as consumers or vehicles for the satisfaction of externally-induced wants.

The capitalist search for profits led to mechanisation and 'industrialism'. For Gandhi machines relieved drudgery, created leisure, increased efficiency and were indispensable when there was a shortage of labour. Their use must therefore be guided by a well-considered moral theory indicating how men should live, spend their free time and relate to one another. Since the modern economy lacked such a theory and was only propelled by the search for profit, it mechanised production without any regard for its wider moral, cultural and other consequences. Machines were introduced even when there was no obvious need for them and were in fact likely to throw thousands out of work. This was justified either in the name of increased leisure without anyone asking why it was important and what to do with it, or of cheaper goods, as if man was only a passive consumer and not an active moral being for whose sanity, self-respect and dignity the right to work was far more important than the febrile gratification of trivial wants.[15] Treated with the veneration and awe accorded to the gods in primitive societies, machines had come to cast a magic spell on modern man and followed their own will. For Gandhi the mechanisation or fetishism of technology was closely tied up with the larger phenomenon of industrialism, another apparently self-propelling and endless process of creating larger and larger industries with no other purpose than to produce cheap consumer goods and maximise profit.[16] He argued that since modern economic life followed an inexorable momentum of its own, it reduced men to its helpless and passive victims and represented a new form of slavery, more comfortable and invidious and hence more dangerous than the earlier ones.

Based on the belief that life was continuous motion and movement, that unless one was constantly on the move one was not alive and that the faster the tempo of life the more alive one was, modern civilisation was inherently restless and intolerant of stability. It aimed to conquer time and space and developed increasingly speedier modes of transport and communication. Cars were replaced by trains, and the latter by planes, but no one asked why one needed to travel so fast and what one intended to do with the time saved. Thanks to its restlessness and 'mindless activism' incorrectly equated with dynamism and energy, modern civilisation undermined man's unity with his environment and fellow men and destroyed stable and long-established communities. In the absence of natural and social roots and the stable and enduring landmarks which alone gave man a sense of identity and continuity, modern man had become abstract, indeterminate and empty. He was not internally or organically related to others and his relations with them were not grounded in the sentiments of fellow feeling and good will. Everyone was a stranger to everyone else and no one cared for or knew how to behave towards others.[17]

As a result people's moral life suffered a profound distortion. First, it became as abstract as the men it was supposed to relate, and was reduced to a set of self-consciously followed and externally legislated and enforced impersonal rules. Other men mattered not because one cared for them but because the moral rules so required. Second, rather than an expression and fulfilment of man's nature, morality was seen as a necessary but painful and widely resented restriction of freedom, a kind of tax he had to pay in order to be able to enjoy his residual freedom unhindered. It was therefore reduced to the barest minimum, requiring little more than what was needed to prevent men from destroying one

another. Third, a society of basically amoral and internally unre-
lated beings was characterised by a climate of suspicion, fear,
hostility and tension. Each perceived the rest as actual or potential
enemies who impinged on his consciousness only when and
insofar as they posed a threat, and amongst whom he could hope
to survive only by sheltering behind carefully planned and fiercely
guarded physical, emotional and moral fortifications.

Fourth, since in the absence of the nourishing soil of the sentiments of good will and mutual concern the moral life lacked roots
and vitality, it had to depend on the non-moral motive of fear.
Modern man took care not to harm others lest they should harm
him, and he did a good turn to them as an investment for the
future. Morality was reduced to reciprocal egoism or enlightened
self-interest and was sustained by fear. Since self-interest was not a
moral principle, Gandhi argued that enlightened self-interest was
not one either. In modern civilisation morality was a form of
prudence, a more effective way of pursuing self-interest, and was
virtually exorcised out of existence. Finally, modern civilisation
denuded morality of its vital internal dimension or what he called
the quality of the soul. Jealousy, hatred, meanness, ill-will, perverse pleasure at another's misfortunes and sordid thoughts and
fantasies were moral impurities reflecting an ill-developed soul.
Moral growth consisted in overcoming these deficiencies and developing a beautiful and noble soul. Although this had been long
cherished by Christianity, modern man felt threatened by it. Being
only concerned to get on in the world and lead a comfortable life,
he not only saw no value in the purity of the soul and the quality of
his motives but found such concerns a hindrance. Not an intro-
spective, reflective, self-critical, sensitive and tender-hearted but a
tough, aggressive, ambitious and suspicious man was the ideal
and the necessary basis of modern civilisation.

Modern man, Gandhi went on, spent most of his energy trying
to steady himself in a hostile and unsteady environment. He had
neither the inclination nor the ability to slow down the tempo of
his life, relax, compose himself, reflect on his pattern of life and
nurture the inner springs of energy. He lived outside himself and
exhausted himself physically and spiritually. Predictably he
needed to depend on such ultimately debilitating sources of instant
energy as intoxicating spirits, tea and coffee, in order constantly to
whip himself into action. Inwardly empty and frightened to be
alone with himself, he was always busy, turning to one activity

after another, easily bored and feverishly looking for new sources of amusement. Gandhi thought that modern civilisation had a depressing air of 'futility' and 'madness' about it and was likely to destroy itself before long.[18]

In Gandhi's view the exploitation of one's fellow men was built into the very structure of modern civilisation. Consumers were constantly manipulated into desiring things they did not need and which were not in their long-term interest. Workers were made to do boring jobs at subsistence wages under inhuman conditions and given little opportunity or encouragement to develop their intellectual and moral potential. The poor were treated with contempt and held responsible for their own misfortunes. The weaker races were treated as if they were animals and bought and sold and brutally exploited. The weaker nations were conquered, mercilessly oppressed and used as dumping grounds for surplus goods and as sources of cheap raw material. For Gandhi imperialism was only an acute manifestation of the aggressive and exploitative impulse lying at the very heart of modern civilisation and at work in all areas of human relationships.

It was therefore hardly surprising that modern civilisation rested on and was sustained by massive violence. It involved violence against oneself. In a society of ambitions, competitive and mutually fearful men, no one could survive without developing a regimented and militant psyche, suppressing his tender feelings and doubts and becoming like a mobile weapon of destruction ready to hurt itself on the slightest provocation. It also involved violence against other men at both the personal and collective levels. Since each felt threatened by others and desperately sought to keep them at a manageable distance, he had to rely on the use or threat of verbal, emotional, moral and even physical violence ultimately backed up by the concentrated violence of the modern state. The realtions between organised groups, classes and states were even more tense and aggressive and scarred by open or cold wars. Modern civilisation also involved an egregious amount of violence against nature, which was largely seen as man's property to do with it what he liked. Its resources were ruthlessly exploited and its rhythm and balance disturbed, and the animals were freely killed or tortured for food, sport, fancy clothes and medical experiments. In Gandhi's view violence 'oozed from every pore' of modern society and had so much become a way of life that modern man could not cope with his relations with himself or other men without translating them into the military language of conflict, struggle, mastery, subjugation, domination, victory and defeat. Deeply rooted in violence man felt suffocated in its absence.

For Gandhi a civilisation properly so-called placed man at its centre and measured its greatness in terms of its ability to produce men and women possessing such distinctively human powers as self-determination, autonomy, self-knowledge, self-discipline and social co-operation. Modern civilisation did the opposite. By encouraging them to alienate their powers to large organisations run by experts, it rendered men passive, helpless and heteronomous. Gandhi took the example of medical science, the pride and glory of modern civilisation.[19] Ideally it should aim at two things. First, it should help people acquire a greater understanding and control of their bodies by explaining to them the causes and aetiology of their ailments, how to prevent them and how they were integrally related to their ways of life. Second, since the body was not an inert machine but a living organism with its own rhythm and built-in intelligence, medical science should mobilise its internal resources and wisely activate them where necessary by external help. Modern medicine did neither. Every time someone complained of an ailment, he was required to hand over the custody of his body to the experts to do what they liked with it, as if it was a contingently related appendage about which he needed to know nothing and for which he bore no responsibility. Predictably the patient learned nothing from his ailment, developed it again, was treated the same way the next time around, and the vicious cycle went on unabated. Thanks to their training the medical experts were unable effectively to deal with the body unless they enjoyed an unchallenged monopoly over it. For his part heteronomous modern man was only too willing to alienate his body and abdicate all control over it. The silent collaboration between the two spawned the huge medical establishment enjoying and closely guarding its monopoly of medical knowledge. It was as if all the bodies in a society were abstracted from their human bearers, nationalised and bureaucratically managed by this organised body of experts.

Medical science also showed little respect for the integrity of the body and was suffused with the spirit of violence characteristic of modern civilisation. It did not see the ailment as the overworked and undisciplined body's plea for rest and discipline, but rather as an unacceptable interference with its hectic routine, requiring an immediate and effective response. The body was not allowed to cope with illness at its own pace and by means of its own judiciously activated resources; instead its sluggish rhythm was aggressively manipulated by bombarding it with powerful chemical agents which ended up doing it grave long-term harm. Like the other form of violence, medical violence too was subject to an inflationary spiral. Once the 'enemies' invading the body developed 'defences' against one set of drugs, more potent ones were invented doing yet greater violence to it and to the animals on whom they were first tried out. The poor body became a battlefield where powerful armies fought out a deadly contest in which it was itself often the first casualty.

Gandhi thought that the same dehumanising phenomenon was evident in the field of law.[20] Men were intelligent and moral beings capable of resolving their differences by discussing them in the spirit of charity and good will or by seeking the arbitration of widely respected men and women in their community. Instead, every time he failed to get what he thought was his due, modern man rushed to the court of law where trained experts in the esoteric body of legal knowledge conducted expensive and incomprehensible debates about him without his participation. Just as the medical establishment reduced him to a passive object, the legal establishment reduced him to a case to be discussed as if he were a child to be tutored into what to say about his own actions and incapable of participating in their evaluation. Even as medical science did little to develop the body's own resources, the legal system did little to develop and mobilise man's moral impulses and capacities for reflection and introspection. Instead it required him to alienate them to a central agency telling him how to run his life and conduct his relations with others, including his own neighbours, wife, ex-wife and children. Gandhi found it strange that modern man, who talked so much about his self-respect and dignity, did not find all this deeply humiliating.

Gandhi argued that the highly centralised and bureaucratic modern state enjoying and jealously guarding its monopoly of political power was a necessary product of modern civilisation. Competitive and aggressive men ruthlessly pursuing their own interests could only be held together by a well-armed state. Since they were all strangers to one another and lacked the bonds of good will and mutual concern, their relations could only be regulated by impersonal rules imposed and enforced by such a powerful external agency as the state. The centralisation of production in the modern economy created social and economic problems of national and international magnitude, and again required a centralised political agency to deal with them. Unemployment, poverty and the social and economic inequalities created by the modern economy led to acute and legitimate discontent and required a well-armed state to deter its desperate citizens from resorting to violence. 'Shorn of all the camouflage the exploitation of the masses of Europe is sustained by violence', Gandhi argued. The centralised modern state was also necessary to protect international markets and overseas investments.

For Gandhi the state dehumanised its citizens in more or less the same ways as the medical, legal and other institutions. It had a vested institutional interest in monopolising all initiative and fostering a state-centred political culture. The more its citizens became 'addicted' to it and the more they felt helpless without it, the safer it felt. Accordingly it systematically nurtured the illusion that the problems of society were too complex and intractable to be solved by ordinary citizens acting individually or collectively, and were best left to the state and its official agencies. It felt threatened by active and independent-minded citizens determined to participate in the conduct of their affairs and worried lest they should be morally compromised by what it did in their name. It therefore denied them access to vital information and opportunities for political participation, and discouraged independent and vibrant local communities capable of challenging its decisions.

Even as the state monopolised all political power, it tended to monopolise all morality. Since its atomic and morally depleted citizens lacked organic bonds and the capacity to organise and run their social relations themselves, the state was the sole source of moral order. It alone guaranteed civilised existence and saved society from total disintegration. As such it came to be seen as the highest moral institution, whose preservation was a supreme moral value. Whatever was prejudicial to its interests was immoral and whatever promoted them was moral. All moral sentiments were sucked into it, all moral energies were appropriated by it, all moral norms were judged in terms of its interests, and its laws were deemed to be the sole determinants of collective morality. Dying for the state was a supreme virtue, and fighting in its wars the highest duty. Disobeying its laws was strongly disapproved of and all attempts to weigh them in the highest moral scale were discouraged on the ground that political life was either amoral or governed by its own distinct morality. The human being was thus reduced to the citizen, and the latter in turn to a passive and uncritical subject.

Gandhi argued that, although the state claimed to be a moral institution transcending narrow group interests and pursuing the well-being of the whole community, it was in fact little more than an arena of conflict between organised interests manipulated and controlled by the more powerful among them. Since men of independent spirit and honour generally avoided it, it was largely in the care of men and women forging convenient alliances with powerful interest groups and using it to serve their interests. Gandhi thought that in these respects the democratic governments were no better than the undemocratic and belonged to the 'same species'. They were just as vulnerable to the pressures of the dominant class and just as 'ruthless' and ready to use violence in the pursuit of its interests. In its actual practice a democracy was basically a form of government in which a 'few men capture power in the name of the people and abuse it', a 'game of chess' between rival parties with the people as 'pawns'.[21] Although the fact that democratic government was periodically elected by and account-able to ordinary people made a difference, it also served as a 'camouflage' hiding the basic fact that the masses were often 'exploited by the ruling class . . . under the sacred name of democracy'.[22] Democracy thus veiled and conferred moral legi-timacy on the reality of exploitation, and had only a marginal moral edge over fascism.

Gandhi contended that the British parliament, the mother of parliaments and the home of democracy, was not much better than its counterparts elsewhere.[23] It was largely a 'talking shop' capable neither of exercising much control over the government nor of pursuing the national interest. It was dominated by political parties whose sole concern was to capture and remain in power by manipulating public opinion and subserving powerful economic interests. Its members meekly followed the party line, rarely re-signed on matters of principle and had 'neither real honesty nor a living conscience'. Although generally immune to crude forms of financial corruption and bribes, Gandhi thought that they were open to the 'subtler influences' of honours, offers of government posts and political patronage.[24] They claimed to be patriotic but had little real love of the country, which consisted not only of the privileged few but the 'whole people' the pursuit of whose well-being must therefore be the true test of patriotism. So long as the masses were exploited, confined to mindless and poorly-paid jobs, and felt impotent and powerless, Britain could not be called a democracy or its politicians patriotic.[25]

Gandhi did not think much of the British electorate either. Unable to look beyond their narrow self-interest, the voters cared little for the long-term interest of their country and the problems and suffering of their less privilged fellow citizens and joined and voted for the parties most likely to promote their interests. They took little interest in the way their country was governed and lazily accepted the biased information and opinions peddled by the newspapers. Gandhi observed:

> To the English voters their newspaper is their Bible. They take their cue from their newspapers which are often dishonest. The same fact is differently interpreted by different newspapers, according to the party in whose interests they are edited.[26]

In Gandhi's view the much-vaunted independence of the press was largely a myth. The press was owned by the capitalists who saw it as yet another industry for manufacturing and selling opinions and who had little regard for their grave moral responsibility. It was not concerned with truth but propaganda, not the education but manipulation of public opinion. Rather than strengthen democracy it corrupted and subverted its very basis.

Although convinced that the foundation of modern civilisation was 'rotten', Gandhi did not dismiss it altogether and praised what he took to be its three great achievements. First, he admired its scientific spirit of inquiry. He observed:

> I have been a sympathetic student of the Western social order, and I have discovered that underlying the fever that fills the soul of the West, there is a restless search for Truth. I value that spirit. Let us study our Eastern institutions in that spirit of scientific inquiry.[27]

Not that the scientific spirit was unknown in the pre-modern West or ancient India. Rather it was muted and denied the full scope it had received in the modern age. For Gandhi the scientific spirit meant the spirit of rational inquiry, 'the spirit of search for the truth in place of being satisfied with tradition without question', and implied intellectual curiosity, rigorous pursuit of truth and critical examination of established beliefs. Gandhi's admiration of the scientific *spirit*, however, did not extend to the scientific *culture*. In his view modern civilisation was right to give pride of place to reason, but wrong to make a 'fetish' of it and ignore its limitations. Such areas of human experience as religion raised matters transcending reason and requiring faith. In some other areas of life, such as morality and politics, reason was inherently inadequate and needed to be guided and supplemented by wisdom, conscience, intuition and moral insight. Since it was essentially an analytical and discursive faculty and its conclusions were necessarily tentative and liable to be subverted by superior arguments, it was inherently unstable and could never form the basis of human life. It certainly had an important role to play in social life, but a society that relied on it alone would not last a day. Gandhi thought that as in the other areas of life, modern civilisation had grasped an important truth but turned it into a falsehood by ignoring its limits.

For Gandhi the second great achievement of modern civilisation consisted in understanding and bringing the natural world under greater human control. Being body-centred it had concentrated most of its energies on improving the material conditions of life. It had developed the ability to anticipate and control natural calamities, eliminate diseases, improve health and public hygiene, prolong life and reduce or relieve human drudgery. It had also developed new means of transport and communication, brought the world closer, increased human comforts and improved the material quality of life. Gandhi contended that since these and other achievements were secured within a fundamentally flawed framework, they had suffered a profound distortion. It was important to preserve and prolong life, but modern civilisation had turned it into the highest value and cultivated a morbid fear of death. Medical science was a great human achievement, but it showed little respect for the human body, drained its indigenous resources, weakened self-discipline and treated the animals as mere means to human well-being. Machines had a place in life, but modern civilisation had turned them into autonomous agents following their own will. Industries were desirable, but modern civilisation had made them the very basis and centre of society. In short, since it lacked a balanced theory of man, many of the achievements of modern civilisation had become forces for evil and harmed rather than helped men.

Third, in Gandhi's view modern civilisation had greatly contributed to the organisational side of life. It had cultivated civic virtues, respect for rules, the capacity to subordinate the personal to the collective interest, public morality, mutual respect and punctuality. Gandhi argued that although he had 'thankfully copied' many of these 'great' qualities without which his personal and especially political life would have been poorer, modern civilisation had once again misinterpreted them and ignored their limits. It had reduced morality to enlightened self-interest and undermined its autonomy. It had rightly subordinated the individual to collective interest, but failed to provide sufficient room for diversity. It rightly stressed the value of organisation, but it over-institutionalised men and left no space for conscientious objection and the lonely dissenter. It was right to emphasise rules, but wrong not to realise that they could never exhaust moral life and were precarious unless grounded in finer human impulses.

For Gandhi, then, modern civilisation was a highly complex human achievement, and the response to it had to be equally complex. Its foundation was shaky but it had genuine achievements to its credit. Unlike his predecessors, Gandhi argued that its achievements could not be abstracted and promiscuously combined with those of Indian civilisation. Since they were secured within a fundamentally mistaken framework and vitiated by their provenance, they had to be purged of their distortions and 'purified' before they were fit to be incorporated into a different framework. For example, it was not enough to say that mechanisation was bad but the machines were good, or that rationalism should be rejected but the spirit of rational inquiry retained. Modern machines, invented within the context of the materialist civilisation that determined their nature, place in life and mode of operation, were not culturally neutral. A differently constituted civilisation had to use the available scientific knowledge to develop different kinds of machines and put them to different uses. The other achievements of modern civilisation had to be subjected to a similar critical and 'cleansing' process.

Before concluding the chapter we might make a few general comments on Gandhi's critique of modern civilisation. Although bearing a strong resemblance to the criticisms of such writers as Rousseau, Ruskin, Carlyle, Tolstoy, Nietzsche and Marx, Gandhi's critique contained original and important insights derived from the two great advantages he enjoyed over them. First, as a colonial native belonging to a despised race and an oppressed country, he experienced the darker side of modern civilisation not directly accessible to them. Second, as an heir to the rich and differently structured Indian civilisation, he brought to his critique an intellectual perspective and moral sensitivity not available to its Western critics.

Gandhi saw that despite all its egalitarian pretensions, modern civilisation was deeply racist and placed non-whites more or less outside the pale of common humanity. He saw too that despite its commitment to human dignity, it was inherently exploitative and had not the slightest hesitation in oppressing other countries and trading in human beings whether in the morally outrageous form of slavery or the slightly less inhuman form of indentured labour. Unlike its Western critics Gandhi saw that these and other evils were not mere aberrations but inherent in the structure of modern civilisation. Its flawed theory of man profoundly distorted its interpretations of such moral values as human dignity, liberty and equality and prevented it from appreciating their true nature and realising their full moral potential. It did not value the full range of human freedom but largely the freedom to pursue self-interest, not the equal development of all men but the equal right to pursue self-interest, not the dignity of all men but only of those satisfying a conveniently biased definition of man. Gandhi also saw that a civilisation that ill-treated outsiders could hardly avoid ill-treating its own people. He was thus able to link up the exploitation and degradation of its internal and external victims and locate them in a global perspective.

As one deeply grounded in another civilisation Gandhi brought to his critique of modern civilisation a fresh perspective. Thanks to his Indian background he was intensely sensitive to the fact that, although apparently civil and non-violent, modern civilisation was suffused with the spirit of aggression and violence which it had learned to contain but had not at all mastered. In his view the colonial, the European and the two world wars could not be conveniently dismissed as mere accidents or products of human folly and miscalculation. No civilisation could launch, live with and periodically unleash such devastating and brutal wars without being able to justify them to itself, and Gandhi could not see how it could do so except on the basis of a distorted system of values and blunted moral sensibilities. Again, he saw that self-determination and autonomy remained fragile without moral self-discipline and that in the absence of an adequate moral basis the modern doctrines of liberty and equality provided flimsy defences against exploitation and oppression. The intense sense of moral responsibility which Gandhi derived from his culture alerted him to the way large organisations swallowed up modern man and stifled his individuality and capacity for dissent. As an outsider he saw too that modern civilisation contained a deep tension. At one level it claimed to be and was Christian; at another it was anthropocentric, obsessed with the satisfaction of material wants, propelled by greed and essentially irreligious. Its two conflicting tendencies naturally rendered it schizophrenic and unstable. No civilisation could live with such a tension without trying to find ways of resolving it. Gandhi thought that for all practical purposes modern civilisation had jettisoned Christianity and only used it to cover up and justify its aggressive pursuit of narrow self-interest. Although Tolstoy, Ruskin, Marx and others had highlighted this, few matched the clarity and penetration of Gandhi's criticism.

Gandhi's advantages were also his disadvantages. Since he largely concentrated on the darker side of modern civilisation, he overlooked some of its great achievements and strengths. And since he saw it from the outside he oversimplified it and did not fully understand its complex structure. As a colonial subject deeply sensitive to the economic damage it had caused in India, he concentrated on its exploitative tendencies and equated it with industrialisation and capitalism. He was therefore unable to appreciate the full range and moral depth of the new vision of man inspiring and informing it. Although preoccupied with the satisfaction of ever-increasing wants, it was at a deeper level guided by the search for personal independence and autonomy, a non-hierarchical social structure, the passionate concern to understand the world and man's mastery over his own environment and destiny. It did foster selfishness and greed, but it also stressed human unity, individuality, equality, liberty, creativity, rationality and man's all-round development. And although it conveniently misdefined and restricted some of these values to the privileged few and failed to tap their full moral potential, that neither diminished their world-historical importance nor detracted from the fact that they represented a collective human heritage. Materialist at one level, modern civilisation also had a spiritual dimension.

Since Gandhi viewed it as an undifferentiated whole, he was unable to distinguish and analyse the complex pattern of relationship between its different components such as capitalism, imperialism, industrialisation, the egoistic view of man and modern science, all of which he regarded as part of the same general phenomenon. He was therefore unable to see that industrialisation need not be accompanied by either capitalism or the egoistic view of man, that imperialism was not inherent in industrialisation, and that modern science was only contingently related to imperialism and the egoistic view of man. He could not provide a satisfactory theory of imperialism either, and naively imagined that every country embarking on large-scale industrialisation was bound to become imperialist. More importantly, his inadequate understanding of modern civilisation limited his intellectual options and compelled him to reject far more than he needed to. Since he thought that nearly all its evils sprang from large-scale industrialisation, he remained deeply hostile to it and neither appreciated the economic aspirations of his countrymen and the dynamics of the economic reality unfolding before him, not offered a viable alternative.

Ghandi's analysis of modern civilisation also made it difficult for him to give an adequate account of what he took to be its three major achievements. He could not explain the rise of the scientific spirit and the development of what he called the organisational side of life, and treated them as if they were accidental products of modern civilisation. He failed to notice that they were vital to the very existence of the modern industrial society and could not be developed outside it. Gandhi was thus caught up in the paradoxical position of wanting to appropriate part of the 'spirit' of modern civilisation while rejecting the very institutions and the social structure that embodied and nurtured it. Like other religious thinkers he abstracted the spirit from the body and thought that the former could survive without the latter. As we shall see, this was one of the major sources of many of his difficulties.

2

Indian Civilisation and National Regeneration

In India as in the other colonies those critical of their ruler's civilsation tended to be uncritically defensive about their own. Gandhi was convinced that this seductive but suicidal trap had to be scrupulously avoided. Colonial experience highlighted two fundamental features of the colony. First, the very fact that it had fallen prey to foreign rule indicated that it had become degenerate and left something to be desired. Second, the fact that it had existed before its conquest as an autonomous community surviving crises to which all human associations are heirs indicated that it was viable and had a considerable reservoir of strength. Its past was just as real as its present, and it should under no circumstances allow the colonial experience to blind it to either. It must in Gandhi's view avail itself of its current predicament and take a patient and critical look at itself, identify its weaknesses and use its internal resources to overcome them. The fact that the self-examination was conducted in a colonial context and under the vigilant and hostile stare of the colonial rulers created obvious dangers. It was likely to be distorted by the prevailing sense of gloom and diffidence, the terms of political discourse set by the rulers and by the understandable temptation to say things palatable to them. The dangers must be fully recognised and each community must find its own ways of coping with them. It was in this spirit that Gandhi embarked on a comprehensive examination of India's past and present.

Like the other Indian leaders, from Rammohun Roy onwards, Gandhi was awed by the sheer survival of Indian civilisation.[1] In the long history of mankind such great civilisations as the Babylonian, Syrian, Persian, Egyptian, Greek and Roman, had come and gone but the Indian civilisation buffeted by stormier waters than them had somehow managed to survive. Many times in the past the 'sons of India were found wanting' and their civilisation was in great jeopardy. Yet almost in spite of them the 'ancient India is still living'. The Indians were like the Jews, 'irrepressible in spite of centuries of oppression and bondage'.[2] The fact that their civilisation had lasted so long and more or less remained whole 'proved' its 'immeasurable' strength and vitality and showed that more than any other it was based on some of the eternal truths of human existence.[3]

Confronted with the arrogant British claim that the Indians were an uncivilised or semi-civilised people, the earlier generations of Indian leaders had worked out an ingenious response. They contended that they were not uncivilised but differently civilised and that, unlike the materialist European civilisation, theirs was essentially spiritual. Although based on a misreading of the character and history of the two civilisations, the response had obvious political advantages and enjoyed considerable support in India. It established a relationship of parity and complementarity between the two civilisations, allowed the Indians to 'borrow' European ideas and institutions without feeling nervous or guilty about it, and legitimised their dream of a grand synthesis of the two as their great contribution to mankind.

With some reservations (to be discussed later), Gandhi shared this view. That man was essentially a spiritual being was in his view the most important truth India had grasped. It had discovered many others as well, but this was the basis of them all. India was a 'truly spiritual nation', 'predominantly the land of religion'. Its best minds, no less curious and creative than their modern European counterparts, had devoted their energies to the cultivation of the 'science of the spirit' and made 'most marvellous discoveries' far more impressive than the 'wonderful discoveries in things material' made by Europe. Although Gandhi nowhere listed them, he had in mind such 'discoveries' or beliefs as that the cosmic spirit informed and structured the universe; that man was not separate from but identical with it; that every man was uniquely constituted and came to terms with himself and the world in his own unique manner; that all men, all life and indeed all creation was one; that man's true happiness and fulfilment lay in overcoming his sense of individuality and opening himself up to the presence of others, and that non-violence to all living beings was the highest moral principle. Unlike many earlier writers Gandhi did not think much of *yoga* and the traditional Hindu repertoire of spiritual exercises and hold them up as monuments to India's spiritual creativity.

For Gandhi the ancient Indians knew that mind and body were seats of desires and threw up temptations that distracted man from his supreme goal of *moksha*. Hence they condemned self-indulgence and argued that his fulfilment lay in restricting his wants and controlling his desires. Not that they ignored the legitimate demands of the human body, rather these were located within the larger framework of and regulated by his moral and spiritual nature. The theory of the four *purushārthas* sanctioned the pursuits of *artha* (wealth) and *kāma* (pleasure) provided they were guided and regulated by *dharma*. Unlike modern civilisation Indian civilisation developed a well-considered theory of man which enabled it to determine the objectives and limits of human activities and to assign them their legitimate place in life. No activity or area of life was allowed to transgress its boundaries and dominate the rest. Indian social and moral life therefore had a balanced structure, each of its elements standing in a clearly defined relationship with the rest.

Gandhi argued that the ancient Indians, who knew how to invent machines and develop industries, decided 'after due deliberation' to impose limits on their growth. They knew too that happiness was 'largely a mental condition' in no way dependent on external conditions, and restricted the pursuit of wealth. As he put it,

> Observing all this, our ancestors dissuaded us from luxuries and pleasures. We have managed with the same kind of plough as existed thousands of year ago. We have retained the same kind of cottages that we had in former times and our indigenous education remains the same as before.

What was for many of his contemporaries a cause of India's decline and a proof of its lack of dynamism was for Gandhi a source of its wisdom and moral courage. Indian civilisation in his view knew nothing of the soul-destroying cities and was based on self-governing villages within whose warm and communal framework their members lived cultured and stable lives.

For Gandhi Indian civilisation was essentially plural and non-dogmatic. From the very beginning it had realised that the ultimate reality was infinite and inexhaustible and that different individuals grasped different aspects of it. None was wholly wrong and none wholly right. Everyone was therefore left free, even encouraged, to live out the truth as he saw it and discover for himself its limits and possibilities. This was why, in his view, Hinduism did not believe in a one-off and definitive divine self-revelation and allowed its adherents full freedom of choice between different religious texts, conceptions of God and forms of worship. It did not regard its religious texts as incorrigible and final but open to new interpretations in the light of new experiences. Such authority as they possessed was based not on faith but on the knowledge that they embodied insights acquired by the spiritual scientists after years of systematic research and were capable of being confirmed by anyone prepared to undertake the required training. Gandhi thought that the much-maligned caste system too was, in its original and 'pure' form, a result of years of research into the nature of man and society and designed to create a social order based on the inelimin-able differences in the human temperament and level of moral and spiritual evolution.

In Gandhi's view Indian civilisation was not only plural but pluralist, that is, committed to pluralism as a desirable value; not just a collection of different ethnic, religious and cultural groups but a unity-in-diversity. Since it held that different men perceived the ultimate reality differently and that a richer view of it could only be attained by a dialogue between them, it not only tolerated but respected and welcomed diversity and encouraged discussion between its constituent groups. It was an open civilisation with permeable boundaries allowing new influences to flow in and vitalise the old, so that the new became part of the old, the old was discarded or vitalised, and the whole civilisation renewed itself. Over the centuries, Gandhi went on, the Indians 'blended with one another with the utmost freedom' and made India a microcosm of the world.[4] Their civilisation was a 'synthesis of different cultures', a happy family whose members, different in temperaments, habit and mode of thought, enjoyed a relaxed relationship and shared enough in common to wish and be able to live together in harmony.[5] It was not wholly Hindu, Muslim or Christian but a 'fusion' of all of them. Thanks to its history of tolerance and synthesis, a unique 'spirit' had grown up in India and become an integral part of its way of life. Indeed India had developed an unusual faculty, the 'faculty for assimilation', and an 'amazing tolerance of opposite ideas'.[6] When any new religion or culture appeared, it did not have to fight for survival or claw out a quiet corner. Instead all the others moved a little and gave it a secure space for growth. Not surprisingly even the most intolerant among them did not remain aggressive and exclusive for long. The 'dominant spirit' of Indian civilisation subtly and imperceptibly loosened their rigidity, smoothed their sharp edges and brought them in harmony with the rest.[7] For Gandhi to be on Indian soil was to breathe the refreshing air of infinite diversity and to watch with admiration and delight the most ingenious ways in which men and groups skilfully negotiated their relations, and the social order spontaneously adjusted itself to their demands without central co-ordination.

Gandhi had some difficulty explaining how India had acquired the synthetic spirit. Sometimes he pointed to its history and geography and thought that a vast and divided country subject to waves of foreign invasions could not help developing it as a very condition of its survival. More often, however, he attributed it to India's pluralist epistemology. Since it sincerely believed that truth was infinite, that all human perceptions of it were necessarily limited and partial and that respect for his moral integrity required that every individual should live by the truth as he saw it, India developed the spirit of not just tolerance but also mutual respect, curiosity and dialogue. Gandhi was convinced that epistemological pluralism was unique to India and had saved it from the dogmatism and arrogant proselytisation that had disfigured many great religions. He did not explain why India alone had succeeded in discovering and making it the basis of its way of life.

For Gandhi its epistemological pluralism was the key to India's long survival and its ability to come out not only unscathed but positively richer from the three 'mighty assaults' it had faced in its history, namely Buddhism, Islam and Christianity. In each case India imbibed 'whatever was good' in the three religions and emerged refreshed 'as one would rise out of a hot bath with a warm glow'.[8] Buddhism was an attack from within India and challenged many of the Hindu beliefs and practices. Initially it provoked a measure of hostility and even some resistance and violence. However, the traditional spirit of adjustment and reconciliation quietly set about bringing the two together, especially as the Buddhists relied on discussion and argument and the moral force of the 'very pure conduct of its preachers', both of which

greatly appealed to the Indian mind. Over time Hinduism reformed itself, Buddhism mellowed, and the two established a
relationship of trust and mutual respect.

Unlike Buddhism, Islam came from outside India and had a
'more profound' impact. It was dogmatic and aggressive and not
given to rational discussion. That alienated and limited its appeal
to the Indian mind. In desperation it used force which frightened
and alienated the Indians yet further and stifled the traditional
spirit of reconciliation and dialogue. Islam, however, had one great
advantage in its strong commitment to equality in both theory and
practice, and that had great attraction both for the Indian mind
which had long preached though rarely practised equality and
especially for the lower caste Hindus who had been denied basic
human dignity. Unlike many other Indian leaders Gandhi thought
that, although some of the Hindu conversions were forced, most
were voluntary. He observed:

> The key-note of Islam was, however, its levelling spirit. It
> offered equality to all that came within its pale. . . . When,
> therefore, about 900 years after Christ, his followers descended
> upon India, Hinduism stood dazed. It seemed to carry every-
> thing before it. The doctrine of equality could not but appeal to
> the masses, who were caste-ridden. To this inherent strength
> was also added the power of the sword.[9]

Gandhi's assessment of Muslim rule was less hostile than that of
many other Indian leaders. He agreed that the early Muslim
invaders and rulers had been oppressive, tyrannical and brutal,
but insisted that over time they had been won over by the synthetic
spirit of Indian civilisation. As they settled down, they entered into
a dialogue with their subjects, cultivated tolerance and absorbed
many a Hindu belief, value and social practice. This was facilitated
by the fact that most Muslims were converted Hindus and carried
the pluralist spirit to their new religion. Over time Islam became
'Indianised' infused with the 'spirit of the soil', and shed some of
its alien and aggressive features.[10] The Hindus 'flourished under
Moslem sovereigns and Moslems under the Hindus'. Not only at
the religious but also at the political level, the two communities
came close and forged common bonds of loyalty and sentiments.
'It was Hinduism that gave Mahomedanism its Akbar.'[11] Gandhi
conceded that they had fought from time to time but thought that

these had been basically 'quarrels between the brothers', born out of simple misunderstandings and lack of sensitivity. He argued that their quarrels had become more frequent and vicious since the second half of the 19th century, largely because of the British policy of 'divide and rule' and could be easily brought under control in independent India. Even when communal carnage raged all around him in the 1940s, Gandhi refused to reconsider his view. To have admitted that it had deeper and wider roots would have impugned the validity of his thesis about the synthetic spirit of Indian civilisation.

Gandhi explained Christian influence in similar terms.[12] When Christian missionaries first came to India, they were sincere men trying to spread their religion and in no way connected with the Raj. Their 'pure' lives, often better than those of their own religious leaders, deeply impressed the Hindus, and their message of love and brotherhood had a great attraction for them, especially the lower castes. Not surprisingly many Hindus, including some from the higher castes, converted to Christianity.[13] Once the British had consolidated their rule and the Christian missionaries came to be closely associated with it, they forfeited their moral authority and had to rely on force and bribes. Gandhi thought that, like the other two religions, Christianity stimulated internal reforms within Hindu society and religion and had on the whole a salubrious influence.[14] Like the others it too was bound over time to lose its alien features and become Indianised.

Gandhi's highly abstract and simplified account of Indian history was informed by several assumptions, of which four are relevant to our discussion. First, as a religious man himself he saw Indian history almost entirely in religious terms and neglected the momentous political and economic changes that had had a much greater impact. Even when he discussed the three religions he took little account of the large political upheavals associated with them and of which they were but a small part. Second, consistent with his belief that truth always prevails and derives its power and authority from the personal examples of those living by it, he attributed much of the influence of the three religions to their doctrines and the allegedly pure lives of some of their preachers. He ignored the far more decisive role played by such other factors as political and economic pressure, subtle and crude coercion, systems of patronage and the social tensions and political rivalries within Hindu society. Gandhi therefore could not explain why a large number of Hindus, including the lower castes, did *not* convert to Islam and why the conversions occurred in some parts of India but not others. He could not explain either why the conversions to Islam and Christianity followed different patterns and had very different consequences. Third, since most of the conversions had occurred among the lower castes who were desperately yearning for social equality, Gandhi concluded that they were the most volatile sections of Hindu society and could not be kept within the fold without a radical transformation of the Hindu moral and social order. For reasons we shall discuss later he also, however, thought that the caste system had not only held Hindu society together during trying times and in general served it well, but was basically good. Accordingly he argued that it should be retained but purged of its hierarchy and exclusiveness, an inherently self-contradictory and impracticable enterprise. Fourth, Gandhi's account of Indian civilisation and history equated India with Hindu India. The three 'assaults' he talked about were all on Hinduism, and the pluralist epistemology in which he located the essence of Indian civilisation was basically Hindu. The spirit of the soil was really the spirit of Hinduism. To be sure, Hinduism itself underwent great changes in response to the various challenges and both influenced and was in turn influenced by the other religions. However, it was the basis of the Indian identity as Gandhi saw it. As we shall see later his limited conception of Indian civilisation made it difficult for him to deal with the demand for the partition of the country.

In Gandhi's view every civilisation had its own distinctive natural and social basis. Modern civilisation was born and could only survive in the cities, and was naturally carried all over the world by the commercial classes. Indian civilisation had, by contrast, been cradled and nurtured in the villages, and only the rural masses were its natural custodians. So long as their way of life was intact, its integrity and survival was guaranteed. If the villages were to disappear and their traditional moral and social structure was to be shattered, it would lose its socio-geographical basis and its fate would be sealed for ever. Since the civilisations that had so far come to India were all rural and thus posed no threat to it, it was easily able to accommodate and enter into a dialogue with them. Modern urban civilisation presented a deadly and unprecedented challenge and required a most discriminating and cautious response.

Until Gandhi left South Africa for good, he had only a limited knowledge of the rural masses of India. He had little contact with them in his native Kathiawar, and his social and political life in South Africa was largely confined to the traders and to a lesser extent to indentured labourers. Like Nehru and many other Indian leaders his 'discovery of India' began on his return in 1915. He embarked on *'Bhārata-darshan'*, a voyage of spiritual discovery involving not only getting to know the country's people and problems but capturing a 'vision' of its innermost spirit and catching 'glimpses of India', as Nehru was to put it later. Given his view of Indian civilisation Gandhi brusquely pushed aside the illusory and glittering *māyā* of urban India that had long concealed its soul and decided to 'open up' and 'penetrate' the villages. During his travels, or rather pilgrimage, he came 'face to face' with and attained the *Sākshātkār* of the 'great people of India'. As he listened to them and organised their movements, he found that they 'overflowed with faith', had a 'deep reservoir of spirituality' and a 'profound knowledge of *dharma*' and manifested a quiet inner strength and a deep sense of contentment. 'The moment you talk to them . . . you will find that wisdom drops from their lips'.[15] He went on, 'an age-old culture is hidden under an encrustment of crudeness. Take away the encrustation, remove his chronic poverty and his illiteracy, and you will find the finest specimen of what a cultured, cultivated free citizen should be'. Although occasionally he got carried away, Gandhi could not avoid noticing that the peasants were not paragons of virtue. Leading a monotonous and 'awful' life which rarely stimulated their intellectual faculties, they had become 'like bullocks' and needed to be lifted 'from the estate of the brute to the estate of man'. He was, however, convinced that once their economic and educational conditions were improved, their dormant moral and spiritual resources could be 'awakened' and mobilised.[16]

Gandhi saw a 'living example' and 'direct demonstration' of the 'spiritual soul' of India in 1918 during the strike of the Ahmedabad textile workers, most of them first generation rural migrants. When they broke their solemn pledge to continue the strike until their demands were met, Gandhi appealed to their pride and moral values by deciding to fast, whereupon they were shaken, 'burst into tears' and reaffirmed their resolve whatever the cost. As he put it, they 'awoke to the reality of their soul, a new consciousness stirred in them, and they got strength to stand by their pledge. I was instantly persuaded that *dharma* had not vanished from India, that people do respond to an appeal to their soul'. Gandhi thought he had now discovered how to stir the deepest recesses of the Indian soul and tap its latent energies.

Gandhi argued that although Indian civilisation was still living and fundamentally sound, it was inevitable that a country so old and subjected to centuries of foreign rule, depriving it of the opportunities for healthy development, should develop serious 'defects' and 'excrescences'. As someone who loved it and wished to see it flourish, he thought he had a duty to expose and remedy them. He was deeply disturbed by the widespread tendency among his countrymen to gloat over their past achievements and either remain complacent about their current predicament or blame it all on the British and hope that their eventual departure would restore them to their ancient glory. Gandhi knew he had to counter this tendency if he was to create a space for national self-examination.

Commenting on the familiar list of achievements of the ancient Indians canvassed by a large array of writers from Rammohun Roy onwards, Gandhi argued that some of these were pure fantasies, products of an understandable but dangerous self-deception, and that even if they were all real, nothing followed. The past glory did not redeem the current degeneration. To the very contrary the greatness of their ancestors made the present generation of Indians look even more degenerate and heightened their sense of shame. The past glory was 'only humiliation and in the nature of a burden'.[17] Gandhi was even more scathing about the tendency to blame the British for India's sorry state. The degeneration had long preceded British rule and was largely responsible for the ease with which they had been able to conquer India. Furthermore, so long as the Indians held the British responsible, they were unlikely to do anything about it and it was bound to grow worse. Gandhi also argued that no individual or group could oppress, rule or exploit another without the latter's co-operation and that the victims were never wholly innocent. Whenever there was a coward, there was bound to be a bully. Rather than blame and hate the bully, the coward should more profitably turn his attention inward.

Gandhi drew up a lengthy catalogue of Indian defects covering the national character and Hindu society, culture and religion. Some of these had long been identified and campaigned against by the earlier generations of leaders; the others were new. Unlike them he was primarily concerned with the Indian character and concentrated on it. In Gandhi's view the Hindu social structure had become degenerate and thrown up both a plethora of excessively rigid and morbidly self-conscious castes obsessed with dietary and other taboos, and a cluster of such ugly practices as untouchability, child marriage, polyandry, sacrificial violence, a ban on foreign travel and temple prostitution. Hindu culture had become callous and the old experimental spirit that had once led to remarkable discoveries and vitalised it for centuries had suffered a decline. Hindu religion had become highly formal and rigid, grossly distorted by effete sentimentalism and replete with mindless rituals and ceremonies.[18] Gandhi was particularly exercised about the degeneration of the Indian, especially Hindu, character.[19] He had raised this question in South Africa and it remained his lifelong concern. 'The first thing we have to do is to improve our national character. No revolution is possible till we build our character'.[20]

For Gandhi courage was one of the highest human virtues and the Hindus had become woefully deficient in it. They lacked the physical courage to face dangers and stand up to a bully. 'I have been travelling all over India these days . . . It has not a particle of [the] courage it should have.'[21] The dacoits terrorised the villagers at will; if a wild animal appeared they ran to the government officer rather than deal with it themselves; they were even unable to defend their wives and children from robbers and bullies and passively prayed for mercy.[22] In Gandhi's view the Indians also lacked the intellectual courage to criticise and deviate from the established customs and conventions and to strike out on a lonely path of their own.[23] Gandhi particularly lamented the absence of moral courage, by which he meant the courage to stand up for what one considered to be right, irrespective of the consequences. In his view the Indians were so frightened to die or suffer injury that rather than dare their opponents to do their worst, they acquiesced in all manner of indignities and humiliations, including the violation of their self-respect and personal dignity. They 'would not fearlessly walk to the gallows or stand a shower of bullets and yet say, "we will not work for you"'.[24] Even in their ordinary social relations they were afraid to say 'no' lest they should offend others. 'I would have us treasure Lord Willingdon's advice and say "no" when we mean "no" without fear of consequences,' Gandhi advised his countrymen.[25]

The Indian's lack of courage was one of the important sources of his several other failings.[26] Like any other human being he had a clear notion of what was due to him and felt hurt when it was denied. However, since he was afraid to fight for it and content to live 'like a worm', he was constantly trampled on. He naturally resented this, and so he sulked and resorted to cynical and devious ploys to get his way. Afraid to offend others he rarely spoke his mind, dissimulated and resorted to hypocrisy. Gandhi thought that cowardice bred suspicion, distrust and jealousy. 'What I would rid ourselves of is distrust of one another and imputation of motives. Our besetting sin is not our differences but our littleness . . . It is not our differences that really matter. It is the meanness behind it that is undoubtedly ugly'.[27] Thanks to their jealousy and mutual distrust the Indians were most 'uncharitable to one another', and blaming others rather than themselves for their mistakes had 'become a second nature' with them.[28]

In Gandhi's view the Indians tended to be insensitive to the needs and feelings of others, especially those outside the narrow orbits of their families and castes. 'Selfishness dominates our action.' He had noticed this in Natal when the Indian traders were busy getting their licenses by 'underhand dealings' rather than launch a collective struggle against the discriminatory Licensing Act.[29] In his view the East India Company had been able to establish and consolidate its rule because the different groups of selfish Indians had done separate deals with it. 'And so have we remained more or less – more rather than less – up to today.' In Gandhi's view selfishness and insensitivity were also evident in such habits as the lack of punctuality, throwing rubbish on the road, careless use of public places, people relieving themselves in public and talking loudly.

Thanks to their preoccupation with narrow personal interests and mutual distrust, the Indians lacked the capacity to pursue a common cause. Everyone went his own way and resisted the discipline of a common organisation. They were 'like children in political matters . . . [who] do not understand the principle that the public good is also one's own good'.[30] They did not take a long-term view of their interests and appreciate that these were best secured within a larger organisational framework whose preservation benefitted them all. In Gandhi's view they only acted in a concerted manner when inspired and organised by great leaders and broke up into loose atoms once the latter disappeared.

Gandhi also pointed to the absence of a social conscience among his countrymen. They were 'callous' about the conditions of the poor and the underprivileged.[31] Their doctrine of the unity of man had remained merely 'philosophical' and was rarely practised, which is why a large number of lower-caste Hindus had embraced such egalitarian religions as Islam and Christianity. It was true that they had a deep reverence for life, but much of this was 'all sentimentalism'. It grew out of a 'superstitious horror of bloodshed' rather than a genuine love of men. Not surprisingly they avoided taking life but did 'little' to preserve and nurture it. The Jains, who talked so much about the sanctity of life and protested against killing animals, did little to help the poor and the weak and showed little mercy towards their enemies. Gandhi observed, 'We are all guilty of having oppressed our brothers. We make them crawl on their bellies before us, and rub their noses on the ground. With eyes red with rage we push them out of railway carriages. Has the English government ever inflicted anything worse on us?'[32]

Gandhi contended that, contrary to the general impression, there was a deep streak of violence in Indian culture. He chided his close friend C. F. Andrews for arguing that non-violence was the central theme of major Hindu scriptures. 'I see no sign of it in *Mahābhārata* and the *Rāmāyana*, not even in my favourite Tulsidas.' Gandhi admitted that these works could be read differently as he was himself to do later, but insisted that he was not thinking of their 'spiritual meanings' but the way they appeared to the average Indian reader. Rama and Krishna were 'certainly bloodthirsty, revengeful and merciless' and used all sorts of tricks to defeat their enemies. Although he read the *Gita* differently, he admitted from time to time that it too sanctioned extensive violence. Manu justified the use of violence against the lower castes, and even Shankaracharya used 'unspeakable cruelty in banishing Buddhism out of India'.[33] And so far as the Indian people were concerned, Gandhi saw 'no warrant' for the belief that non-violence had taken 'deep root' among them, as otherwise they would have shown 'some compassion' in their treatment of the poor, the lower castes and the untouchables.[34]

To avoid misunderstanding, Gandhi did of course say that non-violence was central to Indian civilisation in a way that was not true of any other. By this he meant four things. First, Indian civilisation cherished the ideal of non-violence and gave it pride of place in its hierarchy of moral virtues. Second, a small group of sages and seers had experimented with and successfully practised it in all its rigour and left behind examples of truly non-violent lives. Third, non-violence was widely practised in *ancient* India and formed the basis of its social structure. And fourth, although non-violence in the positive sense of active compassion was not much noticeable among the ordinary Indians of his time, it was present to some degree in the negative and passive sense of refraining from causing harm to living beings. Notwithstanding the general impression to the contrary, Gandhi rarely said that either Indian society or the bulk of the Indian people of *his time* were non-violent in the *active* and *positive* sense.[35] For him non-violence consisted in refraining from exercising the power to hit back and was a virtue of the brave. Those lacking in courage and bravery could be no more non-violent than a mouse in its relation to the cat. In urging his countrymen to adopt non-violence Gandhi was asking them to *return* to their ruptured tradition. For polemical purposes and in order to render his doctrine of non-violence more easily acceptable, he occasionally presented it as an integral part of the contemporary Indian way of life. He was, however, too shrewd to be seduced by his own rhetoric.

Gandhi summed up his assessment of the contemporary Indian character and society in the following brutally frank passages which deserve to be quoted in full.

What are our failings, then, because of which we are helpless and cannot stop the profuse flow of wealth from our country, and in virtue of which our children get no milk, three crores of our people get only one meal a day, raids occur in broad daylight in Kheda district, and epidemics like the plague and cholera cannot be eradicated in our country while they can in others? How is it that the haughty Sir Michael O'Dwyer and the insolent General Dyer can crush us like so many bugs and the priest in Simla can write unworthy things about us; how is it that an intolerable injustice has been done to us in the Punjab?

The reason is our inveterate selfishness, our inability to make sacrifices for the country, our dishonesty, our timidity, our hypocrisy and our ignorance. Everybody is selfish, more or less, but we seem to be more selfish than others. We make some self-sacrifice in family matters, but very little of it for national work. Just look at our streets, our cities and our trains. In all these, we can see the condition of the country. How little attention is paid to the convenience of others in streets, in the town as a whole and in trains? We do not hesitate to throw refuse out of our courtyard on to the street; standing in the balcony, we throw out refuse or spit, without pausing to consider whether we are not inconveniencing the passers-by. When we are building a house, we take little thought of the inconvenience that may be caused to our neighbours. In cities, we keep the tap open, and thinking that it is not our water which flows away, we allow it to run waste. The same thing is seen in the trains. We secure a seat for ourselves by hook or by crook and, if possible, prevent others from getting in. No matter if others are inconvenienced, we start smoking. We do not hesitate to throw banana skins and sugar-cane peelings right in front of our neighbours. When we go to draw water from a tap, we take little thought for others. Many such instances of our selfishness can be listed.

Where so much selfishness exists, how can one expect self-sacrifice? Does the business man cleanse his business of dishonesty for the sake of his country? Does he forgo his profit? Does he stop speculation in cotton for his country's sake? Is any effort made to keep down milk prices by giving up the profit from its export? How many give up a job when necessary, for the sake of the country?

Where are the men who will reduce their luxuries and adopt simplicity and use the money so saved for the country? If it is necessary for the country's sake to go to jail, how many will come forward?

Our dishonesty is there for all to see. We believe that business can never be carried on honestly. Those who have the chance never refuse a bribe. We have the worst experience of corruption in the railways. We can get our work done only if we bribe the railway police, the ticket master and the guard. Even for securing a railway ticket, we have to use dishonest means or shut one's eyes to them. The contents of railway parcels which can be opened ever so slightly, if not of those which are well-packed, are sure to be pilfered.

Our hypocrisy is only a little less than that of the British. We have experience of this every moment. In our meetings and in all other activities of our lives, we try to show ourselves other than what we are.

We have made cowardice especially our own. Nobody wants

bloodshed in connection with non-co-operation, and yet it is out
of this fear of bloodshed that we do not want to do anything. We
are possessed by the fear of the Government's armed might that
we dare not take any step. And so we submit to force in every
matter and allow dacoits to plunder us in broad daylight.

What shall I say about our hypocrisy? It has increased in every
field. Weakness is always accompanied by hypocrisy. Moreover,
where the people want to be upright but cannot be so, hypocrisy
will naturally increase; for, if we are not upright, we are anxious
to seem so and thus we add another moral weakness to the one
which we already possess. Hypocrisy had entered our religion as
well, and that so fully that the marks which we put on our
forehead, the rosary and things of that kind have ceased to be
tokens of piety and become signs of impiety.[36]

Like most of his predecessors Gandhi was strong on diagnosis
but weak on explanation. Since for a long time he saw nothing
wrong with the caste system and refused to blame Muslim rule, his
difficulty was greater. Some, especially the Hindu fundamentalists
had argued that India's degeneration dated from its acceptance of
the Buddhist teachings, above all the doctrine of non-violence.
Gandhi vehemently rejected this 'fashionable' view both because it
was 'untrue' and impugned the validity of his own message.
Sometimes he blamed such popular religious leaders as Swaminar-
ayana and Vallabhacharya for 'robbing us of our manliness' and
encouraging emotional self-indulgence. However he also said that
the other Vaishnavite leaders had the opposite influence. Sometimes he blamed the unworldliness of Hinduism, but on other
occasions he thought that it was not inherent in it and represented
a biased Brahmanic reading. He was not clear either about when
the Indian degeneration had begun. On one occasion he said that
Indian society had been in a 'rut almost since the days of the
Guptas', which was nearly 16 centuries ago! On other occasions
he argued that like every other society India had had its ups and
downs and that the current degeneration was relatively recent and
unlikely to last long. Gandhi had too little knowledge of Indian
history to be able to trace the sources and development and even
identify the character of Indian degeneration. More to the point, he
was far more interested in how to reverse it than what caused it,
and did not appreciate that the answer to the latter might throw
some light on the former.

For Gandhi then Indian civilisation, although fundamentally sound, had become degenerate and needed urgent attention. The national character had to be improved, the social structure made more just, religion reformed and its central values reinterpreted and related to the needs of the modern age. Following the earlier writers he sometimes called this 'national regeneration'. More often he preferred to use the historically evocative term *ātmashud-dhi*, a process of 'purging' the Indian soul of its limitations by means of a great national *tapasyā* or *yajna*. The theme of national regeneration had been in the air since at least the beginning of the 19th century, and different leaders had canvassed different ways of bringing it about. Some advocated a return to an unspecified golden age in the past, some others proposed a wholesale or subtantial adoption of Western civilisation, whereas most urged a creative synthesis of the two civilisations. Gandhi was out of sympathy with all three. He rejected the first because he could not see the relevance of the past. Every *yuga* or age had its own distinctive problems and needed to come to terms with them in its own way. For him as for Hindus in general the past was a source of inspiration and self-confidence, never a model or a blueprint for the present. One learned from it *how* to reinterpret the central insights of Indian civilisation and go about determining the *yugadharma*, not *what* the *yugadharma* for one's own age consisted in.

In Gandhi's view national regeneration could not be brought about by adopting modern civilisation either, not so much because the latter was inferior (although he thought it was), as because a civilisation must fit a society and represent its truth. It was not enough for it to be good *in itself*; it must also be good *for* the society concerned. Indian civilisation has grown up with the Indian people and reflected their unique and historically acquired *swabhāva*. It was woven into the structure of their soul, and the alternative of rejecting it in favour of the modern was simply not available to them.

Gandhi argued that although India could not and should not adopt modern civilisation, there was 'much' that it could 'profit-ably assimilate' from it. Since his position was often misunder-stood, he observed:

My resistance to Western civilisation is really a resistance to its indiscriminate and thoughtless imitation based on the assumption that Asians are fit only to copy everything that comes from the West.[37]

Gandhi was, however, most fearful of the eclectic adoption of Western values, institutions and practices. Unless Indians knew what to adopt or 'borrow' and why, the adoption was bound to be 'indiscriminate' and lead to the 'corruption' and eventual erosion of their civilisation. And they would not know what to borrow and how unless they had first acquired a full and unbiased knowledge of themselves. Gandhi shared the old Hindu fear of *varnasankara* or 'confusion' of castes resulting from people doing things to which they were unsuited and which they could not easily integrate into their ways of life and thought. In addition to the familiar form of *varnasankaratva* already occurring as a consequence of industrialisation, Gandhi also saw developing all around him a new variety of it. Enamoured of a civilisation wholly different to their own, his countrymen were indiscriminately borrowing its various elements and promiscuously combining them with their own. The result was *sanskritisankaratva* or *sanskārasankaratva*, a confusion of civilisations and hybridisation of national character threatening to produce a profound cultural schizophrenia. In Gandhi's view even the best and the most discriminating conservatives had unwittingly fallen prey to this. Tilak, for example, deeply loved and knew his ancestral culture and intended to reaffirm its central values. In actual fact he had swallowed a large dose of European civilisation. As Gandhi put it, Tilak

> has written on the inner meaning of *Gita*. But I have always felt that he has not understood the age-old spirit of India, has not understood her soul . . . Deep down in his heart he would like us all to be what the Europeans are. As Europe stands on top at present, as it seems, that is, to those whose minds are steeped in European notions, he wants India to be in the same position. He underwent six years' internment but only to display a courage of European variety, with the idea that these people who are tyranising over us now may learn how, if it came to that, we too could stand such long terms of internment, be it five years or twenty-five . . .[38]

Gandhi felt that even Pandit Madan Mohan Malaviya, one of the finest students and champions of Indian civilisation, had 'not properly understood the soul of India in all its grandeur' and unwittingly borrowed many a Western value and practice that really subverted its very basis.[39] He thought even less of such religious leaders as Dayananda Saraswati and Savarkar who had 'all too hastily' accepted some of the central values of modern civilisation, read them back into their own and subverted the very civilisation they claimed to defend.[40] Although some of them claimed otherwise, they were all infatuated with modern civilisation and thought that India's salvation ultimately lay in imitating it.

Gandhi did not think much of the grand project and cultural synthesis advocated by both the liberal and conservative leaders. The two civilisations had very different orientations and could not be integrated. Besides, since Indians lacked self-confidence and self-knowledge and were involved in an unequal relationship with the West, all attempts to synthesise the two were bound to end up in redefining their civilisation in terms of the modern. To talk of a synthesis, further, was to assume that they occupied an archimedean standpoint from where they were free to decide what to choose from which civilisation. This was absurd, for they were deeply rooted in their own, which they could certainly enrich but never transcend or treat as something external to them.

For Gandhi the only proper and realistic course of action open to India was to take a careful and critical look at itself in a 'discriminating conservative spirit'.[41] For the past few centuries India had become static, 'asleep', 'inert'. Thanks to its welcome contact with the West, it had both 'awakened' and gained access to the scientific spirit of inquiry. It must now turn inward, identify and critically reinterpret the central principles of its civilisation in the light of modern needs and use them as the basis of its carefully planned programme of regeneration. A dialogue with another civilisation should 'follow, never precede' an appreciation and assimilation of our own'. By reversing the process Indians risked looking at themselves through the distorting prism of the assumptions and categories of an alien civilisation and forming a wholly distorted and derivative view of themselves. When they had formed a clear and unprejudiced view of their heritage and identified its moral and cultural resources, they were in a position to decide what aspects of modern civilisation were good for them and capable of being integrated into their own. Once they felt convinced that some of its values and institutions met the requirement, they should courageously adopt them without in the least feeling guilty or nervous about doing so. This was not an act of 'imitation' or 'copying' widely condemned as a sign of the 'de-nationalised' Indian's sense of inferiority, nor of 'borrowing' widely criticised for its mechanical approach to social life, but of 'adaptation' to the constantly changing world, of 'growing' by learning from others.[42] 'Adaptability is not imitation. It means power of resistance and assimilation.'[43] Learning from others involved discrimination, deciding what to reject and resist as well as what to accept and assimilate. Assimilating some European ideas and practices did not amount to 'Europeanisation', the constant target of conservative Hindus. Europeanisation meant adopting the European way of life in preference to one's own; assimilating *some* of its values and practices *because* they were *freely* judged by Indians to be in their best *interest* was very different. Such an assimilation was an act of free choice and did not compromise India's moral autonomy; it was done in full knowledge of what India could easily absorb and hence not inauthentic; it was consistent with the synthetic spirit of its civilisation; above all it was in harmony with India's history, for only by remaining true to itself while learning from others had it managed to survive intact for over three millennia.[44]

For Gandhi Indian regeneration was an urgent and vital task. As he repeated on countless occasions, the British had not taken India; rather it had offered itself to them. Since *this* was the 'truth' behind the *māyā* of British rule, its self-regeneration was the *sine qua non* of its independence. Invoking the medical analogy of which he was very fond, Gandhi argued that even as a diseased body kept falling prey to new diseases and only the healthy organism had the capacity to resist foreign bodies, only the regenerated and healthy India had the capacity to shake itself free of foreign rule. So long as it remained weak and degenerate, it could not become independent and, if it somehow did, its inherently fragile independence was bound to remain vulnerable to new foreign invasions, external manipulation and internal unrest. Gandhi pointed to the ease with which the colonial government had exploited the indiscipline and internal divisions of Congress and the communal conflicts to weaken and frustrate the Non-Co-operation Movement of 1920. He felt convinced that India not only could not but *should* not become independent until it had, if not completely, at least substantially regenerated itself. He put the point well in *Navajivan* in 1922:

I am positively shaking with fear. If a settlement were to be

made, then where are we to go? Although I will miss no
opportunity of settlement, still after having come to know the
strength of India I am afraid of the settlement. What will be our
condition if settlement is made before we have been throughly
tested? It would be like that of a child prematurely born which
will perish in a short time. In Portugal, the Government was
changed in a moment as the result of a revolution, and in that
country, new revolutions are constantly occurring, and no one
constitution endures. In Turkey when all of a sudden the government was changed in the year 1909, congratulations came
from all sides, but this was only a nine days' wonder. The
change was like a dream. After that Turkey had to suffer much
and who knows how much more suffering is still in store for that
brave people. On account of this experience, I am often plunged
in anxiety.[45]

Gandhi's programme for Indian regeneration was highly complex
and involved a cluster of interrelated strategies of which cultivating
the *swadeshi* spirit, *satyāgraha* and the Constructive Programme
were the most important.[46] *Swadeshi*, a complex Hindu concept
with a long history, had been revived and widely used since at
least the Partition of Bengal in 1905. Gandhi took it over and so
redefined it as to offer an Indian alternative to the European
doctrine of nationalism.

For Gandhi every man was born and grew up in a specific
community with its own distinct ways of life and thought evolved
over a long period of time. The community was not a mere
collection of institutions and practices but an ordered and well-knit
whole informed by a specific spirit and ethos. It provided its
members with an organised environment vital for their orderly
growth, a ready network of supportive relationships, a body of
institutions and practices essential for structuring their otherwise
chaotic selves, foci for sentiments and loyalties without which no
moral life was possible and a rich culture. In these and other ways
it profoundly shaped their personalities, modes of thought and
feeling, deepest instincts and aspirations and their innermost
being. Every community in turn was inextricably bound up with a
specific natural environment within which it had grown up, which
had cradled and nursed it and in the course of interacting with
which it had developed its distinctive customs, habits and ways of

life and thought. The natural environment was not external to it but integrated into its history and culture and suffused with its collective memories, images, hopes and aspirations. As Gandhi put it, a community's culture or way of life constituted its soul or spirit and its natural habitat its body. The two formed an indissoluble unity and the inescapable basis of human existence.

Gandhi used the term *Swadesh* to refer to this unity, *swa* meaning one's own and *desh* the total cultural and natural environment of which one was an inseparable part.[47] *Desh* was both a cultural and an ecological unit and signified the traditional way of life obtaining within a specific territorial unit. The territorial reference was as important as the cultural. *Desh* did not mean a state or a polity for a way of life might not be organised in such a manner; nor a mere piece of territory unless it was inhabited and culturally appropriated by a community of men sharing a common way of life; nor a cultural group unless it occupied a specific territorial unit and its cultural boundaries coincided with the territorial. The castes, religions and cultures constituting the Indian mosaic were not *deshas*; India, a civilisational-cum-territorial unit, uniting them all in terms of a common way of life was. In classical Indian political thought every territorial unit distinguished by a distinct way of life was called a *desh* and India was a *desh* composed of smaller *deshas*, each a distinct cultural and ecological unit but united with the others by a shared civilisation. Gandhi agreed except that he thought of the constituent units as *pradeshas* or subordinate or *quasi-deshas*.

The *swadeshi* spirit which Gandhi variously translated as the community, national or patriotic spirit or the spirit of nationality and sharply distinguished from nationalism, basically referred to the way an individual related and responded to his *desh*.[48] Since he was profoundly shaped by and unintelligible outside it, he should accept the inescapable fact that it was the necessary basis and context of his existence and that he owed his humanity to it. He should show a basic existential loyalty and gratitude to it and accept his share of the responsibility to preserve its integrity. He should recognise himself as an heir to the countless generations of men and women whose efforts and sacrifices made it what it is and cherish his heritage in the spirit of familial piety.[49] Even as he inherits his physical features, bodily constitution and natural endowments and should accept them as facts of life without a sense of shame or arrogance, he inherits his *desh* with all its strengths and limitations and should accept it without self-glorification or self-pity. This did not mean that he should turn a blind eye to or remain uncritical of its limitations any more than self-respect implied indifference to one's weaknesses. Gandhi insisted that since a man imbued with the *swadeshi* spirit loved his community and wanted it to flourish and realise its full potential, he could never be insensitive to its limitations; on the contrary, he was intensely alert to them lest they should cause its degeneration and decline. His was, however, not the criticism of an indifferent or hostile outsider only interested in denigrating or making fun of it, but of one who passionately cared for his community and intuitively understood and accepted responsibility for it. He sought to change it not because he was in love with some other to which he wanted it to conform, but because he wanted it to be true *to itself* and knew that it had the resources to become better. Gandhi's reaction to Katherine Mayo's highly vituperative *Mother India* was a good example of what he meant by the *swadeshi* spirit. He called it a gutter inspector's report which the British rulers should forget but the Indians should always remember.

For Gandhi the *swadeshi* spirit extended to all the elements composing the *desh* and implied a love of not only the traditional way of life but also the natural environment and especially the people sharing it. The integrity of a way of life was inextricably bound up with that of its ecological context and could not be preserved without preserving the latter. A man who claimed to love his *desh* but saw nothing wrong in savagely altering its environment and disrupting its unity was profoundly inconsistent and lacking in the *swadeshi* spirit. The *swadeshi* spirit also required that he should be passionately concerned with the way the other members of his community lived. They were an integral part of his *desh* and bound to him by the deepest bonds. To love his *desh* was to love them. He should therefore identify himself with them, especially the least privileged who most need his attention, eschew comforts and privileges unavailable to them, buy locally produced in preference to foreign goods likely to throw them out of work, and in general do all in his power to create and sustain a decent existence for them. For Gandhi the *swadeshi* spirit was not a sentimental attachment to an abstraction called India or Britain but an active love of the men and women sharing and sustaining a way of life, and had a moral, economic and political content. A man who loved Indian food, customs, traditions and way of life but remained indifferent to the plight of the people who collectively made all these possible was guilty of moral hypocrisy and gravely deficient in the *swadeshi* spirit.[50]

For Gandhi the *swadeshi* spirit did not imply indifference let alone hostility to other *deshas*. As a moral being every individual had a duty to be deeply interested in the problems faced by people in other communities. And even as he cared for his *desh* he had a duty to do all he could to preserve the integrity of their ways of life. Gandhi was, however, deeply wary of abstract internationalism. Every man was a part of a specific community which he under-stood better than he did others and whose members had a prior though not exclusive claim on him. They must therefore remain his primary though not sole concern. Gandhi thought that some form of moral division of labour was inescapable and that each community must look after its own members. He did not see why that should ever lead to the exploitation of or even conflicts of interests with other communities. The earth provided 'enough for everybody's needs but not enough for anybody's greed'. Unless a community demanded more than its legitimate share of the earth's resources, no conflict of interests need occur. Gandhi distinguished between self-interest and selfishness. The former referred to legitimate needs, that is, to those material and other opportunities all men needed in order to realise their human potential and to which they were entitled to make legitimate claims; the latter referred to illegitimate greed, that is, to those opportunities that far exceeded the level of legitimate needs, could not be universalised and could only be secured at the expense of others. The *swadeshi* spirit sanctioned legitimate self-interest but not selfishness.

Gandhi used the term *swarāj* to describe a society run in the *swadeshi* spirit.[51] It meant self-rule or autonomy and implied not only formal independence but also cultural and moral autonomy. A culturally parasitic community living in the shadow of and constantly judging itself by the standards of another might be independent but it lacked integrity, *swadeshi* spirit and *swarāj*. As Gandhi put it, under *swarāj* a community lived by its own truth. It conducted its affairs in the light of its traditions and values while remaining fully alert to their limitations and ready to learn from others. It was both rooted and open, the two ideas recurring with great regularity in his writings. If a society was not rooted, it was swept off its feet by every passing fashion and remained chaotic. If it was not open, it lacked 'fresh air', smelt stale and decayed.

Hence Gandhi often compared *swarāj* to a house with its windows and doors open. One cannot live in the open, but one cannot live in a closed house either. As the *Rigvedic* prayer Gandhi was fond of quoting put it, 'may the noble winds from all over the world blow into our house.'

The *Satyāgraha* was the second important constituent of Gandhi's programme of national self-purification. Since we shall discuss it at length later, we shall only comment here on one relevant aspect of it. When he started campaigning against the racially discriminatory laws in South Africa, Gandhi discovered that his countrymen there lacked personal and communal self-respect, courage and the willingness to organise themselves. In a memorable phrase he urged them to 'rebel' against themselves and warned them that, if they behaved like worms, they should not blame others for trampling on them. It was in this context that he had hit on the method of *satyāgraha*. 'The purpose of *satyāgraha* is to instil courage into people and make them independent in spirit'. On his return to India he found that the problems were even more acute. On the one hand the colonial government was firmly entrenched, arrogant, heavily armed and not at all like the weak governments of Natal and the Transvaal. On the other hand the Indians were much more divided and weak and just as deficient in courage, self-respect, personal and collective discipline and the spirit of self-sacrifice. He seems to have felt that the method he had developed in South Africa was inadequate and needed a radical revision. Non-violence could not be practised by cowards lacking the courage to hit back. Gandhi wondered how courage, manliness, self-discipline and pride could be cultivated among Indians and toyed with the idea of military training. Since the soldier possessed all the qualities he was looking for, he thought that if Indians received military training they too could cultivate them.[52] Even as 'you cannot make a dumb man appreciate the beauty and the merit of silence', you cannot 'teach *ahimsā* to a man who cannot kill'. He went on, 'It may look terrible but it is true that we must, by well-sustained conscious effort, regain this power [to kill] and then, if we can only do so, deliver the world from its travail of *himsā* by a continuous abdication of this power.'[53] Gandhi even thought that war was not an unmitigated evil and had a vital role to play in the development of national character. He realised that his 'terrible discovery' involved him in a contradiction. As a votary of non-violence he wanted his countrymen to fight non-violently, yet he wanted them to undergo a training in violence in order to acquire the required virtues! He appreciated too that war and military training were fraught with dangerous consequences including the fact that once a man was taught to kill he did not fancy dying without a good fight. Not surprisingly Gandhi felt utterly confused and complained to a close friend that the 'hard thinking' he had been doing was wrecking his health.[54]

After considerable reflection he concluded that, if properly refashioned, the method of *satyāgraha* he had discovered in South Africa provided the answer. It had all the advantages and none of the disadvantages of military training and cultivated 'manliness in a blameless way'. It could be conducted at various levels and with varying degrees of intensity, it made flexible demands on the participants ranging from attendance at a protest meeting to the sacrifice of life, women and even children could participate in it and acquire the desired qualities, it relied on the strength of numbers which India had in plenty, and it could easily be withdrawn if found to be getting nowhere. Again it required courage, but not of the heroic kind. It often involved injury, but not necessarily death, and the courage it required was based on the quiet obstinacy and tenacity of purpose characteristic of Indians, especially the rural masses. The *satyāgraha* had the further advantage that it 'never failed'. Since it did not threaten the government, it denied the latter the excuse to use indiscriminate and massive force that would easily frighten and demoralise a nervous and long-supressed people. If the government did become brutal, it forfeited domestic and international good will; if it gave in, the masses gained a sense of power. As Gandhi put it the *satyāgraha* was a 'trump-card' and particularly suited to India. As he put it after his first *satyāgraha* in India, he did not tell the people involved that they were about to stage one; he led the protest along the lines they were used to and told them later that they had in fact launched a *satyāgraha*. Gandhi's method of *satyāgraha* was a fascinating example of the *swadeshi* spirit. Instead of making excessive demands and lambasting his countrymen for lacking certain abstractly desirable qualities of character, he gratefully accepted and built on those they had in plenty. And rather than lament their incapacity to conform to an ideally desirable method of political action, he took over and subtly transformed their accustomed forms of protest.[55]

The third element in Gandhi's strategy of national regeneration was what he called the Constructive Programme.[56] It was 'designed to build up the nation from the very bottom upward' and regenerate India's society and economy. It was a mixed bag of such 'absolutely essential' 18 items as Hindu-Muslim unity, the removal of untouchability, a ban on alchohol, the use of khadi, the development of village industries and craft-based education. It also included equality for women, health education, the use of indigenous languages, the adoption of a common national language, economic equality and trusteeship, building up peasants' and workers' organisations, integration of the tribal people into mainstream political and economic life, a detailed code of conduct for students, helping lepers and beggars and cultivating respect for animals.

Although some of these items were rather trivial and did not measure up to the gravity of the situation, none was without value. For example, the use of *khādi* was intended to provide a national uniform and create at least a measure of outward equality in a highly unequal society, to introduce simplicity in an ostentatious society, to generate a sense of solidarity with the poor, to bring economic pressure on the British government and to reduce foreign imports. The use of regional languages was intended to bridge the vast and widening chasm between the masses and the Westernised elite, to ensure cultural continuity, encourage authenticity of thought and action and to forge indigenous tools of collective self-expression. The development of village industries was intended to help the poor in the villages, to guarantee them not only a livelihood but also employment, to arrest migration to the cities and, above all, to sustain what Gandhi took to be the necessary social and geographical basis of Indian civilisation. Some of the other items were more important and urgent, but Gandhi had little to say that was original or likely to yield the desired results. For example, he naïvely thought that Hindu-Muslim unity could be brought about by 'personal friendship' and each refraining from doing whatever was likely to offend the other. For many years he also thought that untouchability could be eradicated by propaganda and personal example, and that poverty could be removed by persuading the rich to look on themselves as trustees of their property.

Although several items in the Constructive Programme had only a limited practical impact, its symbolic and pedagogical value was considerable. First, for the first time during the struggle for independence, Indians were provided with a clear, albeit limited, statement of social and economic objectives. Second, they were specific and within the range of every one of them. In a country long accustomed to finding plausible alibis for inaction, Gandhi's highly practical programme had the great merit of ruling out all excuses. Third, his constant emphasis on it reminded the country that political independence had no meaning without comprehensive national regeneration, and that all political power was ultimately derived from a united and disciplined people. Finally, the Constructive Programme enabled Gandhi to build up a dedicated group of grass-roots workers capable of mobilising the masses.

As Gandhi understood them *satyāgraha* was primarily concerned with the moral and political, and the Constructive Programme with the social and economic regeneration of India, and the *swadeshi* spirit was the overarching principle inspiring and guiding them. The 'diseased' and weak India required a drastic 'medicine' and a rigorous programme of 'body building', and Gandhi thought that his tripartite prescription provided both. 'He is a true physician who probes the cause of disease, and if you pose as a physician for the disease of India, you will have to find out its true cause.'[57] Dr Gandhi fancied himself as a national physician who had accurately diagnosed India's disease and knew how to restore it to health and build up its strength.

For nearly 30 years Gandhi devoted all his energies to the implementation of his master plan. He knew what he needed and set about achieving it. He required a powerful and united team of men and women with complementary talents, and skilfully identified, nurtured and welded them. He needed a journal to carry his message in his own words, and so he started and edited one himself. He required funds, and so he discovered, cultivated and shrewdly managed India's half dozen richest industrialists. He needed to awaken and unite his countrymen, and so he initiated a series of well-phased and well-planned *satyāgrahas*, each mobilising a clearly targeted constituency. He needed a mass following which he secured by transforming his way of life and evolving an easily comprehensible and highly evocative mode of symbolic discourse. No other leader before him had worked out such a clear and comprehensive strategy for tackling India's problems, and none possessed either his massive self-confidence or his skill in developing the indispensible organisational and communicational tools. It was hardly surprising that Gandhi should have exercised unparalleled influence on Indian political life for nearly a quarter of a century.

3

Philosophy of Religion

Although Gandhi grew up in a devout and educated Vaishnavite family, his knowledge of Hinduism was extremely limited. He had learnt little Sanskrit, was innocent of Hindu philosophy and had not even read the *Gita* until persuaded to do so in England by two theosophists. It was only when he went to South Africa that he began to take serious intellectual interest in Hinduism. As he admitted to a lay preacher, 'I am a Hindu by birth. And yet I do not have much knowledge of where I stand and what I do or should believe and intend to make a careful study of my own religion.' His employer Abdulla Sheth pressed Islam on his attention, and he read the Koran and several commentaries on it. Finding that he was troubled by and unable to offer a coherent defence of his religious beliefs, some of his enthusiastic Christian contacts sought to convert him. Gandhi dutifully read all the books they gave him, even attended the church and participated in discussions on the comparative merits of the two religions. The book that most impressed him was Tolstoy's *The Kingdom of God is Within You* before whose 'independent thinking, profound morality and truthfulness' all other religious books 'seemed to pale into insignificance'. The three qualities he found in Tolstoy's book give a fairly good idea of what he then and all his life looked for in a religion. Although deeply impressed by Christianity, Gandhi remained 'utterly' unpersuaded by it. As he put it,

My difficulties went deeper. I could not swallow the belief that Jesus Christ alone was the son of God and that only those believing in him could attain salvation. If God could have Sons, then we are all His sons. If Jesus was like God or indeed God himself, every man is like God and can become God. The intellect simply cannot literally accept the view that the sins of the world can be washed away by the death or blood of Jesus, although metaphorically the view may contain truth. Again,

65

according to the Christian belief only the human beings have souls, not the other living beings for whom death means total extinction. My own belief was quite different. I could accept Jesus as a renouncer, a great soul, a devine teacher, but not as one without an equal. His death was a great example to the world, but I could not accept that there was some mysterious or miraculous power in it. I did not find anything in the pure lives of the Christians that I could not find in those of the adherents of other faiths. I have seen their lives changing in just the same way as those of the Christians. So I did not see anything extraordinary in the Christian principles. So far as the spirit of renunciation was concerned, I thought the Hindus had an edge. I could not accept Christianity as a perfect or the greatest religion. Even as I could not accept Christianity, I could not make up my mind either about Hinduism being the perfect or greatest religion. Its limitations were clearly evident to me. If untouchability was really a part of Hinduism, then it was certainly an excrescence, and a corruption. I could not make sense of the multiplicity of sects and castes. What could be the meaning of saying that the Vedas were divinely inspired? And if they were so inspired, why not also the Bible and the Koran.[1]

It was in this state of confusion that Gandhi wrote to Raichand-bhai, the only man who came close to being his *guru*, and to several other religious leaders in India. Like many Hindus, Gandhi thought that religion was a matter of conduct not doctrines, and turned for guidance to those who in his view had tried to live by rather than written books about it. He asked Raichandbhai 24 questions, all metaphysical and indicative of his perplexed and diffident state of mind. Some related to the meaning and basis of Hindu beliefs, whereas others solicited his views on several crucial Christian doctrines. It would seem that his Christian friends had successfully challenged the Hindu concept of *moksha*, for in nearly a quarter of the questions he asked to know what it meant and how he could be sure that he was progressing towards it. Raichand-bhai's reply 'pacified' him, especially his conviction based on a 'disinterested investigation' of 'all' religions that Hinduism excel-led them in its philosophical profundity, the analysis of the nature of the soul and the spirit of compassion. Gandhi read the books on Hinduism and Jainism he had sent him, but not yet the basic philosophical texts and the epics, only some of which he managed to read later in life. Over time he read and deeply reflected on the literature of all the major religions, especially Hinduism and Christianity, the two religions to which he was most attracted, and developed a fascinating philosophy of religion. For Gandhi religion was essentially concerned with how one lived, not what one believed. Accordingly he experimented with whatever religious ideas appealed to him, rigorously tested their 'truth' in the crucible of daily life and explored their existential potential and limits. His philosophy of religion was born out of sustained reflection on his experiences. It was theoretically untidy but had the authenticity of a lived reality.

Gandhi's conception of God was extremely complex and unintelligible outside the framework of the Indian religious tradition by which it was profoundly influenced. It would be useful therefore to begin with a brief and inevitably sketchy outline of the latter. Before we do that a brief note of caution is in order.

The concept of God is deeply problematic, not only because it is difficult to assign clear meaning to it but also because it is differently defined in different religious traditions. The difficulty becomes particularly acute in the case of the Indian religious tradition which is not amenable to the categories abstracted from or developed within the framework of the monotheistic semitic religions. The early Christian missionaries discovered this but learnt little from it when they asked the Hindu *pandits* whether they believed in one God or many. The latter rejoined that the question was blasphemous and absurd. Even as colour, gender, height, size and such other qualities did not apply to God, the quantitative categories could not be applied either. He was both one and many, yet also neither. To insist that He *must* be one was to reduce Him to the limited proportions of the human mind and thus to detract from His dignity. Furthermore the question was predicated on the unsubstantiated assumption that God was a being or a person. If he was conceived instead as power or energy, the question made as much sense as whether air, energy or light was one or many. The Hindu pandits, many of whom were trained in the formidable Buddhist logic, went on to argue that since the entire universe was regulated and pervaded by God, everything in it was divine or God-like. There was therefore nothing improper in calling it a god, a limited manifestation of the supreme God, and using it as a way of reaching up to Him. Even the Christian view that the human soul represented a spark or a particle of God implied that every man was a god. The obvious lesson of this fascinating exchange is that every religious tradition must be understood in its own terms and asked questions growing out of its own structure of thought.

Almost right from its recorded beginning Indian religious tradition conceived the supreme power or God in both personal and impersonal terms. The *Vedas* conceived it as both *rta*, the objective and impersonal law regulating the universe, and *Vishvakarmā*, the supreme creator of the universe.[2] The Vedantic philosophy, consisting of the *Upanishads*, the *Brahma Sutras* and the *Gita*, collectively known as *Prasthanatrayi*, also subscribed to both views, albeit in a much more refined form. Although Indian religious tradition enjoined on the commentators on the three bodies of texts an obligation to stress their unity and distil a common set of doctrines, the texts gestured in different directions and gave rise to different schools of thought founded by such men as Saṁkara, Rāmānuja, Nimbārka, Mādhava and Vallabha. The schools differed greatly on the nature of the supreme power. However, they all showed sympathy for both the personal and impersonal conceptions of it.

For Samkara the *Brahman* or the supreme power was *nirguna*, or without qualities. Since the qualities qualified and limited their bearer, and since they were conceived and attributed from a specific point of view and relativised it, he argued that they could not be attributed to the *Brahman* who could therefore only be described negatively, as 'not this, not this'. It was beyond good and evil, indifferent to human concerns, uninvolved in the affairs of the world and a disinterested, dispassionate and detached witness. It was embodied in man in the form of *ātman*, loosely and inaccurately translated as soul. The *ātman* was not a particle, spark or part of the *Brahman*; it was the *Brahman*. As the Upanishadic philosophers put it, *Tat Tvam Asi* (Thou Art That) and *Aham Brahmasmi* (I am the *Brahman*). For Saṁkara the *Brahman* could not be an object of prayer or worship because worship presupposed both a Being to be worshipped, which the Brahman was not, and a conceptual distance between the worshipper and the worshipped, which did not obtain when the *ātman* and the *Brahman* were one. For Samkara, it was exceedingly difficult for the limited human mind used to the world of qualities to grasp the concept of the quality-free *Brahman*. It could not also avoid asking who created the universe and seeking guidance from a transcendental source. The result was *saguna Brahman*, the quality-bearing or personalised

Brahman, the *Brahman* seen from the practical and worldly stand-point or *vyavahārika-drsti*. Samkara's distinction between the two conceptions of *Brahman* was formally somewhat like Spinoza's distinction between substance and God and Hegel's between the Absolute and God.

The critics of Samkara found the concept of impersonal God challenging but indeterminate and abstract. Accordingly they stressed the *saguna Brahman* or personal God and such related notions as creation, divine grace (*prasād*), love, mercy, worship, devotion, self-surrender (*saranāgati*) and resignation to the divine will (*ārta-prapatti*). However, none of them was able to reject the *nirguna Brahman* altogether. Rāmānuja, the most powerful critic of Samkara, had to concede that the attribution of personality and person-like qualities to the *Brahman* limited and relativised it. He also realised that the concept of *saguna Brahman* made it exceedingly difficult for him to establish an internally differentiated but substantive unity between the *Brahman*, man and the world. If God was a person, Ramanuja could not show how the *jiva* could be wholly dependent on Him, and his distinction between the *para* and *apara* only compounded his difficulties. Vaishnavism had fully developed in his time and he sought to give it *Vedantic* legitimacy. Within the *Vedantic* framework some form of *advaita* metaphysic was inescapable, and not surprisingly the concept of *nirguna Brah-man* or impersonal God lurks behind Rāmānuja's brave synthesis. Mādhava and Vallabha faced similar difficulties at different levels and fared little better.

Indian thinkers then were attracted to both the *nirguna* and *saguna Brahman*, to what I have for reasons of convenience called impersonal and personal conceptions of God. Although most of them were convinced that no inconsistency was involved in hold-ing both, different writers demonstrated the consistency in dif-ferent but related ways.[3] For many of them the impersonal con-ception of God was extremely difficult to grasp; the personal God made its comprehension easier and was a necessary stepping stone to it. Some argued that man was endowed with both the head and the heart, the intellect and feeling, and each had its distinct requirements and way of comprehending God. The *nirguna Brah-man* alone was a philosophically coherent concept and satisfied the intellect, whereas the *saguna Brahmana* alone met man's religious need and satisfied the heart. Some writers argued that thought and action represented different points of view and entailed different conceptions of God. Thinking required detachment from the object thought about, and hence *qua* thinking being man was inescapably attracted to the 'passionless' and impersonal *Brahman*; by contrast action required faith, energy, passion, hope and solace in moments of despair, and only the *saguna Brahman* provided these. Some others argued that man was an ambiguous being who could not avoid looking at the world both from the human point of view and, as a being endowed with the capacity for self-transcendence, *sub specie eternitatis*. The former generated the concept of the *saguna*, the latter that of the *nirguna Brahman*. For yet others the *Brahman* was the only ultimate reality and man was really the *ātman*. Since, however, man was an embodied being and thought of himself as a person or an independent self, he endowed the *Brahman* too with personality. The more he transcended the consciousness of self-hood, the more unsatisfactory he found the personal *Brahman*.

Like most Indian thinkers Gandhi subscribed to both the impersonal and personal conceptions of God. His language, however, was all his own. Although he sometimes used the term *Brahman*, he was somewhat uneasy with its historical associations and preferred to use such terms as eternal principle, supreme consciousness or intelligence, mysterious force and cosmic power, spirit or *shakti*.[4] Later in life he preferred to call it *Satya* or Truth and thought that this was its 'only correct and fully significant' description. Following Indian philosophical tradition, Gandhi used the term *satya* to mean the eternal and unchanging, what alone persists in the midst of change and holds the universe together. For a long time he had said that 'God is Truth', implying both that Truth was one of God's many properties and that the concept of God was logically prior to that of Truth. In 1926 he reversed the proposition and said that 'Truth is God'.[5] He regarded this as one of his most important discoveries and thought that it crystallised his years of groping. The new proposition implied that the concept of Truth was prior to that of God, and that calling it God did not add anything new to it but only made it more concrete and comprehensible to the human mind. Although Gandhi's reversal of the earlier proposition has given rise to much discussion and speculation, it was really a self-conscious and belated recognition of the distinction central to Indian religious tradition and coincided with his greater understanding of it. Following the long line of Indian thinkers he intended to distinguish between the impersonal and personal conceptions of God, and preferred to call the *nirguna Brahman* Truth. Since the term Truth is likely to create confusion I shall use the more familiar terms cosmic spirit or power.

For Gandhi the *Brahman*, Truth or cosmic spirit was *nirguna*, beyond all qualities including the moral. As he put it. 'Fundamentally God is indescribable in words . . . The qualities we attribute to God with the purest of motives are true for us but fundamentally false.'[6] And again, 'beyond the personal God there is a Formless Essence which our reason cannot comprehend.' The Formless Essence or cosmic spirit was not a 'personal being', and to think that it was represented a mistaken and 'inferior' conception of its nature.[7] Although the cosmic power was without qualities, including personality, Gandhi argued that such a limited being as man found it difficult to avoid attributing them to and personalising it.[8] First, the human mind was so used to the world of qualities that it did not find it easy to think in non-qualitative terms. Second, man was not only 'a thinking but also a feeling being and the 'head' and the 'heart' had different requirements.[9] The quality-free cosmic power satisfied the head but was too remote, abstract and detached to satisfy the heart. The heart required a being with heart, one who could understand and respond to the language of feeling.[10]

Gandhi articulated the nature of the cosmic spirit in the following terms.[11] First, it was a 'pure' or non-embodied consciousness, not the consciousness of some *Being*, for the latter would then have to be other than consciousness, but rather consciousness *simpliciter*. Second, it acted in a law-like manner in the sense that it was never arbitrary or capricious.[12] Third, it was active and represented infinite *shakti* or energy. Fourth, it pervaded, informed and structured the universe. Fifth, it was 'benevolent'. Since the cosmic spirit is supposed to be beyond good and evil, it is not entirely clear what Gandhi meant by calling it benevolent and whether he could consistently so describe it. He seems to have thought that although it was beyond good and evil in the conventional moral sense and its actions were not amenable to moral evaluation, the very facts that the universe functioned in a stable and law-like manner, made life possible, was conducive to the well-being of all living beings and offered the necessary conditions for a good life showed that it had a structural bias towards good and was regulated by a well-meaning spirit. When its actions appeared cruel in human terms as in the case of natural calamities, they should not be hastily judged but accepted as part of an incomprehensible but basically benevolent design. Finally, the cosmic power was 'mysterious' in the sense that although men could acquire some knowledge of it, they could never fully grasp or describe its nature and manner of operation. When Gandhi said that he believed in Truth or cosmic spirit, he meant to say that an active, all-powerful, benevolent and partially comprehensible intelligence operating in a law-like manner was at work in the universe. Since the cosmic spirit was not a person or a Being, Gandhi sometimes referred to it as 'it'. Since it was not inanimate and represented intelligence, he also referred to it as 'He'.

Like most Hindu thinkers Gandhi defined the eternal principle in non-volitionalist terms and largely as a rational principle of order or *rta*. It was not a Being but a Law, an active and self-powered Law, an intelligent principle of order. As Gandhi put it, 'there can be no manner of doubt that this universe of sentient beings is governed by a Law. If you can think of Law without its Giver I would say that the Law is the Lawgiver, that is God.' And again, 'He and His Laws are one. The Law is God'.[13] Cosmic power structured and regulated the universe by means of natural laws. At one level, the laws were natural or 'mechanical'; at another they were 'rational' in the sense that they represented and embodied the cosmic spirit. As Gandhi put it, there was a 'spiritual law behind natural laws'. The fact that the natural laws were unchanging and conducive to the preservation of the universe indicated that they were not 'blind' but vehicles of an intelligent principle. The spiritual law did not and could not override the natural laws as the cosmic spirit would then be guilty of contradicting Himself. Indeed, that He cannot disregard His own laws is 'an indispensible condition of His very perfection'. This was why Gandhi rejected miracles and thought that the religions that stressed them diminished God's rationality and dignity.

The distinctive nature of Gandhi's conception of cosmic power would become clearer if we compared it with the better known Christian view of God. In its standard and popular version, the latter stresses His three features. First, God is an extra-cosmic being who pre-exists and is outside the universe. Second, He creates and imposes laws on the universe and ensures its orderly existence. Third, He is not only infinitely loving but also infinitely powerful, for to create and impose laws on the sun and the stars and the seas is obviously a dazzling and awe-inspiring display of power. The three features are closely related. As the creator of the universe, God is necessarily extra-cosmic, and power is obviously one of the most striking qualities of the creator and regulator of a vast universe.

Like many Hindu thinkers, Gandhi viewed cosmic power differently. Since the universe for him was eternal, the question was not one of creating but ordering and structuring it. His God was therefore not a creator but a principle of order, a supreme intelligence infusing and regulating the universe from within. Unlike a supreme Being who can and perhaps must be extra-cosmic, a principle of order cannot be. As Gandhi put it, 'God is not some person outside ourselves or away from the universe, He pervades everything, . . . [is] immanent in all things'. Like most Hindus, further, Gandhi was puzzled not so much by the material world as by living beings, not by the rhythmic and orderly movement of the stars and the seas but the baffling phenomenon of life with its 'mysterious' origins, immensely diverse forms and their ingenious and complex mechanisms. It is worth noting that the term *Brahman* itself is derived from the root *brh*, meaning to grow, to spread out, to burst forth, and the *ātman* originally meant breath or life force. Gandhi was fascinated by the facts that the world should throw up life at all and that living beings should adapt themselves to their environment with such ease. Not surprisingly he sometimes described the cosmic spirit as the 'totality' or the 'sum-total of life'.

Gandhi's starting point then was quite different from that of Christianity. That was why, although he was deeply influenced by its moral thought, he took no interest in and a rather dim view of its cosmological theories. God's awe-inspiring powers and dazzling feats did not impress or even interest him. In fact he thought that to stress them was to distract from His spiritual nature and to inspire fear and awe rather than love and intimacy. Instead Gandhi stressed the cosmic spirit's intelligence, subtlety, skill and energy. For him He was not a Hercules bending the mighty universe to His will but an intriguing magician subtly permeating and guiding it from within. He did not *impose* laws from the outside and *create* order, rather He infused the universe and gently and skilfully evolved order from within it. Gandhi's was basically a non-violent God holding the universe together by means of love which Gandhi saw at work in the forces of gravitation, mutual attraction and natural sympathy.

Gandhi's reasons for believing in the existence of the cosmic spirit were varied and complex. He agreed that it could not be perceived by any or all of the five senses, but did not see the point of the argument. The cosmic spirit was not a *physical* entity, so the fact that it could not be sensually perceived was not a valid argument against its existence. It was pure spirit or consciousness, and could only be grasped by a human spirit equipped after proper training to hear its silent utterances and feel its presence. We shall return to this complex argument later.

Gandhi agreed too that the existence of the cosmic spirit was incapable of rational demonstration, but disagreed about its implications.[14] By itself reason could not prove the existence of anything, not even chairs and tables. And therefore if it were to be the sole criterion of existence, we would have to deny the existence of the world itself. Furthermore, Gandhi could not see why only what satisfied reason should be deemed to exist. He rejected the view that it was man's highest faculty. If it was the highest because it said so, the argument was circular. And as for the other faculties, they said no such thing.[15] Gandhi went further and rejected the very idea of any human faculty being the highest. The human mind was an essentially plural, federal and non-hierarchical structure of autonomous and interacting faculties, each with its own distinctive mode of operation and way of knowing the world. All knowledge was a product of their co-operative effort, each making its unique contribution and correcting and being corrected by the others. Gandhi could not see why the other human faculties should be required to conform to and be judged by the standard of reason.[16] It was obviously one of man's important faculties and should be assigned its due place in life, but it could not be made the sovereign arbiter of all the others. Obviously every belief must 'pass the test' of reason, but that did not mean that it could not 'transcend' or 'go beyond' it.[17] Reason laid down the minimum, not the maximum, and specified what men may not believe, not what they *must* believe. Though belief in God should not *contradict* reason, it need not be confined to or demonstrated and proved by it.

Gandhi agreed that to go beyond observation and reason was to enter the realm of faith, but saw nothing wrong in this.[18] Men went beyond faith in most areas of life and simply could not live without it, be it in friends, in their capacity to achieve the desired goals, in their belief that the sun will rise and the world will not come to an end tomorrow. Even the hard-headed scientists relied on the faith that the universe was governed by laws, had a rational structure and was amenable to human understanding. Although their faith was rational and fully justified, it was nevertheless an act of faith and not a matter of rational demonstration. The important and the only legitimate question therefore was not whether but when faith was 'justified' and how to separate 'rational' from 'blind' faith. Neither reason nor faith alone but rational faith was the only valid basis of life.

Although Gandhi nowhere stated them clearly, he seemed to invoke the following four criteria of rational or justified faith. First, it should relate to matters falling outside the purview of observation and reason. Whether or not elephants could fly or there were flowers in the sky was amenable to empirical verification and could not be a matter of faith.[19] Second, faith should not contradict observation and reason. Faith that the world will not end tomorrow was justified because both observation and reason indicated that the opposite was a wholly unlikely event. Third, faith was a leap, an act of going beyond what could be observed and demonstrated. One must therefore show that it was called for by and had a 'basis' or 'warrant' in experience. Finally, faith was a calculated gamble in a situation where the available evidence was inconclusive. One must therefore show that it not only had a basis in experience but was also likely to lead to beneficial consequences.

Gandhi contended that faith in the existence of the cosmic spirit satisfied the four criteria. The cosmic spirit was not amenable to observation and rational demonstration. At the same time belief in His existence did not contradict observation and reason, and had a warrant in experience. The order and regularity observable in the universe could not be explained in terms of natural laws alone, for there was no obvious reason why the universe should be governed by laws at all and not be in perpetual chaos, or governed by those that were stable and hospitable to life. Matter by itself could not create life, nor could its laws explain the most sophisticated ways in which even the minutest living beings adjusted to their often hostile environment. Gandhi also found it mysterious that life persisted in the midst of destruction.[20] Such destructive forces as earthquakes, floods and storms could have easily snuffed out life a long time ago. Yet it has continued to persist, flourish and throw up increasingly higher forms. Again, although both good and evil existed in the universe, good not only survived but triumphed in the long run. In the short run and in individual cases, it might not. However, 'if we take a long view, we shall see that it is not wickedness but goodness which rules the world'. Indeed, evil itself could not last unless sustained by good. Gangs of murderers might go about killing everyone in sight, but they must trust and help one another. Good was self-sufficient, whereas evil was parasitic, and it was basic to life in a way that evil was not. The fact that the universe had a structural bias towards good and was not amoral could not be explained without postulating a cosmic spirit.

Gandhi claimed that his own experiences of unexpected divine guidance in the form of an 'inner voice' in times of great crises pointed to the existence of a cosmic power.[21] Such experiences were not unique to him but attested by countless men and women over the centuries. These were all 'real', although obviously they could not be tested in a laboratory and supported by 'hard' evidence. The evidence in such matters was necessarily soft and could not be dismissed simply because it did not conform to an *a priori* and arbitrary standard of evidence. Indeed it was inherently improper to judge spiritual experiences by the criteria of evidence drawn from the physical world. Even natural scientists talked about a number of entities they had never seen and will never see. We accept their existence because we have confidence in the intellectual calibre and honesty of the scientists and in the rigour of their methods. For Gandhi the spiritual world was 'exactly' like this. It too involved 'search' and 'research', and had its own 'methods of investigation', 'experiments' and ways of rigorously 'training' the 'spiritual scientists'. Over the centuries scores of highly intelligent men had cultivated the 'science of spirit', undertaken rigorous research and unanimously arrived at the view that God exists. They included, among others, Jesus, Moses, Zoroaster, Mohammed, Kabir, Nanak, the great Hindu sages and seers, the Buddha, Mahavira, Ramkrishna and Raichandbhai. They could not all be dismissed as deluded and confused for their 'conduct and character' had been 'profoundly transformed' for the better by their spiritual experiences, and mere delusions could never have had such a lasting impact.[22]

Turning now to the fourth criterion of rational faith, Gandhi contended that faith in the existence of the cosmic spirit was a better guide to life than its opposite. It made it easier to bear the burdens of life, encouraged men to trust one another and guarded them against the cynicism provoked by the ingratitude and meanness of their fellows. It helped them resist the temptations to bend moral rules to suit their narrow personal interests, inspired them to great acts of sacrifice and gave them the strength to launch struggles and take risks they otherwise would not. Although one could not be *absolutely* certain of the existence of the cosmic spirit, belief in it had beneficial consequences and was a 'better hypothesis' than its opposite.[23]

We may comment on two important features of Gandhi's arguments for believing in the existence of the cosmic spirit, especially as they are central to Hindu religious tradition. First, unlike the other religious traditions Hinduism takes great pride in its 'scientific' character. Most religions stress man's inability to comprehend God's nature and mode of operation, and rely on Him to reach out to man and reveal Himself through a prophet or His chosen son. Hinduism takes an optimistic view of human powers and believes that man can discover and 'see' God by following a rigorous and carefully worked out programme of spiritual training and meditation. When the young and sceptical Swami Vivekananda asked Ramkrishna Paramahansa, a great 19th-century Hindu *yogi*, if he had seen God, the latter replied, 'yes, I have seen Him more vividly than I see you, and you can see Him too'. The history of Hindu religious thought contains many such examples. Hindus therefore claim to offer a direct and experiential proof of God's existence and define religion not in credal but experimental terms, not as a body of beliefs but as a search for spiritual experiences culminating in the state of bliss consequent on the realisation or *sākshātkāra* of God.

This may partly explain why Hindus have not evinced much interest in arguments about the existence of God. Since God can be and indeed has been seen or experienced by those with the courage to embark on the arduous spiritual journey, they do not see the point of relying on arguments. A sceptic is asked to undertake the journey and discover for himself how wrong he is. After all a dispute about whether or not there is a cat in the next room is pointless when one can easily ascertain the fact for oneself. This manner of reasoning has had an enormous influence on the Hindu mind. It is bewitchingly simple for, rather than 'merely' argue about God and waste time and energy in 'hair-splitting' debates, it makes sense to ask a genuinely interested person to follow the prescribed or his own special programme of spiritual quest. It also appeals to our sense of fairness for we cannot really dismiss as mad or liars those who undertook the arduous search and sincerely claimed to have realised God. The Brahmanic tradition took advantage of this and silenced many an agnostic and atheist voice. Although he did not claim to have discovered God, Gandhi too claimed to 'hear' his voice, 'feel' His presence and periodically catch 'glimpses' of Him.

In the history of Hindu religious thought, there have been periodic attacks on this line of argument. The Buddha took up the challenge, undertook an intense and rigorous penance and, despite his refusal to talk about God, seems to have found nothing. Mahavira Jain reached a similar conclusion. The Cārvaka and Lokāyata schools challenged the argument on different grounds. They demanded to know why anyone should be asked to embark on the spiritual journey at all for, unless one had already assumed the existence of God, it was a thoroughly pointless self-infliction of pain and a sad waste of time and energy. They therefore asked for the reasons for believing in His existence. And since for the most part they were offered none save the self-authenticating and incorrigible experiences of a few, they rejected the whole approach. All religions ultimately rely on the testimony of some individuals, Hinduism on that of those claiming to have 'seen' God, most of the others on that of those claiming to be His messengers or specially chosen sons. Each has its characteristic strengths and weaknesses.

Second, Gandhi's arguments for believing in the existence of the cosmic power contain a powerful pragmatic element, which too is characteristic of Hindu religious tradition. Historically Hindu pragmatism has taken two forms. Some argued that if a belief had desirable consequences and caused no obvious harm, there was nothing wrong in subscribing to it. For others the fact that it had such consequences meant that it was true, for truth alone was the source of goodness. In either case the consequences were taken to justify the acceptance of a belief provided, of course, that it was plausible and permitted by reason. Although Gandhi's thought points in both directions, for the most part it is informed by the first kind of pragmatism. The difficulties of his position are obvious. While claiming to take full account of reason, he really assigns it a limited place. He defines reason in extremely narrow terms and more or less equates it with common sense. So long as a belief does not violate common sense or is patently absurd, it is deemed to be consistent with or permitted by reason. In this view there is no effective check on what beliefs one may hold, and even belief in ghosts and witches cannot be ruled out. On a more rigorous view of reason one would reach a different conclusion to Gandhi's. If one defined reason in terms of the available body of scientific knowledge about the nature of the universe, belief in the existence of God would appear highly problematic and certainly not as self-evident as Gandhi maintained. The order and regularity in the universe and the emergence of life can be explained without postulating God, and the alleged victory of good over evil in the natural and human world has only a limited basis in fact.

For Gandhi then the cosmic spirit constitutes the ultimate reality or Truth of the universe. Although it is impersonal and without qualities, the limited human mind guided by inescapable moral and emotional considerations cannot avoid conceiving it in personal and moral terms. For Gandhi every human being has a unique psychological and spiritual constitution. He cannot leap out of it any more than he can jump out of his body. Every God is therefore someone's God, that is, his or her way of understanding the cosmic spirit. No individual can avoid looking at the cosmic power through his own eyes and conceptualising it in terms of his uniquely personal dispositions, tendencies and needs. Since the very idea of a personal God owes its origin to man's moral and emotional needs, and the latter vary from individual to individual, Gandhi insists that one cannot consistently accept the legitimacy of a personal God and deny each individual's right to form his own distinctive conception of Him.

Religion represents the way man conceives and relates himself to God.[24] Since Gandhi postulates both the impersonal and personal God, he distinguishes two different kinds or levels of religion. The 'formal', 'customary', 'organised' or 'historical' religions centre on the personal, and the 'pure', 'true' or 'eternal' religion around the impersonal God. Even as the different conceptions of personal God are grounded in and share in common the impersonal God which they conceptualise differently, organised religions are all grounded in the eternal religion of which they are so many different articulations. For Gandhi Hinduism, Christianity, Judaism, Islam and the other religions are all based on specific conceptions of a personal God. They involve distinct forms of prayer, worship, rituals and beliefs about His nature and relation to the world, and are all 'sectarian'.[25] The 'pure' or 'true' religion lies beyond them, and has nothing to do with organisation, beliefs and rituals. It consists in nothing more and nothing less than recognising that the universe is pervaded and governed by a cosmic power and organising one's entire life accordingly. It is basically living in the constant, intimate and unmediated presence of the cosmic spirit, and represents the purest form of spirituality. The true religion 'transcends [but] does not supersede' organised religions and constitutes their common 'basis' and connecting 'link'.

For Gandhi a specific conception of God forms the basis of every religion. Since conceptions of God vary from man to man, he argues that there are as many religions as men, each man relating himself to God and worshipping Him in his own way. Like most Hindus Gandhi has considerable difficulty coming to terms with organised religion and the single conception of God and the uniform structure of beliefs lying at its basis. He acknowledges that men might find sufficient similarities between their conceptions of God to induce them to belong to a common religion. However, he is convinced that since men are naturally different, their conceptions and ways of relating to Him can never be completely identical. Every organised religion must therefore remain a loose fellowship of believers and accommodate, even encourage, individual diversity. Insistence on total credal conformity denies their individuality, violates their spiritual integrity and leads to untruth.

For Gandhi every major religion articulates a unique vision of God and emphasises different features of the human condition. The idea of God as a loving Father is most fully developed in Christianity, and the emphasis on love and suffering is also unique to it. 'I cannot say that it is singular, or that it is not to be found in other religions. But the presentation is unique.' Austere and rigorous monotheism and the spirit of equality are 'most beautifully' articulated in and peculiar to Islam. The distinction between the impersonal and personal conceptions of God, the principle of the unity of all life and the doctrine of *ahimsā* are distinctive to Hinduism. Every religion has a distinct moral and spiritual ethos and represents a wonderful and irreplaceable 'spiritual composition'. To a truly religious man all religions should be 'equally dear'.[26]

Gandhi argues that since the cosmic power is infinite and the limited human mind can grasp only a 'fragment' of it, and that too inadequately, every religion is necessarily limited and partial.[27] Even those claiming to be directly revealed by God are revealed to men with their fair share of inescapable human limitations and communicated to others in necessarily inadequate human languages.[28] To claim that a particular religion offers an exhaustive or even definitive account of the nature of the cosmic spirit is to imply both that some men are free from inescapable human limitations and that God is partial, and thus to be guilty of both spiritual arrogance and blasphemy. Since no religion is final and perfect, each can greatly benefit from a dialogue with other religions.[29] Unlike Rammohun Roy, the Brahmos and the other Hindu leaders, Gandhi does not think that the purpose of inter-religious dialogue is to distil their common or complementary insights and create a new and higher universal religion. Rather its purpose is threefold. First, it cultivates humility and enables each religion to understand the *others* better and to feel relaxed enough to assimilate from them whatever it finds worth accepting. Second, it enables each to understand *itself* better and to appreciate both its uniqueness and similarities with the others. Third, it lifts each religion above the superficial level of beliefs and rituals, deepens its spirituality and enables it to catch a glimpse of the eternal religion lying beyond all religions.

For Gandhi every religion centres on the spiritual experiences of its founder, and its scriptures embody his spiritual insight. Over time those inspired by his example embark on a similar journey, both confirm and deepen his experiences and insights, and build up a religious tradition. The founder is a guide and the first explorer, not a saviour, a unique son of God or the final spiritual authority. To hold on to his every word and not to encourage new spiritual discoveries and experiments is to misunderstand, even betray, his example and arrest the growth of his message. Gandhi observes:

> The priest has ever sacrificed the prophet. *Vedas* to be divine must be a living word, ever growing, ever expanding and ever responding to new forces. The priest clung to the letter and missed the spirit.[30]

The priest is concerned with theology, the prophet with religion. Theology freezes religion, treats it as if it were merely a matter of belief and builds abstract systems rather than exploring new ways of living by its central principles. As Gandhi puts it:

> Amongst agents of the many untruths that are propounded in the world one of the foremost is theology. I do not say that there is no demand for it. There is a demand in the world for many a questionable thing. But even those who have to do with the-ology as part of their work have to survive their theology. I

know two good Christian friends who gave up theology and decided to live the gospel of Christ.[31]

Since Gandhi believed that all religions charted the identical spiritual terrain from different directions, he thought that they had much to say to each other. Accordingly he made it a practice to read passages from different religions at his prayer meetings and encouraged his followers to make a 'reverential' study of their basic texts. When he was reading the New Testament with the students of Gujarat Vidyapith, there was a public protest. He replied:

I regard my study and reverence for the Bible, the Koran and the other scriptures to be wholly consistent with my claim to be a staunch sanatani Hindu . . . My respectful study of other religions has not abated my reverence for and my faith in the Hindu scriptures. They have broadened my view of life. They have enabled me to understand more clearly many an obscure passage in the Hindu scriptures.[32]

Gandhi read the *Gita* in terms of the basic message of the Sermon on the Mount and claimed to discover new meanings in its central passages. Sometimes this resulted in their original and creative reinterpretation; on other occasions it led to gross distortions, as when he read in it the doctrine of the dignity of manual labour.

While all religions are 'equally valid' for Gandhi, he thinks it is possible to compare them in terms of the degree to which they realise the essential nature of religion. He works out four criteria. First, religion is ultimately a matter of how one lives, not what one believes, and beliefs are important only in so far as they inspire morally desirable conduct. A religion that makes beliefs the sole or primary basis of salvation or of corporate membership is therefore inferior to one that emphasises the development of character and conduct. Second, since all religions are inherently partial, the more open and tolerant a religion and the more it welcomes a dialogue with the others, the better it is. Third, since each individual is unique and relates to God in his own way, the greater the 'scope for self-expression' offered by a religion, the better it is. Finally, since God creates and loves all living beings, a true religion must be based on the twin principles of the unity of all men and of all life. 'The greater the scope for compassion in a way of life, the more religion it has', Gandhi argues.

Gandhi thinks that judged by these criteria Hinduism has an edge over other religions. It is 'most tolerant', 'most free' of dogmas, gives the 'largest scope' for self-expression and offers the 'highest expression and application' to the principle of universal compassion.[33] He readily concedes that Hindu practice in some areas leaves a good deal to be desired, but argues that he is concerned with its central values and general ethos. Since he derives his criteria from Hinduism, Gandhi's conclusion is hardly surprising. Like the Christian missionaries who, using their religion as the model of a 'proper' religion, dismissed Hinduism as not really a religion at all, Gandhi universalised the Hindu conception of religion and naturally found the others difficient. Unlike them, however, he did not think unfavourably of other religions or refuse to call them such.

Gandhi finds the idea of religious conversion profoundly irreligious and offensive. In his view it rests on three false assumptions. First, it assumes that a particular religion represents the final truth. We saw earlier why Gandhi considers such a view incoherent and blasphemous. Second, conversion consists in changing a man's beliefs and assumes that religion is solely or primarily a matter of belief rather than conduct. Gandhi rejects this view of religion on the ground that God is interested in how a man lives and relates to Him and other men, not in what he believes. Third, conversion assumes that all men have identical moral and emotional needs so that what is good for one is necessarily good for all. As we saw, Gandhi rejects this too.

For Gandhi every man is born into a particular religion. Since no religion is wholly false, he should be able to work out his destiny in and through it. And if he feels attracted to some aspects of another religion, he should be at liberty to borrow them. Gandhi cannot see why a man should ever need to give up his religion. That situation only arises when a religion is mistakenly organised like the modern state in whose jealously guarded territory no-one may settle without first giving up his old citizenship and acquiring a new one. When Madeleine Slade expressed a desire to become a Hindu, Gandhi advised her against it. She should, he insisted, live by her own faith and absorb into it whatever she liked in Hinduism. Merely changing over to a new religion would not improve her conduct or way of life, the only thing that ultimately mattered. When they were overwhelmed with doubts, Gandhi encouraged his Christian friends to draw new inspiration and strength from their own religion. An American missionary, Stanley Jones, spoke for many of them when he said that Gandhi had reconverted him to Christianity. In a different context he told his friend Mrs Polak that she need not 'become' a Christian in order to 'be' one. She could draw inspiration from Jesus' life and teachings and live like a Christian without ceasing to be a Jew. Hinduism gives its adherents an amazing degree of freedom to believe what they like so long as they conduct themselves in a socially required manner. Since the connection between belief and conduct is therefore looser and logically different from that in almost all other religions, like most Hindus Gandhi had great difficulty understanding the phenomenon of religious conversion and the way changes in belief might sometimes transform conduct.

For Gandhi a truly religious man should aim to live at three levels, representing increasingly higher forms of spirituality. First, his own religion is his necessary starting point, and he should endeavour to live by its central values. Second, he should respect, enter into a dialogue with and assimilate from other religions whatever he finds valuable.[34] Third, he should eventually seek to go beyond all organised religions and practise the 'pure' religion in which prophets, priests, images, beliefs and rituals are all transcended. Gandhi's own religious evolution followed this pattern. He was born and for a time lived as a Hindu; he later generously borrowed from other religions and enriched his own; over time he evolved and practised a religion bearing a strong resemblance to what he called 'pure' religion. His first Christian biographer summed up his religious thought well:

> A few days ago I was told that 'he is a Buddhist'. Not long since a Christian newpaper described him as 'a Christian Mohammadan', an extraordinary mixture indeed. His views are too closely allied to Christianity to be entirely Hindu, and his sympathies are so wide and catholic that one would imagine he has reached a point where the formulae of sects are meaningless.[35]

4

Spirituality, Politics and the Reinterpretation of Hinduism

Much of the Western philosophy of man is anthropocentric in the sense of regarding man if not as the centre of the universe at least as the highest being on earth. The anthropocentric tendency goes back to the Sophists, was forcefully articulated by Plato, endorsed with several reservations by Aristotle and, with the exception of the Natural Law theorists, shared by the other Greek and Roman thinkers. It lies at the basis of the Judeo-Christian tradition for which man is the crowing glory of creation enjoying under the lordship of God a privileged ontological position and almost unlimited rights over the non-human world. As God receded further and further in the modern age and the cosmic dimension of human existence dropped out of sight, man moved in to occupy the resulting vacuum and the anthropocentric tendency acquired unprecedented domination. His relation to the increasingly desacralised nature was released from the different kinds of constraints imposed by the earlier writers and societies, and it was reduced to a mere resource to be exploited as he pleased.

Since the anthropocentric approach assigned man a highly privileged position in the universe, it needed to show that he was radically or qualitatively different from the non-human world. The determination of his constitutive and distinguishing features or what was clumsily called his nature or essence therefore became a fundamental problem for Western philosophy and in one form or another the starting point of all moral and political inquiry. Since man was abstracted from the rest of the universe, his essence obviously lay not in the quality of his relationship with it but his properties or capacities, that is, in something internal to him. It was the philosophical basis of his claim to absolute superiority, and

85

obviously had to be exclusive and unique to him and capable of clear and unambiguous definition. His essence thus excluded all that he shared in common with the rest of the non-human world, especially his nearest cousins, the animals, and was located in such abstract, highly specific and narrowly defined capacities as rationality, whether theoretical, practical or both, speech, self-consciousness and self-determination. As in any centric approach, the anthropocentric approach could not avoid neatly dividing the universe into the human and the non-human or man and nature, and grading the constituents of the latter in terms of their distance from him.

Following much of the Indian philosophical anthropology, Gandhi approached the question differently. Not man but cosmos was his starting point. The cosmos consisted of different orders of being ranging from the material to the human, each autonomous and standing in a complex pattern of relationship with the rest within a larger framework. It was polycentric and without a dominant centre to which the rest of the universe could be instrumentally related. Since man represented only one order of being, obviously he could not be the centre of the universe. And since Gandhi conceived the cosmic spirit as a principle of order and not as a creator, it too lacked the separateness, transcendence and independence necessary to constitute one. Man was an integral part of the cosmos, tied to it by a million bonds and incomprehensible outside of it. Since he was internally and necessarily related to the rest of its members, Gandhi saw him not as a bearer of properties but as a world of relationships, a whole, and a member of such increasingly wider wholes as the family, the caste, the community, mankind, the sentient world, the material world and the all-encompassing cosmos. Each whole was self-contained but not self-sufficient, and both autonomous and pointing to the larger whole of which it was a part. In Gandhi's favourite metaphor the cosmos was not a pyramid of which the so-called nature or material world was the basis and man the apex, but a series of ever-widening circles.

As man for him was not the centre of the universe, Gandhi did not divide it into the human and the non-human world or man and 'nature'; indeed such a classification struck him as arrogant and blasphemous. Since, further, man did not occupy a supremely privileged position, Gandhi did not see the need radically to mark him off from the rest of the universe and lay excessive stress on his uniqueness. If he had seen man as the lord and master of the universe, he would have considered it crucially important to show that he belonged to a totally different and superior species or race. For Gandhi such a hierarchial mode of thought did not remain confined to man's relation to nature but spilt over into his relations with his fellow-men. If nature had no dignity and was a mere means to human self-interest, women, non-white races and the poor, who on a convenient definition of rationality could be presented as living close to nature or like animals, were fair game for those fancying themselves as fully rational. Gandhi, who had himself been a victim of much racial arrogance and well knew how oppressive systems justified themselves, had not only a philosophical but also a political reason for rejecting the anthropocentric view of the universe. Since he refused to see man's relation to the universe in imperialist terms, he did not feel it necessary either to stress man's uniqueness or to distinguish him from the non-human world in sharp and unambiguous terms. No harm was done in his view and no vital human interests were damaged if man and animal turned out to have overlapping properties and could not be qualitatively and hierarchically separated. Gandhi did, of course, need a conception of man. However he did not have to articulate it in terms of his differences from the non-human world, nor to stress them at the expense of the obvious similarities, nor to establish man's radical discontinuity. The point will become clearer as we proceed.

Gandhi maintained that since the cosmic spirit informed and structured the universe, all creation was divine and one. It was one in both the substantial and systemic sense, the former because it shared a common spiritual essence, the latter because it constituted an organically interdependent system and formed a coherent whole.[1] For Gandhi the universe was a 'partnership' between its constituent parts and their common heritage. Even as man was sacred, so was the rest of the cosmos and could not be viewed as his property to be used as he pleased. Since his very survival required it, he might take from the universe what he needed to live in moderate comfort but no more and only under certain conditions. He had no right to violate the integrity of the other orders of being and disturb their balance and rhythm. Since nature constantly reproduced and replenished itself, he might draw on its resources but had no right to undermine its regenerative capacity. To pluck a flower or a fruit or to cultivate land in harmony with its natural propensities was to accept the spontaneous offerings of nature. To pollute, poison or unleash destructive forces, to render land infertile and barren, or ruthlessly to exploit and deplete natural resources betrayed a contempt for nature, and was an act of cosmic sacrilege.

Following the *Gita* Gandhi saw the universe as one vast *yajna*, a system of uncoerced and interrelated offerings.[2] Every member of it offered its services, contributed to the maintenance of the whole and took what it needed from the contributions made by others. The earth generously offered its hospitality and products to living beings who in turn, but not as a return, enriched it by contributing organic waste. The sea spontaneously offered itself in the form of rain which sustained the vegetation which in turn made possible the rain that filled the sea. The universe was held together by the spirit of service, not self-interest or contract. The services freely offered by each collectively created a rich and orderly environment from which they all benefitted. Their relations were mediated by their membership of the whole and were not bilateral and based on direct exchanges.

For Gandhi human society was similarly structured. It was a product of the spontaneous sacrifices of thousands of men over hundreds of years, and represented a collective *yajna* to which each individual brought the offering of his unique gifts. Nature continually went through a protracted and painful process to provide man with his means of sustenance; his parents made countless sacrifices in order to bring him into the world and raise him as a sensitive and sane human being; hundreds of sages, seers, saints, scholars and scientists struggled over the centuries to create a civilisation without which his life would have remained poor and brutish; and millions of unknown men and women worked hard, thought little of their comforts, fought wars, even gave up their lives and created an orderly and stable society so vital for his existence and growth. In short every man inherited a world to the creation of which he had contributed nothing. As Gandhi put it, every man was 'born a debtor', a beneficiary of others' gifts. This was the most basic fact about human and indeed all existence; in the interdependent universe things simply could not be otherwise. The ancient Indians had distinguished five basic *runas* or debts incurred by every man at birth, namely to parents, ancestors, the creators of his civilisation, the universe and the gods. Although

Gandhi did not classify them in this way, his view was not very different.

The inherited debts were too vast to be repaid. Even a whole lifetime was not enough to pay back what a man owed to his parents, let alone the others. Furthermore the creditors were by their very nature unspecifiable. Most of them have long been dead or remained anonymous. And those alive were so numerous and their contributions so varied and complex that it was impossible to decide what one owed to whom. To talk about repaying the debts thus did not make sense except as a clumsy and metaphorical way of describing one's response to unsolicited but indispensable gifts. Since the debts could never be 'repaid' and the favours 'returned', all a man could do was to accept them with grace and gratitude, 'recognise the conditions of his existence' and continue the on-going universal *yajna* by accepting his full share of collective responsibility. The only adequate response to the fact that he was born in and constantly sustained by *yajna* was to look upon his own life as *yajna*, an offering at the universal altar, and to find profound joy in contributing to the maintenance and enrichment of both the human world and the cosmos. '*Yajna* having come to us with our birth we are debtors all our lives, and thus for ever bound to serve the universe.'

Since mankind constituted an organic whole and men were necessarily interdependent, every human action was both self- and other-regarding. Directly or indirectly, visibly or invisibly, it affected the collective ethos and shaped the quality of the prevailing pattern of human relationship. 'We cannot see this, near-sighted as we are,' but it remains an inescapable feature of the necessarily interdependent world.[3] 'Rot in one part must inevitably poison the whole system.' When a man rose, he awakened others to their potentialities and inspired, encouraged and raised them as well. If he fell, others fell as well. Even a trivial crime was enough to create a general sense of insecurity, heighten mutual suspicions and lower the moral tone of the entire community. 'I believe that if one man gains spiritually the whole world gains with him, and if one man falls the world falls to that extent.'[4] For Gandhi humanity was indivisible, and no man could degrade or brutalise another without also degrading or brutalising himself, or inflict psychic and moral damage on others without inflicting it on himself as well. This was so in at least three ways. First, to degrade others was to imply that a human being may be so treated, and thus to lower the expected level of the moral minimum due to every human being from which all alike suffered. 'To slight a single human being is . . . to harm not only that human being but with him the whole world.' Second, to degrade and dehumanise others was to damage their pride, self-respect and potential for good, and thus both to deny oneself and the world the benefits of their possible contributions and to add to the collective moral, psychological and financial cost of repairing the damage they were likely to do to themselves. Third, as a being endowed with a moral sense and a capacity for reflection, no man could degrade or maltreat others without hardening himself against their suffering and cries for help, building up an elaborate and distorted system of self-justification and a coercive apparatus to put down discontent, and thus both coarsening his moral sensibility and lowering his own and the collective level of humanity. As Gandhi put it, no man 'takes another down a pit without descending into it himself and sinning into the bargain'. Since humanity was indivisible and vital human interests were identical, every man was responsible to and for others and should be deeply concerned about how they lived.

For Gandhi this was the central message of the Indian doctrine of *advaita* and its three basic principles. The principle of the *unity of man* was not a mere rhetoric, a pious sentiment or a moral postulate but the deepest *truth* about human existence. It conveyed the profound insights that men necessarily rose and fell together, that no man could ever benefit at the expense of another and that his relation to himself and to others, his internal and external world, formed part of a single pattern. At a different level the principle of the *unity of life* made the same point that in harming other living beings man harmed himself as well. Violence to them coarsened his sensitivity, rendered him insensitive to their well-being and could not but affect his relations with his fellow-men. At a yet higher level the principle of the *unity of creation* made the point that in violating the rhythm and harmony of the cosmos, man damaged the basic conditions of his existence and sooner or later paid a heavy price.

Gandhi's principle of indivisible humanity formed the basis of his critique of systems of oppression and exploitation. Such dominant groups as the whites in South Africa, the colonial governments in India and elsewhere and the rich and the powerful in every society naïvely imagined that their exploitation and degradation of their respective victims did not in any way damage them as well. In fact they suffered as much as their victims and sometimes even more. The white South Africans could not deprive the blacks of their livelihood and basic human dignity without suppressing their doubts and tender feelings, damaging their capacities for critical self-reflection and impartial self-assessment and becoming victims of moral conceit, morbid fears and irrational obsessions. In brutalising the blacks they brutalised themselves and were only prevented by their arrogance from noticing how sad, empty and pitiable their lives had become. They might have enjoyed more material comforts, but they were neither happier nor better human beings. The colonial rulers met the same fate. They could not dismiss the natives as 'effeminate' and 'childlike' without thinking of themselves as tough, hypermasculine and unemotional adults, a self-image to which they could not conform without distorting and impoverishing their potential. In misrepresenting the natives, they misrepresented themselves and fell in their own traps. They also took home the attitudes, habits and styles of government acquired abroad, and corrupted their own society. Colonialism did promote their material interests, but only at the expense of their larger and infinitely more important human interests. Material interests had only an instrumental significance and were positively harmful when they hampered man's moral and spiritual development.

For Gandhi then the cosmic, including the social, order was created and maintained by every member making its or his own proper contribution to the collective *yajna*. If one of them failed to do its or his part, the whole became disturbed and all the parts including the delinquent suffered. The cosmic order was not created by the cosmic spirit working independently of them but was a co-operative product based on its partnership with them. The cosmic spirit *depended* on and was helpless without them. The non-human world was so structured that it naturally and necessarily played its part. Man had a capacity for free will and should contribute to the maintenance of the cosmic order as a matter of *duty* discharged in the *spirit of co-operation* with the cosmic spirit. 'Absolute Truth has no power unless incarnated in human beings.'[5] This was Gandhi's answer to the persistent Indian query as to why men should lead an active rather than a contemplative life and how they could do so without becoming over-involved in the world. For Gandhi men should lead a life of action because the ceaselessly active cosmic spirit needed their co-operation. And they could avoid its moral and spiritual perils by acting in the spirit of *yajna*, that is, by viewing their actions as grateful offerings at the cosmic altar and themselves as witnesses addressed by and disinterestedly responding to the call of events. Actions so done were 'free' in the threefold sense that they did not spring from an inner compulsion or a frenetic urge to act, were not means of self-projection and self-gratification, and did not generate a binding attachment to their consequences and to the world. Indeed, although actions in one sense, they were non-actions in another, and their agents led a life of action but not an active life.[6]

Following Hindu philosophical tradition Gandhi distinguished between the self and the *ātman*.[7] Every man had a distinct self, that is, an unique 'psychological and spiritual constitution' consisting of distinctive dispositions, propensities, tendencies and temperament inherited at birth. It was a product of his actions in his previous lives and shaped but did not predetermine his subsequent development. Unlike the body and the *ātman* which have no history, the self had nothing but history encompassing several life-spans and largely beyond racall. Every man was uniquely and solely responsible for all he was, and had to work out his ultimate spiritual destiny himself.

For Gandhi man was also *ātman*, which was nothing but the *Brahman* or cosmic spirit manifested in him in all its totality. Although following other writers we shall translate it as soul, it is important to note that the two differ in several crucial respects. The concept of soul is, of course, defined differently in different religious traditions, but in most of them, especially Christianity, it is conceived as a spark, part or particle of God, implies separation between man and Him, and is unique to every individual. Within Gandhi's monist framework the *ātman* obviously could not have any of these properties. It was not a particle or a spark but the whole of *Brahman* 'flowing through' every living being; it was not separate or distinct from but one with the Brahman; and it was identical in all men. For Gandhi as for most Hindus, especially the *advaitins*, man did not *have ātman* for he was ultimately nothing but it, and he did not have *an* atman for it was not unique to him or separate from the *Brahman*.

For Gandhi neither the *ātman*, nor the body, but the self was the basis of individuality. The *ātman* was the same in all men and could not provide the principle of individuation. Although separate and distinct, human bodies were so many different anatomical configurations of the identical material substance, were subject to the same laws, displayed the same basic properties and functioned in the same way. The body was the seat of particularity not individuality, a principle of numerical not substantive or essential differentiation. The self, a unique historical product of the individual's own efforts and choices and linking the past, present and future in a single temporal continuum, was the basis of his individuality and personal identity. While man *qua* man was constituted by the *ātman*, *a* man was constituted and defined by his self. Even as he could not leap out of his skin, he could not jump out of his self.

For Gandhi, as for most Hindus, the *ātman* constituted the ultimate reality and defined the character and content of the ultimate goal of life. The goal consisted not so much in what is sometimes called *self*-realisation as in realising, not just cognitively but existentially, that man was really the *ātman* and thus *Brahman*. Following tradition Gandhi called it *moksha*, liberation from *samsāra* or the unending cycle of rebirths. Since man *was Brahman*, the pursuit of *moksha* consisted not in becoming something he was not but in being what he really was, and involved the negative task of shedding the illusory consciousness of separateness or individuality and transcending selfhood.

Since each individual was unique and possessed a distinct spiritual and psychological constitution, he had to work out his *moksha* in his own unique manner, at his own pace and by following the path best suited to him. The goal was the same for all men; the paths varied. The *ātman* defined the destination, the self the path. Since the self was the basis of individuality, it was also the basis of freedom. For Gandhi man needed freedom to live and act as he liked not because he alone or best knew his moral and spiritual interests, for these were common to all men and capable of being articulated by the spiritual elite, but for two related reasons. First, he was the sole architect of his self and uniquely responsible for his actions. Since the law of *karma* was inexorable and each individual had to reap the consequences of his actions in this life as well as the next, his actions must obviously reflect his own choices. Second, every man was uniquely constituted, had distinct moral and spiritual capacities, and necessarily saw and came to terms with the world in his own manner. As such he perceived Truth differently from others and arrived at *his* truth or *relative* truth as Gandhi called it.[8] Such truth necessarily formed the basis of his life from which he progressively strove to get as close to the Truth as possible. No man could 'act beyond his capacity' or perceive the world other than through his own eyes. To prevent him from living by *his* truth was to disjoin his belief and conduct, to create untruth in him, to violate his integrity – the worst form of violence for Gandhi. He could, of course, be profoundly mistaken, but had to discover his mistakes himself. Since, thanks to the law of *karma*, he would have to suffer the inexorable consequences of his mistakes, he had every interest, and greater than anyone else could possibly have, in avoiding them. As men were responsible for one another, they had a duty to reason with and persuade him out of what they took to be his errors. However they also had a duty to respect his integrity or truth and must ultimately leave him alone to work out his destiny himself unless, of course, his truth interfered with their right to live by their truths and threatened the social order.

Gandhi's theory of the self was the basis of his epistemological, moral and social pluralism. Since their selves were differently constituted, all individuals necessarily perceived the world and had a right to live in their own unique manner. In Gandhi's moral theory the selves created the spiritual civil society and provided the principle of differentiation and freedom, whereas the *ātman* created the spiritual state and furnished the overarching framework of order. Without the *ātman* his radically individualist conception of the self would have created unmanageable chaos and rendered society impossible. Without the self his conception of the *ātman* would have created a highly authoritarian society and left no space for freedom and individuality. It was not easy to integrate the two, and predictably Gandhi's moral theory contained a deep and unresolved tension.

Every social order requires a basic agreement on its organising principles or what Gandhi would call a minimum body of agreed 'truths,' as otherwise it lacks unity and the means of resolving inevitable human disagreements and conflicts. Gandhi not only paid little attention to how such common principles were to be arrived at but also tended to underestimate the magnitude and difficulty of the task. For the most part he relied on the institution of *varnadharma* to sustain the social order and on the method of *satyāgraha* to resolve disagreements. He was convinced that the caste system, freed of its 'historical excrescences,' rested on some of the profoundest truths discovered by the ancient Hindu sages after years of reflection and experimentation. Although Gandhi later came to see its grave limitations and even its impracticability in modern society, he desperately hankered after some form of *varna* system. It would appear that he saw no other way of holding together a collection of radically individualistic men morally entitled to live by their own truths. Vivekananda once remarked that Hindu society gave such an amazing degree of religious freedom to its members that it could not create the necessary order without a relatively rigid social organisation. His remark throws much light on Gandhi's dilemma. As for Gandhi's method of *satyāgraha*, its capacity to resolve fundamental disagreements was considerably limited and could not play the pivotal role he assigned it in his social theory. We shall return to this later.

For Gandhi then the highest goal in life was to attain *moksha*, to become one with or dissolve oneself into the cosmic spirit. As a being endowed with the body and the self, an unique physical and psycho-spiritual constitution, man was prone to the illusion that individuality was the ultimate reality. He saw his fellow human beings as separate from him, divided the world into the self and the 'Other' and constantly strove to preserve, protect and assert himself as a distinct individual. Accordingly he constructed all manner of high protective walls around himself and spent his time and energy guarding them against the world, viewing their slightest weakening as a mortal threat to his identity. *Qua ātman* man belonged to the cosmos, as it did to him. Being heir to such a vast treasure, he felt deeply anguished by the mean poverty of the self. *Moksha* consisted in shedding the illusion of individuality, seeing through the *māyā* of the subtle and ingenious forms through which it perpetuated itself and dismantling the protective walls. In the ultimate analysis it signified infinite openness and a blissful release from the ontologically suffocating and claustrophobic world of individuality.

Since the self and the Other were interdependent polarities, each creating and being in turn created by the other, *moksha* involved the complementary processes of dissolving the self by eliminating desires and dissolving the Other by attaining total identification with all creation. Hindu religious tradition had stressed the former and Gandhi did not add much to it. The way he defined the latter and related the two contained novel insights and represented his great contribution.[9]

Following Hindu tradition Gandhi argued that desire was a form of self-projection and self-maintenance. A desire presupposed a self, its seat or bearer, and its gratification involved the gratification and confirmation of the self and perpetuated the illusion of individuality. The self, itself a creation of desires, projected itself into the world and endured in time by means of desires. In the ultimate analysis it was nothing but a cluster of interrelated desires and could not be dissolved without eliminating the desires altogether. Its dissolution consisted in mastering the senses, overcoming the 'bondage of the flesh' and cultivating total detachment or desirelessness.

The second aspect of *moksha* was a relatively novel departure, and Gandhi arrived at it by means of a series of important steps. Since the cosmic spirit was manifested in all living beings and did not exist independently of them, unity with it consisted in total identification with all living beings; 'realisation of Truth is impossible without a complete merging of oneself in and identification with the limitless ocean of life'.[10] And again, the 'only way to find God is to see Him in His creation and be one with it. I cannot find Him apart from the rest of humanity'.[11] For Gandhi identification with the cosmic spirit involved the three increasingly higher levels of identification with all men, all living beings and finally all creation. Although he stressed all three, he tended to concentrate on the first two.

Gandhi argued that love was the only way of indentifying oneself with other living beings. It implied opening up oneself to their presence, relieving them of their otherness and making them part of oneself. As love deepened the distance between the two decreased, and at its highest love culminated in total identification. Universal love was the only way to attain identification with all living beings. It involved infinite openness, breaking down all the barriers between the self and others, letting them flow into one's being and suffuse one's thoughts and feelings with the deepest concern for their well-being.

The concept of love was relatively new to Hinduism and caused Gandhi some difficulty. The Hindu philosophical, especially *advaita*, tradition had been deeply suspicious of it, largely on the grounds that being an emotion it compromised the agent's autonomy, was liable to become addictive, created desires, built up attachments to the person loved, and in these and other ways stood in the way of total detachment. Gandhi was fully aware of

this and, since he also shared the traditional ideal of total detachment, he had to show how it was compatible with his untraditional
emphasis on love. He attempted to resolve the tension by redefining both love and detachment.[12] Although his views are not
easy to follow, he seems to have thought that love was not an
emotion but an objective concern for others' well-being, not a
subjective feeling but a sentiment or spirit of good will. As for
detachment it did not mean indifference but absence of attachment, not lack of interest but of self-interest. Gandhi thought that
when so understood love and detachment were not only compatible but interdependent. To love one's fellow-men was to be guided
by consideration for their well-being, not by any reference to one's
own interests and desires. To help others because one could not
bear to see them suffer or because helping them had become a
powerful *craving* or desire was not an expression of love but a form
of self-assertion, even of self-indulgence.[13] True love must be
totally self-less, not only in the ordinary sense of being unselfish
but in the profound sense of not involving the self in any form at all
and being wholly non-self-referential. It thus required dissolution
of the self and total detachment. Gandhi thought that God's love
for the world was of this kind; deep and warm yet non-emotional,
serene and detached. At a different level a surgeon operating on a
patient in agony exemplified it to some extent. He was caring,
reassuring, full of good will and concerned to do all he could to
help his patient, but also detached, calm and emotionally uninvolved. Indeed, he could only operate on him if he remained
detached and unperturbed by his pain.

Although ingenious and insightful, Gandhi's attempt to reconcile love and detachment remained unsuccessful. As he understood it love implied total identification, whereas detachment
necessarily involved a measure of separation and distance. Further, although non-emotive, love for him was not just a matter of
doing good to others but also a *sentiment* or a spirit of good will,
and implied at least some degree of attachment. It is difficult to see
how one could be deeply concerned about others and not feel
worried about them or avoid becoming involved in their lives.
Gandhi himself constantly complained that he had great difficulty
reconciling his intense love for his countrymen with his ideal of
total detachment. When he saw the suffering of the poor and the
untouchables and the intensity of inter-communal hatred and
violence, he felt lacerated and could barely restrain his anger and

resist an occasional tear. He saw this as a limitation, a failing, and kept blaming himself. At the same time he also knew that the total detachment of the ancient *rishis* had rendered them utterly indifferent to human suffering, and wondered if such a state of mind in which nothing 'moved' the agent did not really lead to motionlessness and inaction. Until the end of his life he kept struggling to reconcile the irreconcilable.

Gandhi argued that to love someone was to wish him well and help him grow and flourish. It implied, negatively, that one did not wish to cause him the slightest harm or injury and, positively, that one actively promoted his well-being and offered every help he needed. Indian thinkers, including Buddha, had generally defined *dayā* and *karunā* in negative terms. Gandhi took a very different view and insisted that love was essentially a positive concept involving active service. Service was positive love, 'love in action' or 'active love'. Universal love meant placing oneself at the service of all living beings and devoting all one's energies to 'wiping every tear from every eye'.

Gandhi argued that active service of his fellow-men was necessarily limited by the agent's capacity, knowledge of their needs and the opportunities at his disposal.[14] On the basis of his theory of the organic self and the concommitant principle of *swadeshi* discussed earlier, Gandhi contended that since every individual was an integral part of a specific community of whose members he had an instinctive understanding, with whom he enjoyed intimate daily contact and who had built up legitimate expectations of him, its well-being had the first moral claim on him. To try to serve strangers of whom he knew nothing and ignore his own people was to harm both. Moreover, to take on himself the care of all mankind was to imply that the other parts of the world were bereft of the likes of him and that he was indispensable to the universe, and to betray overweening moral conceit. He should, of course, hold himself ready to respond to their call for help, but must at all costs avoid becoming a global *guru*. Although he thought that he had a universal message, it is worth noting that Gandhi devoted all his attention to India, leaving it to others to decide if his experiments there had any relevance for them.

For Gandhi service to one's fellow-men was not a separate and independent activity, but was expressed in and informed all one did. Every man was a husband, a father, a son, a friend, a neighbour, a colleague, an employer or an employee. These were not so many discrete roles, each governed by its own distinct norms and values, but different ways of realising his humanity and relating to his fellow-men. He should define, reconcile and inte- grate them into a coherent pattern of life governed by the general principle of social service.[15] As a neighbour, for example, he should not only refrain from making a nuisance of himself but also help those in need, take an active interest in their well-being and the quality of their surroundings, help create a vibrant local com- munity and join them in their fights against injustice. A similar spirit of service and humanity should infuse his manner of earning his livelihood, which he should look on as a *yajna*, as his form of participation in the preservation and development of mankind and of which the monetary reward was not the purpose but an inciden- tal though necessary consequence.[16] Gandhi thought that by bringing to his every activity the 'sweet smell of humanity', every man could in his own small way help transform the quality of human relationships and contribute to the creation of a world based on love and goodwill. Such a 'quiet, unostentatious service' as wiping the tear of a widow, educating a neighbour's child, nursing a sick relation and helping a poor or an untouchable family live in peace and dignity, and thus 'picking up one clod of earth' from the entire mass of human unhappiness, was just as important as the more glamorous forms of social service and sometimes had even more lasting and beneficial results.

Every age and every country, Gandhi went on, had its own distinctive forms and sources of suffering, and hence the nature and content of social service varied. In earlier ages when India was a happy and just society, the *rishis* were perhaps justified in retiring to the forests. By contrast modern India was deeply scarred by acute poverty, vast social and economic inequalities, foreign rule and extensive moral degeneration, and the active service of its people consisted in fighting against these evils. Gandhi observed:

> *Yajna*, *dāna*, *tapas*, are obligatory duties, but that does not mean that the manner of performing them in this age should be the same as in ancient times. *Yajna*, *dāna*, etc., are permanent prin- ciples. The social practices and the concrete forms through which they are put into practice may change from age to age and country to country. The right gift which a seeker of *moksha* in this country and this age may make is to dedicate his all, body, intellect and possessions, to the service of the country. And,

likewise, the right *tapas* for this country and this age consists in burning with agony at the suffering of countless untouchables and others who are starving for want of food or because of famines. Anyone who performs these three important duties certainly becomes purified and he may even have a vision of God's cosmic form which Arjuna had.[17]

For Gandhi the modern age was the age of politics *par excellence*. Almost all aspects of individual and social life were directly or indirectly organised and administered by the state. Its presence was ubiquitous, and all human relationships were politically mediated. He thought this was particularly true of India and all other colonies.[18] Since politics was so pervasive, Gandhi advanced the fascinating thesis that it was the central terrain of action in the modern age. In a politcally dominated age it was impossible to serve one's fellow-men and eliminate social and economic ills without active political involvement. Gandhi thought that if political life could be spiritualised, it would have a profoundly tranformative effect on the rest of society. In every age a specific area of life was the unique testing ground of religion and morality and offered them a unique opportunity to revitalise themselves. In the modern age it was politics, and no religion could be taken seriously that failed to address itself to its political challenges. In the modern age and especially in India, political action was therefore the only available path to *moksha*, a truly revolutionary view in the Indian context.[19] The fundamental principles of Hinduism were being weighed in the political scale, and its only chance of regenerating itself lay in reaffirming them on the political plane. As Gandhi put it:

Every age is known to have its predominant mode of spiritual effort best suited for the attainment of *moksha*. Whenever the religious spirit is on the decline, it is revived through such an effort in tune with the times. In this age, our degradation reveals itself through our political condition . . . Gokhale not only perceived this right at the beginning of his public life but also followed the principle in action. Everyone had realised that popular awakening could be brought about only through political activity. If such activity was spiritualised, it could show the path of *moksha*.

. . . In this age, only political *sannyāsis* can fulfil and adorn the ideal of *sannyāsa*; others will more likely than not disgrace the *sannyāsi's* saffron garb. No Indian who aspires to follow the way of true religion can afford to remain aloof from politics. In other words, one who aspires to a truly religious life cannot fail to undertake public service as his mission, and we are today so much caught up in the political machine that service of the people is impossible without taking part in politics. In olden days, our peasants, though ignorant of who ruled them, led their simple lives free from fear; they can no longer afford to be so unconcerned. In the circumstances that obtain today, in following the path of religion they must take into account the political conditions. If our *sadhus, rishis, munis, maulvis* and priests realised the truth of this, we would have a Servants of India Society in every village, the spirit of religion would come to prevail all over India, the political system which has become odious would reform itself.[20]

For Gandhi then every Indian had a duty in the modern age to become politically involved. The purpose of political engagement was to regenerate India along the lines discussed earlier. Political involvement therefore took a number of forms and occurred at a variety of levels. Although participation in the struggle for independence was obviously important, it was not the most important and could itself take different forms. Since independence was merely formal and had no meaning without national regeneration, 'true politics' in Gandhi's view consisted in revitalising Indian society, culture and character by working in the villages, fighting against local injustices, helping people acquire courage and self-respect, building up their organised strength and in general devoting oneself to any of the 18 items of the Constructive Programme. Every activity that contributed to India's regeneration and made it just and cohesive was political in nature. Politics was not necessarily connected with, let alone exhausted in, the state. Indeed, the fact that it should be so understood showed the extent of degeneration both in India and elsewhere. The state had become the sole arena of political activity because modern man had surrendered all his moral and social powers to it. His regeneration consisted in regaining his powers and running his life himself in co-operation with others. Since 'true politics' was primarily concerned with man's moral and spiritual development, it involved removing his 'addiction' to the state and necessarily occurred *outside* it.

For Gandhi then the pursuit of *moksha* consisted in self-purification and the active service of all men. Sometimes he called the former spirituality, the latter morality and the two together religion, defining it as spiritually grounded and orientated morality.[21] On other occasions he called both morality, one internal, the other external, and equated it with religion.[22] In either case he was concerned to insist that morality was a matter of *both* the quality of the soul and conduct. It was like a tree whose roots and fruits were intimately connected and equally important. The world only saw and was primarily interested in its fruits or conduct and tended to concentrate on it; the agent alone knew and had struggled to nurture the roots, and had a tendency to emphasise the quality of character or motive alone. Gandhi insisted that each captured only one aspect of morality and that no action was moral that excluded either. Unless a good motive led to action, it was a mere thought and not a motive or a principle of action. If a man really felt well-disposed towards others, he must translate it into action, the only 'test' of whether or not he 'really' felt this way. Conversely, promoting their well-being was moral only when motivated not by consideration of the agent's own worldly and other-worldly interests but by 'pure love'. For Gandhi morality was at once both social and spiritual, both other-directed and self-directed, and a moral being must act on two planes at once, the world as well as his soul.

All religious traditions have perceived a potential conflict between the concerns of the soul and the world, and warned against excessive preoccupation with the latter even in the morally acceptable form of social service. Gandhi disagreed and argued that the traditional view rested on three false assumptions; first, God was separate from the world as, otherwise, His service could not conflict with that of the world; second, his own salvation was every man's sole or highest concern; and third, his salvation might conflict with and be hampered by worldly involvement.

For Gandhi God was not separate from but identical with the totality of living beings, and there was therefore no question of His service conflicting with theirs.[23] Since all men were manifestations of the cosmic spirit and thus one, their salvation, like their humanity, was indivisible. The concept of personal salvation was therefore philosophically incoherent. Indeed, since it rested on the mistaken belief that the self and others were separate, the concept of personal salvation was precisely the illusion every spiritual aspirant should shed. Finally, Gandhi contended that far from being a hindrance to spirituality, the life of worldly involvement was its necessary training and testing ground. It was only in the course of a life of action that men learned to discipline themselves, resist temptations, cultivate will-power and co-operative impulses, subordinate the personal to social interests and indeed to keep their minds free from 'idle fantasies'. Only 'one in a million' had the inner strength to develop a pure soul without the rigorous discipline of action.[24] Furthermore it was only in the realm of action that men were fully tested and stretched and discovered themselves. Sitting in a forest or a monastry carefully insulated from all possible temptations and provocations, a man could easily convince himself that he had overcome anger, sexuality, selfishness or jealousy. If he dared enter the real world and put himself in trying situations, he might have painful surprises waiting for him. The self discovered itself in all its complexity and grew only in the course of trying to meet the powerful challenges of the world. For Gandhi self-realisation was impossible without worldly involvement.[25]

It would be helpful briefly to recapitulate the apparently obvious but really momentous steps by which Gandhi not only linked but identified the *vita activa* and the *vita contemplativa*, and gave political life a spiritual foundation. First, *moksha* consisted in identification with the *Brahman*. Second, since the *Brahman* was manifested in all living beings, *moksha* consisted in identification with all living beings, especially men. Third, love was the only means of identification, and therefore *moksha* involved universal love. Fourth, love implied active and dedicated service to one's fellow-men, including fighting against inequalities and injustices. Fifth, in the politically-dominated modern age, and especially in a poor and subject country like India, injustices could not be fought without engaging in political action in the wide sense in which Gandhi used the term. Sixth, politics so understood was therefore the only or at any rate the most effective path to *moksha* in the modern age. Strictly speaking only the first of the six premises was an integral part of Hindu religious tradition. The second had some basis in it, but not the way Gandhi defined it. The rest were all new and constituted Gandhi's great contribution.

To be sure, Gandhi's conclusion that politics was a spiritual activity was not novel and had been advanced by a large number of his predecessors such as Gokhale, Tilak, Ranade, B. C. Pal and

Aurobindo. Indeed, the phrase 'spiritualisation of politics' seems to have been first used by Gokhale, and Gandhi himself acknowledged that he had borrowed it from his 'political guru'. Several important differences, however, separated them from Gandhi. First, unlike them he offered well-considered reasons for regarding politics as a spiritual activity. Second, while many of them separated politics and spirituality and talked of spiritualising politics, for Gandhi the two were identical. Politics as he defined it was itself a spiritual activity, and all true spirituality culminated in politics. Third, for most of them spirituality largely meant morality, and politics was spiritual in the sense of being a moral activity. Hardly any of them saw it as a vehicle of *moksha*. Indeed, they would have been horrified by such a view. Finally, many of them generally defined morality in social terms and equated politics with social reform. Gandhi was one of the first to define morality in political terms, and politics in terms of active struggle against injustices and oppression.

Gandhi well knew that his theory of morality represented a radical departure from Hindu religious tradition and that his only hope of getting it widely accepted consisted in criticising and drastically reinterpreting the latter.[26] He distinguished between philosophical and practical or popular Hinduism, the two extremes into which in his view it had become polarised, and contended that they had failed in their own different ways to develop a satisfactory theory of morality.[27]

By philosophical Hinduism Gandhi largely meant the *vedantic* metaphysic, the pride and glory of Indian philosophy and by which he was himself deeply influenced. In his view it had discovered some of the greatest moral principles known to mankind such as the unity of man, life and creation, *ahimsā* and the indivisibility of humanity and of human salvation, and could have constructed a most profound system of morality on their bases. For reasons discussed earlier, Gandhi argued that instead it turned its back on the world and betrayed its powerful insights. Although for obvious political and other reasons he did not launch a frontal attack on it, he stated in no uncertain terms why he was most unhappy with it. First, like all other religions philosophical Hinduism defined salvation in personal terms and encouraged spiritual selfishness. Second, it was 'callous', lacked a 'social conscience' and showed indifference to worldly suffering on the spurious ground that 'material' suffering was spiritually inconsequential and had no claim on the attention of a spiritual seeker. Third, it was 'negative' and 'passive' and had a wholly unjustified 'horror' of action. Although Gandhi appreciated and shared its fear that the active life tended to strengthen the sense of individuality and led to worldly attachments, he thought that the *Gita* had already shown how to act in a spiritually blameless manner. He also argued that the life of action developed and tested the powers of self-discipline and self-control, and had a profound spiritual significance. Fourth, and to Gandhi its most important limitation, philosophical Hinduism failed to develop an adequate theory of morality. It either exorcised morality out of existence by insisting that spirituality was beyond good and evil and that a spiritual seeker should avoid being imprisoned within conventional morality, or it gave it a highly negative and passive content and so emaciated it that it amounted to little more than non-injury to living beings.

For Gandhi popular Hinduism represented the other end of the spectrum and suffered from opposite limitations. Although he greatly admired its simple faith, feel for the pervasive presence of the divine, its sense of *dharma* and the spirit of service and self-surrender, he found it gravely defective. While philosophical Hinduism had become unworldly and was only concerned with the inner life, its popular counterpart had become intensely worldly and was only interested in the external side of life. It had more or less reduced religion to *karmakānda*, rituals, rites, ceremonies, pilgrimages to holy places, feeding the cows and the Brahmins and giving occasional alms to beggars in the hope that these would propitiate the relevant deities and earn the agent religious merit. It had similarly reduced morality to an uncritical observance of caste duties and social customs. It thus eviscerated both religion and morality of their spiritual basis and gravely impoverished them.

Gandhi concluded that both philosophical and popular Hinduism needed radical reform, albeit for opposite reasons. The former stressed the *Brahman* but ignored the world, the latter made the opposite mistake. Since neither grasped the fundamental fact of their identity, they ended up misunderstanding both. Philosophical Hinduism needed to appreciate the importance of the world of morality, its popular counterpart that of the *Brahman* or spirituality. One therefore needed to be given an activist and social, and the other a spiritual and inward orientation. By reinterpreting each in this way Gandhi hoped to reduce their traditional distance and create a common basis on which all Hindus could unite.

Gandhi redefined almost every major category of philosophical Hinduism in activist, social and worldly terms. He gave a radically novel content to the concept of *moksha* and almost equated it with *dharma*. It did, of course, mean to him what it meant to the *Vedantins*, namely the dissolution of individuality into the *Brahman*. However, the dissolution consisted not in a mystical unity with it but in losing oneself in the active service of mankind. Indeed, as we saw, he made politics the only adequate path to it in modern India and gave *karmayoga* a wholly new orientation. In defining *moksha* in this way Gandhi was also led to redefine the state of mind traditionally associated with it. Traditionally it implied *ānanda* or a state of supreme joy. For Gandhi it involved not only *ānanda* but also *dukha* or suffering, for to identify oneself with all men was to suffer for and with them and make their suffering one's own. *Moksha* therefore meant not so much avoidance of or freedom from suffering as finding joy in sharing and ceaselessly striving to relieve it. As Gandhi put it, 'joy comes . . . out of pain voluntarily borne'. It was hardly surprising that he should have described his fasts as sources of both supreme peace and intense agony.

Hindu philosophical tradition had stressed the central importance of *tapasyā* in attaining self-purification.[28] Gandhi agreed, but totally redefined it. '*Tapasyā* does not simply consist in betaking oneself to the forest and sitting down there surrounded by fires. That *tapasyā* may even be the height of folly.' Gandhi's amusing and unkind description of it barely conceals his contempt for it. In his view true *tapasyā* consisted in suffering in the service of one's fellow-men and included *satyāgraha*, voluntary poverty and even fasting. Gandhi contended that *sannyāsa* too meant renouncing not the world but the self.[29] 'A *sannyāsi* is one who cares for others. He has renounced all selfishness. But he is full of sleepless and selfless activity.'[30] He was not a recluse but a selfless worker 'burning with agony' and actively fighting against the injustices of his society. 'A *sannyāsin*, therefore, to be true to his creed of renunciation, must care for *swarāj* not for its sake but for the sake of others.'[31]

Gandhi also redefined the doctrine of *yoga*. Patanjali had elaborated several *yamas* and *niyamas* to be observed by a spiritual aspirant. Gandhi reinterpreted them all and added a few of his own so as to increase the individual's capacity for sustained social service. He replaced the traditional repertoire of spiritual exercises with a wholly new set of his own, including cleaning latrines, living and working among the untouchables and nursing the sick. Cleaning latrines was in his view a better way of acquiring self-discipline, 'reducing oneself to a zero' and learning the dignity of labour than some of the traditional spiritual exercises. And living and working among the untouchables was a far more effective way of learning the unity of mankind than meditation.

Again, to Gandhi *samādhi* meant not leaving the world and engaging in intense meditation for days on end, but temporary withdrawal from the daily routine in order to compose one's thoughts and reflect on the meaning and significance of one's actions. It did, of course, require the temporary 'shelter of a cave'; however, 'I carry one about me if I would but know it'.[32] Like *samādhi, dhyāna* meant periods of silence in the midst of and as a preparation for intense involvement in the world. They were not 'like jewels to be kept locked in a strong box. They must be seen in every act of ours.' Gandhi also changed the traditional concept of *āshram*. Unlike the ancient and modern *rishis*, he located his first *āshram* in India on the outskirts of a major industrial city and used it to conduct experiments in education, spinning, weaving and other productive activities as well as to train a cadre of committed social workers and *satyāgrahis*.

Gandhi gave an inward or spiritual orientation to the central categories of popular Hinduism, and his reinterpretation of them was no less radical.[33] It had confined God to heaven; Gandhi argued that He was present in every living being and to be found not in temples but in the huts of the poor. Prayer did not consist in chanting hymns and devotional songs but serving other men as a way of serving God. *Yajna* consisted not in conducting formal *karmakānda* and rites but in seeing the entire life as one continuous offering at the altar of mankind.[34] The true worship of God consisted not in visiting temples but in nursing the sick, helping orphans and improving the conditions of the poor and the untouchables. Spinning as a way of identifying with the poor was 'the greatest prayer, the greatest worship'.[35] For Gandhi wearing khadi was more sacred than wearing beads and saffron robes. Not the so-called holy rivers and towns but the places where the poor and the untouchables lived were truly holy, and working and living among them in the spirit of a pilgrim was a true pilgrimage. When Gandhi went to Noakhali to reconcile the warring Hindus and Muslims, he called himself a pilgrim and his stay there an act of pilgrimage.

In these and other ways Gandhi profoundly redefined Hinduism and gave it a radically novel orientation. Not God, not Man, but men were made its centre, and self-purification and their active service in the spirit of love constituted its content. Gandhi thus rationalised Hinduism and reduced it to a set of such basic moral principles as love, truth, *ahimsā* and social service. He marginalised the *sāstras* and deprived them of their religious and moral authority.[36] He rarely referred to them to support his views, poured contempt on the endless debates about the meanings of their isolated passages and interpreted them as he thought proper.[37] He thereby undermined the traditional religious basis of Brahmanic authority and liberated Hinduism from their stranglehold. The Brahmins had stressed the authority of the *sāstras*; Gandhi argued that they, including even the *Vedas*, were subject to the test of reason and conscience. They had insisted on the eternal validity of the revealed knowledge; Gandhi contended that every *yuga* had its own unique *dharma* and periodically needed to reinterpret the eternal moral principles.[38] They had concentrated on the ritual and ceremonial aspect of religion; Gandhi made social service its basis. The Brahmins glorified the intellectual and spiritual and condemned manual activities; Gandhi insisted that the latter were an integral part of the cosmic *yajna* and that whoever avoided them was a 'thief' and a 'parasite'. They regarded certain activities and the people engaged in them as polluted; Gandhi rejoined that only those engaged in the 'lowly' activities truly served their fellow-men and made the untouchables, not the Brahmins, the privileged 'children of God'. Gandhi turned Hinduism upside down in a way no-one had done before, and did it with such consummate skill and authority that the Brahmins were thoroughly outsmarted.[39]

The Brahmins' reactions to Gandhi covered a wide range. Some were deeply impressed by his creative reinterpretation of their religion hailed him as a great social *and* religious reformer and gave him their most loyal and enthusiastic support. Some others welcomed his new definition of *yugadharma*, but not the way he arrived at it, and thought that he had misinterpreted the basic concerns of Hindu religious tradition. They welcomed him as a social but not a religious reformer. A small group of Brahmins remained implacably hostile to him. Almost wholly out of sympathy with his social and political message, they argued that he had mischievously *vaisya-ised* and even *sudra-ised* their religion and chartered it in the service of his social and political objectives. Not surprisingly they were his most vocal and virulent critics, spreading more vicious gossip about his personal life and staging more demonstrations against him than any other group of Indians.

Gandhi's Hinduism was an ingenious intellectual construct. There was hardly a Hindu religious category and practice to which he did not give a worldly and secular content. At the same time he respected the integrity of the Hindu religious consciousness and avoided the all-too-common mistake of reducing religion to mere social service or morality. For him religion culminated but was not exhausted in social service, and the latter had a spiritual meaning and significance only when inspired by the search for *moksha*. Gandhi's Hinduism thus had a secular content but a spiritual form, and was at once both secular and non-secular. It therefore both appealed to and alienated his atheist and religious followers. The former were attracted by his passionate concern with social, economic and political issues but felt ill at ease with their spiritual roots; the latter reacted in the opposite manner. Gandhi secularised Hinduism as much as it was possible to do *within* a spiritual framework, an unparalleled achievement in the history of Hindu thought anticipated by several, especially Vivekananda, but accomplished by no other.

5

Theory of the State

Like many other Indian leaders Gandhi had considerable difficulty in coming to terms with the modern state. At one level he understood it better than them. He was trained as a lawyer, had observed it in its developed form in Britain and distorted forms in South Africa and India, and as a leader of the independence movement he had close day-to-day contact with it. He was one of the few to notice that the modern age was unique in assigning the state a most dominant position in society. Having led several anti-racist campaigns in South Africa, he understood the nature of political power and ideology better than most of his contemporaries and well knew how the state was interlocked with dominant interests and upheld the prevailing social order. Gandhi, however, had his severe handicaps. As a votary of non-violence he was obsessed with the coercive aspect of the state and could not appreciate its moral dimension until fairly late in life. He was opposed to large-scale industrialisation and did not much understand the economic role of the state either. As a moralist he was deeply preoccupied with personal integrity and individual responsibility and had great difficulty in coming to terms with the need for collective discipline and the moral compromises required by membership of the state. As a political leader who had spent all his life fighting against it, he could hardly avoid sharing the rebel's deep suspicion and biased view of it. For these and other reasons Gandhi's theory of the state was uneven, in parts refreshingly original and profound, in others ahistorical and naïve.

As we saw earlier, Gandhi was most critical of the modern state. It was impersonal, ruling by rules, functioning more or less like a 'machine' with no human beings apparently in charge of it or accepting responsibility for its actions.[1] Laws were collectively made by the legislature, and no individual member of it felt responsible for them. Civil servants claimed merely to administer

110

them and did not feel responsible for their consequences either. Insofar as it destroyed or at least obscured all sense of personal responsibility and the concomitant feelings of remorse and guilt, the state demoralised and dehumanised man. Gandhi contended that even when it left room for personal responsibility, its structure and manner of operation allowed too many escape routes. A member of parliament who regretted a law convinced himself that it would have been passed anyway or that he had no choice but to follow the party line. A civil servant might regret the consequences of a rule, but pleaded helplessness on the grounds that his duty as an officer left him no alternative. Like almost all other Indian leaders Gandhi thought that the state was inherently inhospitable to personal responsibility and had an anti-human thrust. He was not opposed to rules and institutions whose vital importance he fully recognised, but thought that the modern state relied on them so heavily that it stifled human responsiblity and even 'forgot' that it was an association of human beings. As he sometimes put it, the modern state was organised along 'scientific' lines and had reduced the government to a machine. Gandhi's criticism of it was an integral part of his larger critique of modern science.

For Gandhi the state compromised man's moral nature in yet another way. As we shall see presently, the state was for him a system of institutionalised co-operation sustained by the acts of its citizens. Each of them was therefore partly responsible for what it did in their name. It was, however, so structured and run that it appeared to exist independently of them, obscured the links between its acts and theirs, and dulled their conscience. Without their realising it, they were morally compromised and rendered accomplices to its sometimes immoral deeds.

In Gandhi's view the state also fostered a statist manner of thinking and appropriated man's moral and social powers. Rather than let them run their lives themselves and grow to their full moral stature, it encouraged its citizens to take the easy option of letting it take all their decisions. Over time they became so 'addicted' to it that they were even unable to imagine how they could live orderly lives without being ordered. For Gandhi, further, the state stood above and lorded over society, and was neither in organic and daily contact with nor constantly accountable to it. Its primary concern was to reduce society to a pliable and homogeneous material amenable to uniform rules and bureaucratic management. It was therefore impatient of individual differences and diversity and hostile to strong and independent-minded citizens, groups and communities lest they should become centres of independent initiative and dissent.[2]

Gandhi contended that as a vast and impersonal 'machine' only concerned with administering society, the state was uninterested in and incapable of activating and mobilising the full range of its moral impulses and had no alternative but to rely on fear and force. It was really nothing but 'violence in a concentrated and organised form' and could 'never be weaned away from violence to which it owes its very existence'.[3] Unlike the personal violence of ancient kings, its massive violence was barely visible. It was hidden behind the fabric of rules, never crudely flaunted but nevertheless subtly displayed at regular intervals, officialised such that no specific individual could be blamed for committing it, parcelled out to a number of agencies to administer it on its behalf so that its citizens never grasped its scale and magnitude, and exported abroad and rendered invisible. All this created the dangerous illusion that the modern state had eliminated violence when in fact it had intensified it.

For these and other reasons Gandhi concluded that by its very nature the state was incompatible with man's moral and spiritual nature. Man was really *ātman* or soul; the modern state was a 'soul-less machine'. The two simply could not co-exist. If they really cherished and were genuinely concerned about their moral status, men had to find an alternative way of structuring their organised life.

In addition to his general critique of the modern state, Gandhi contended that it was especially unsuited to India. India had a spiritual civilisation, whereas the state was uniquely a product of materialist civilisation. Non-violence was deeply cherished in India, whereas the state relied on violence. Indian society valued and was based on direct and unmediated relations between men; the modern state was a highly abstract institution. Indian civilisation was plural and tolerated the utmost diversity of customs and ways of life; the modern state required homogeneity. Indian civilisation was essentially rural, whereas the state required an urban civilisation. Indian society valued autonomous and self-governing castes, sects and ehtnic groups; the state imposed a uniform system of laws. Since the task of independent India was to 'purify and stabilise' its civilisation, its polity should be so structured that it could protect and act as its internal critic. In Gandhi's view, far from revitalising Indian civilisation, the modern state was bound to set about replacing it with one conducive to its own ethos and requirements.

The Indian people had over the centuries become degenerate, and the task of independent India was to build up their courage, self-confidence and capacity for initiative and concerted action. Gandhi thought that the modern state with its centralist tendencies was inherently incapable of doing so and was likely to render them even more passive and timid. He was also deeply worried about the enormous amount of power it would have to acquire in order to undertake the massive task of social reconstruction and the threat this posed to people's liberties. He thought, too, that since the Indian state was likely to be dominated by the urbanised and Westernised elite alienated from ordinary people and committed to values profoundly at odds with theirs, it was bound to remain as exploitative as its colonial predecessor.

For these and other related reasons Gandhi argued that independent India should evolve a new type of non-statal polity. Ideally he preferred 'enlightened anarchy' under which socially responsible and morally disciplined men and women never harmed one another and did not need any kind of polity. Since that was, like the Euclidean straight line, inherently unrealisable but to be constantly approximated, Gandhi opted for 'ordered anarchy' under which citizens enjoyed maximum freedom consistent with the minimum necessary order. The guiding principles of such a polity were obvious. It should be based on non-violence; should place man at the centre and help him recover and develop his moral and social powers currently surrendered to the state; build up courage, autonomy and a sense of power among its people; break the statist political culture by fostering strong and vibrant local communities; and it should facilitate the regeneration of Indian society and culture along the lines discussed earlier. India had come to grief in the past because, among other things, it lacked both a central authority strong enough to unite it and a spirit of nationality transcending the narrow ethnic, religious, linguistic, regional and other identities. The new polity should remedy these and other defects without undermining the basic character of Indian civilisation. It should have a central government but not a centralised structure of authority, and it should cultivate a sense of nationality but base it on autonomous and self-governing local communities.

Gandhi sketched such a polity, not as a blueprint to be copied but only as an indication of the general lines along which Indians should think. As he imagined it, the new polity consisted of small, cultured, thoroughly regenerated, well-organised and self-determining village communities.[4] Their affairs were managed by *panchāyats* consisting of five persons annually elected by every literate adult between the ages of 18 and 50, those above 50 being expected to have less interest in the human world and therefore being not qualified to vote. Gandhi insisted on literacy because the problems of the modern world were too complex to be understood by anyone unable to read and write, and also as a way of ensuring that the citizens would put enough pressure on the goverment to eradicate illiteracy. In his view the literacy requirement was not unfair for, being a form of political power, the vote was a public trust and a citizen could legitimately be required to prove his capacity to discharge it by acquiring the necessary qualification.[5] The village *panchāyat* had legislative, executive and judicial powers, and largely relied on its moral authority and the pressure of public opinion to ensure order and harmony. Gandhi thought that the village community would over time build up a 'strong sense of local strength and solidarity', provide 'meaningful' interpersonal relationships, encourage a sense of social responsibility and the spirit of co-operation, and act as a nursery of civic virtues.

Beyond the relatively self-sufficient villages the country was organised in terms of 'expanding circles'. The villages were grouped into *talukas*, the latter into districts, these into provinces, and so on, each governed by representatives elected by its constituent units. Each tier of government enjoyed considerable autonomy and a strong sense of community, both sustained and limited the one above it and dealt with matters of common interest to its constituent communities. Each province was free to draw up its own constitution to suit local requirements and in conformity with that of the country as a whole.[6] The central government wielded enough authority to hold them all together, but not enough to dominate them. Gandhi was opposed to direct elections to the central assembly because they were divisive and encouraged corruption and also because the average voter knew little either about the candidates involved or the large issues of national policy. The polity so constructed was not a collection of isolated atoms but a community of communities, a unity of unities, a whole composed of wholes. As Gandhi put it:

In this structure composed of innumerable villages, there will be every-widening, never-ascending circles. Life will not be a pyramid with the apex sustained by the bottom. But it will be an oceanic circle whose centre will be the individuals . . . Therefore the outermost circumference will not wield power to crush the inner circle, but will give strength to all within and derive its own strength from it.[7]

Gandhi contended that a polity constructed along these lines did not need a vast bureaucracy as much of the decision-making was decentralised. It did not need police either since crime was bound to be minimal in a society where no-one starved and everyone enjoyed face-to-face relations with his fellow-citizens. Such crimes as did occur would be dealt with by the moral pressure of local public opinion and, if necessary, by its members taking turns at policing.[8] Gandhi thought that such a polity did not require an army and could rely on 'non-violent soldiers' trained in the method of *satyāgraha*. There was no danger of civil war, and no foreign country was likely to invade a polity whose fiercely independent-minded citizens would resist it to the death.

Gandhi insisted that only a federally-constituted polity based on vigorous and self-governing local communities was truly democratic. Democracy was based on the recognition of the fundamental fact that men were self-determining moral agents fully capable of regulating their personal and common affairs and the source of all political power. It therefore aimed to organise the conduct of collective affairs in such a manner that the people remained in full charge of them and were never dominated by or at the mercy of their government. To the extent that they were or felt powerless to do the things they wanted to do or to 'bend the government to their will', the form of government was not fully democratic. Democracy was not so much an arrangement of offices or a cluster of institutions, rules and procedures as a way of life geared to developing and actualising popular power. Since the term democracy was generally used to refer to liberal democracy based on the centralisation of power to be used by popularly elected and accountable representatives, Gandhi preferred the term *swarāj* to describe what he called 'true democracy'.

In Gandhi's view liberal democracy remained imprisoned within the restrictive and centralised framework of the modern state and could never be truly democratic. It abstracted power from the people, concentrated it in the state and then returned it to them in their new incarnation as citizens. The result was a triple disaster. First, a good deal of their power seeped away into or was deliberately usurped by the institutions of the state. Second, they, the ultimate source of all political power, now received it as a *gift* from the state and became its creature. Third, political power was given to them on condition that they only exercised it as *citizens* or members of the state, that is, as abstract and truncated men guided by values relevant to and permitted by the state and not as concrete and whole human beings giving expression to the full range of their moral concerns. For Gandhi the state by its very nature emasculated democracy and frustrated its complete realisation. Since liberal democracy was state-centred, it achieved only as much democracy as was possible within the structure of the state and could never be truly or fully democratic. *Swarāj* or true democracy was only possible within a federally constituted non-statal polity in which the citizens conducted their local affairs themselves, delegated only the minimum necessary authority to the successively higher levels of government and kept a constant and vigilant eye on their representatives. As he put it.

> . . . real *swarāj* will come not by the acquisition of authority by a few but by the acquisition of the capacity by all to resist authority when it is abused. In other words *swarāj* is to be attained by educating the masses to a sense of their capacity to regulate and control authority.[9]

Gandhi was convinced that the creation of the new polity or *swarāj* could not be delayed until after independence, as many of his colleagues had argued. Unless its foundations were laid and the necessary institutions and ethos created during the course of the struggle for independence, India was likely to take the lazy and seductive but suicidal option of reproducing the modern European state. As observed earlier, his tripartite strategy of the Constructive Programme, *satyāgraha* and the cultivation of the *swadeshi* spirit was designed to prepare for the new polity. The *swadeshi* spirit was intended to develop an attitude of cultural self-respect and autonomy so that his countrymen did not blindly opt for European ideas and institutions. *Satyāgraha* was intended to involve people in political life, build up their courage and capacity for concerted action, to expose them to common political experiences and create a feeling of collective solidarity and, above all, to help them shed their centuries-old fear of government. On several occasions Gandhi launched *satyāgrahas* not so much because he wanted to put pressure on the government or forestall violence, although the latter determined their timing, as because they were the kind of moral and political exercises the country needed to build up its moral and political muscle. Even when they had failed and were apparently pointless, he therefore sometimes allowed them to go on for a while. Gandhi's Constructive Programme had similar objectives and was part of his larger strategy of building up Indian character and society. Some of his colleagues and the colonial government thought that the Programme was intended to give the independence struggle a mass base. Gandhi made it clear that he had something very different in mind. In order to promote and implement the Programme, he set up several organisations and kept a constant and careful eye on their activities. He persuaded a large number of Congressmen to go to the villages and devote themselves to the 'silent' and 'invisible' but vital task of 'leavening' the 'inert mass'. He thought of them as his 'army for *swarāj*, quietly working behind the back and corroding the basis of the colonial state and preparing for its eventual replacement by a distinctively Indian polity under their leadership.

Within Gandhi's framework of thought the 'Council Entry' naturally looked irrelevant, even diversionary, and he strongly opposed it. It took him some time to realise that entering government could serve at least three important purposes. First, it helped Indians acquire the necessary constitutional and political skills. Second, it gave them an opportunity to criticise and oppose the government, educate public opinion and build up their self-confidence. And third, it helped promote legislation conducive to the Constructive Programme. The first argument never carried much weight with Gandhi; the other two did. He agreed to give the Swaraj party his official blessing on condition that Congress did not attenuate its commitment to or downgrade the importance of his larger strategy, especially the Constructive Programme. He never took much interest in what it did within the government; his interests and affections were largely confined to the implementation of his tripartite strategy.

From about 1930 onwards Gandhi's views on the nature of the state and the functions of government underwent an important change. Although he still continued to plead for a loosely structured polity based on the institutionalised partnership between the people and the government, the latter now began to assume a more dominant role. Hitherto he had thought of the state almost entirely as a 'soul-less machine' based on and sustained by violence and only necessary because the weak human will required the coercive discipline of the law. When such exploited and long-oppressed groups as the untouchables, the poor, the tribals, the agricultural labourers and the landless peasants began to campaign for social and economic justice and threaten the unity of the independence movement, Gandhi had to take serious notice of them. He had always been solicitous about the first two but not the rest, and he also began to appreciate that poverty and untouchability could not be as easily eradicated as he had hitherto thought. The increasing pace of industrialisation created a large class of poor, discontented and organised industrial workers, and he could not ignore them either. He realised that many of these groups were too weak to compete on equal terms with the rest of their countrymen, and that they threatened to unleash violence and tear apart the social fabric of India unless something was done to meet their demands.

Gandhi began to appreciate that the state had a vital role to play in promoting social and economic justice. He put the point well at the Round Table Conference in 1931:

> I am afraid that for years to come India would be engaged in passing legislation in order to raise the down-trodden, and the fallen, from the mire into which they have been sunk by the capitalists, by the landlords, by the so-called higher classes, and then, subsequently and scientifically, by the British rulers. If we are to lift these people from the mire, then it would be the bounden duty of the National Government of India, in order to set its house in order, continually to give preference to these people and even free them from the burdens under which they are being crushed. And, if the landlords, zamindars, monied men and those who are today enjoying privileges – I do not care whether they are Europeans or Indians – if they find that they are discriminated against, I shall sympathise with them, but I will not be able to help them, even if I could possibly do so, because I would seek their assistance in that process, and with-

out their assistance it would not be possible to raise these people out of the mire.

Look at the condition, if you will, of the untouchables, if the law comes to their assistance and sets apart miles of territory. At the present moment they hold no land; they are absolutely living at the mercy of the so-called higher castes, and also, let me say, at the mercy of the state. They can be removed from one quarter to another without complaint and without being able to seek the assistance of law. Well, the first act of the Legislature will then be to see that in order somewhat to equalise conditions, these people are given grants freely.[10]

Gandhi also began to acknowledge that the deeply entrenched social and economic inequalities and injustices could not be removed by moral persuasion alone. As we shall see, he conceded that the capitalists were unlikely to become trustees of their property unless compelled to do so by law. He realised too that independent India could not do without large industries and would have to nationalise many of them 'with or without compensation'. He saw that the state also had an important role to play in the national regeneration of India. Although much of the work was to be done by dedicated voluntary workers, the state could greatly assist their efforts. In some areas its intervention was critical, for example, the preservation of village industries and the spread of basic education; in some others it could act as a facilitator and remove hindrances, for example, the prohibition of alcohol and the removal of untouchability; in yet others it could lend its moral and material help and expedite voluntary efforts, for example, the development of regional languages.

These and other related functions Gandhi now assigned to the state implied that it was an instrument of social and economic justice, a protector and promoter of the public and some aspects of private morality, a custodian of Indian civilisation, and the patron of the grand *yajna* of national regeneration. Indeed when it sought to level up the poor and the oppressed, it did nothing other than put into practice the spiritual principle of active love. He now began to realise that the state was far more complex than he had hitherto imagined, and had a potential for both good and evil. It was not entirely a soul-less machine but also a *moral and spiritual* institution capable of playing a vital role in the moral development of its citizens. It *did*, no doubt, represent concentrated and organised violence; it was also, however, a vehicle of some of their deepest moral aspirations. It *was* a soul-less machine; it was also, however, a custodian of the spirit of Indian civilisation and a vehicle of justice. Although Gandhi appreciated all this, he did not reconsider his earlier theoretical analysis of the nature of the state and continued to talk about it in highly critical terms. Like his theories of *ahimsā* and *satyāgraha*, his theory of the state lagged behind his practice.

If the state was to undertake the large range of functions Gandhi now assigned it, it obviously could not be as loosely structured and uncentralised as he had hitherto maintained. It had to have a fairly strong central government capable of taking and enforcing important decisions in the relevant areas of collective life, an effective bureaucracy, a system of national planning, an institutional structure for articulating public opinion, and a coercive machinery to deal with the discontented vested interests who would have to be dispossessed or carefully regulated. A polity with these and other features was not very different from the modern state! Although Gandhi continued to warn against the state, he increasingly began to appreciate that India could not dispense with it. As independence drew nearer his guidance was sought by his colleagues and followers about whether they should join the new government, fight parliamentary elections and support the new constitution setting up the modern Indian state. Not surprisingly his advice was ambiguous and sometimes confusing. However, there is enough evidence to show that he had come round to accepting the modern state.

When the Constituent Assembly met to determine the profile of the new polity, Gandhi did not press his views on it. When it opted for the modern state, he did not take a public stand against it either. He does not seem to have spoken about it to Nehru or even to such loyal supporters as Patel and Rajendra Prasad either. When his close associates offered to mobilise public opinion and mount pressure against the new constitution, he advised them against it and urged them instead to 'leave it to those who are labouring at it'.[11] No doubt, during those critical months he was deeply involved in arresting the rising tide of communal violence and acutely frustrated by the way his erstwhile colleagues had deserted him. However, he was too tenacious a fighter to give in easily on matters as momentous as the nature of the Indian state. If anything the communal violence seems to have convinced him how much

India needed the modern state to maintain even a modicum of order. The readiness with which he approved of both the despatch of the Indian army to defend Kashmir and the use of the police to put down communal violence points in that direction. His confession towards the end of his life that India under his leadership had never really believed in the principle of non-violence showed how far in his view it had to go before it could dispense with the state.

Although Gandhi seems to have come round to accepting the modern state, he did not lose his suspicion of it nor abandon his theory of partnership between it and the people. Since the state had come to stay, he explored ways of taming and regulating it. He outlined his ideas in a series of speeches and statements, including his moving talk and the subsequent discussion at the *Gandhi Seva Sangh* meeting in 1940.[12] Just before he died he crystallised his ideas in a fascinating proposal based on the dual strategy he had developed during the independence movement. When read together with his earlier statements, it gives a fairly clear idea of the way his mind was working.

He proposed that now the Congress had served its political purpose of attaining independence, it should dissolve itself as a state-oriented body and reconstitute itself as *Loka Sevak Sangh*, a national organisation for the service of the people, perhaps better translated as a national organisation of the servants of the people. Its members were to settle in villages and become *samagra grām sevaks*, all-purpose or comprehensive village workers dedicated to their total regeneration. They were not social workers in the conventional sense of the term but moral and political leaders. In addition to implementing the Constructive Programme and doing 'researches' in the 'post-graduate laboratory' of advanced social work, they were to 'awaken' the people to their rights, sensitise them to the 'wrongs' done to them, mediate between them and the official agencies of the state, help them fight against local injustices and, when necessary, launch *satyāgrahas*.[13] They were also to train local workers and build up active cadres capable of taking over their work. In these and other ways they were to win over the confidence and trust of the people, build up their strength, and set up a structure of moral authority paralleling the legal authority of the 'official' state. Gandhi thought that in the course of the struggle for independence the Congress had acquired moral authority equal, even superior, to that of the state and trained an 'army' of workers whose moral calibre and commitment were far superior to those of the civil servants. It was therefore uniquely equipped to lead the people, regenerate society and provide an effective moral counterweight to the state.

Gandhi seems to have thought that the 'official' state enjoying legal, and the reconstituted Congress enjoying moral, authority formed the basis of the Indian polity, and provided a uniquely Indian alternative to, or rather a uniquely Indian version of, the modern state. Ideally he would have liked India to evolve a more radical alternative and dispense with the state altogether. Since that was not possible he pleaded for a polity articulated in terms of the complementary and mutually regulating institutions of the state and the *Loka Sevak Sangh*. The new polity was to be a partnership between them in the massive task of regenerating India. The state was to draw on the *Sangh*'s grassroots experiences and expertise in formulating its policies and enact facilitating legislation. For its part the *Sangh* was to take over much of the nation-building work of the state and help implement its policies. Gandhi even thought that the state might second some of its ablest civil servants to the *Sangh* to give it the benefit of their administrative skills. He was, however, most anxious that the state and the *Sangh* must retain their distance and respect each other's autonomy. They had different functions which must never be confused, and they were engaged in different types of politics. One was concerned with the 'politics of power', the other with the 'politics of people'; both were necessary in the common task of national regeneration. They also wielded different kinds of authority. One enjoyed legal, the other moral authority, and two had very different bases and orientation. Although not a part of the 'official' state, the *Sangh* was an integral part of the polity or political system. The *Sangh* was to the state what the Brahmins were to the *kshatriyas* in a traditional Hindu polity; co-operative, respectful, willing to advise and help, but also fiercely independent and ready to give a call for disobedience should the occasion so require.

Gandhi was ambiguous about the moral nature of the state and made contradictory utterances on the subject. On the one hand he thought that it *was* a moral institution capable, as seen earlier, of practising active love in the form of economic and social justice, protecting Indian civilisation and contributing to the moral development of its people. On the other hand he thought that since it was based on violence, it could 'never' be a moral institution. Morality was not merely concerned with doing good but doing so voluntarily and in the spirit of good will. Since every action required by the state was shadowed by the fear of punishment, it could never be moral. Gandhi also argued that like the combination of legal and economic power, that of legal and moral authority was extremely dangerous. By its very nature the state wielded enormous legal authority and power and its citizens needed to be deeply suspicious of it. If it were also to be seen as a moral institution invested with moral authority, they would not only feel obliged to obey its laws blindly but also entrust it with the custody of their conscience and thus abdicate their moral responsibility. Gandhi did not resolve the tension. For the most part he viewed the state as an essentially *legal* institution enjoying the authority to make and enforce laws. Moral authority, accruing from the trust and confidence of the people earned by means of their active service, belonged to the *Lok Sevak Sangh*. Like the Brahmins in ancient India the *Sangh*, their modern equivalent, was the conduit through which the citizens freely and daily decided whether or not and when to confer moral authority on the state.

For Gandhi not consent, nor will nor fear but co-operation was the basis of the state. Every state, democratic or otherwise, depended on the co-operation of its citizens, be it silent or vocal, passive or active, willing or unwilling.[14] Since the state was an agency of action, co-operation with it consisted in rendering it specific services such as carrying out its orders, paying taxes, fighting wars and obeying laws.[15] The state did not exist independently of its citizens and was ultimately nothing more than a system of institutionalised co-operation between its members. Its actions were not only made possible by *their* own actions, but they, as self-conscious moral agents, all were ultimately accountable for its activities.

Since the state was a vast and complex organisation involving thousands of conscious and unconscious acts of daily co-operation among millions of citizens, they did not usually notice that they in fact sustained it and were morally responsible for its actions. And if they did, they excused themselves on the grounds that each of them was only an insignificant cog in a mighty wheel which would relentlessly roll on irrespective of what any of them did. Gandhi considered this a most dangerous fallacy. A mightly river was made up of individual drops, each of which contributed to its creation; the state was no different. Further, as a moral being, every citizen had a duty to ask how he personally contributed to the maintenance of the state and whether he was happy about it. He was responsible for his actions, and the responsibility was in no way diminished by what others did or did not do. In Gandhi's view it was wrong to say that what an isolated individual did had no wider consequences. Every action at least influenced those known to the agent, who in turn influenced others, and thus a ripple produced by it silently covered a long distance.[16] In any case no individual could know in advance how his actions would affect others.

For Gandhi it was the citizen's sense of moral responsibility for his actions that ultimately determined the character of the state. Every government was tempted to misuse its power, and the democratic goverment was in that respect no different from the autocratic. What distinguished the two was the fact that one did and the other did not succumb to the temptation. And this was so because unlike the autocratic, a democratic government knew that if it did, its citizens would refuse to co-operate with it. Notwithstanding all its institutional checks and balances, a democratic government could easily turn evil if its citizens became apathetic or vulnerable to corruption and manipulation. The virtues and vices of a government were not inherent in it but derived from those of its people. It was the coward who created the bully, and the worm who encouraged others to trample on it. As Gandhi put it:

> Rulers, if they are bad, are so not necessarily or wholly by reason of birth, but largely because of their environment. But the environment are we – the people who make the rulers what they are. They are thus an exaggerated edition of what we are in the aggregate. If we will reform ourselves, the rulers will automatically do so.[17]

Discussing the demoralisation of Indians under British rule, Gandhi observed:

> We are all puppets in their hands. But it would be wrong and foolish to blame the authority. That authority does not compel us to be puppets. We voluntarily run into their camp. It is therefore open to any and every one of us to refuse to play the British game.

As a moral being a citizen had a duty to decide to whom he

should give his loyalty and support, under what conditions and when he should withdraw it. His self-respect and dignity required that his loyalty should not be unconditional or taken for granted. Gandhi observed:

> Most men do not understand the complicated machinery of the government. They do not realise that every citizen silently but nevertheless surely sustains the government of the day in ways of which he has no knowledge. Every citizen therefore renders himself responsible for every act of his government. And it is quite proper to support it so long as the actions of the government are bearable. But when they hurt him or his nation, it becomes his duty to withdraw his support.[18]

When a law was just, a citizen had a 'sacred duty' to give it his fullest co-operation and 'willing and spontaneous obedience'. The duty had a dual basis.[19] As a moral being he had a general duty to do or support good. And as a citizen he had a specific moral duty to help sustain the community into which he was born and rooted, by which he was profoundly shaped, whose benefits he had enjoyed and to whose members he was bound by ties of mutual expectation. If a law was unjust or morally unacceptable, he had the opposite duty. To obey it was to 'participate in evil' and to incur moral responsibility for its consequences. It was a 'mere superstition' and an attitude worthy only of a 'slave' to think that all laws, however unjust, deserved to be obeyed or that a citizen was somehow exempt from the duty to judge every law before obeying it.[20]

Gandhi agreed that a law could not be judged in isolation from the general character of the state concerned. If the state was 'intrinsically' or 'mainly' good, it deserved the fullest co-operation of its citizens and its occasional 'lapses' should not be judged too harshly. All men made mistakes and no citizen had a right to magnify those of the state. Furthermore a good state was unlikely to want to act badly, and deserved the benefit of the doubt. Again, the state represented 'compulsory co-operation' and no-one could be its member on his own terms. Respect for his fellow-citizens demanded that he should generally respect their views and go along with them.

Gandhi argued that even in a well-constituted state, serious and unacceptable lapses might sometimes occur. Since it was a good state, a citizen also felt entitled to judge it by higher than normal standards. After taking full account of its general character, the views of the majority and his own fallibility, a citizen might decide that he could not in good conscience obey a particular law. If this was how he felt, he had a duty to disobey it on two conditions.[21] First, his disobedience should be 'civil'; that is, it should be public and non-violent; he should show why he finds the law unacceptable and how it violates his integrity or truth; he should be prepared to enter into an open-minded dialogue with the government and his fellow-citizens and to accept an honourable compromise; and he should voluntarily submit himself to the prescribed punishment. Second, he should have earned the *adhikār* or moral right to disobey the law. Civil disobedience or non-cooperation with an otherwise good government was a serious matter with potentially grave consequences and required mature deliberation. Only those were entitled to resort to it who had as a rule obeyed its laws, demonstrated their loyalty to the state and proved their moral maturity by not turning every disagreement into a matter of principle. When such reflective, loyal and law-abiding citizens disobeyed a law, their 'respectful disobedience' deserved attention and a reasoned response. Rather than ridicule, harass or ruthlessly put them down, the government should appreciate that such acts nurtured the citizen's sense of moral responsibility and built up a moral capital bound to be useful to it in the long run. They also saved the government from falling prey to the all-too-easy temptation to abuse its power, and acted as a safety valve for popular discontent.

Although Gandhi nowhere elaborated the criteria for evaluating the law and the state, he invoked one or more of the following whenever he felt compelled after careful consideration to disobey a law or withdraw his loyalty to the colonial state.[22] For Gandhi a law was bad if it satisfied one or more of the following criteria. First, it 'demeaned' and 'degraded' its subjects 'in their own or others' eyes', 'insulted their manhood' and required them to behave in a manner inconsistent with human dignity. Gandhi thought that apartheid in South Africa and slavery fell within this category.

Second, it was against a citizen's 'conscience' or 'deepest convictions'. The convictions might be profoundly mistaken, but Gandhi thought that the risk had to be taken. If a citizen felt strongly that he could not live with a law, that it violated his truth and that obeying it created an unacceptable hiatus between his beliefs and conduct, he had a duty to disobey it and pay the price. Gandhi, of course, thought that the state should respect his conscience and not punish him. In return he had a reciprocal obligation to ensure that his convictions were not based on mere prejudices or rationalisations of self-interest, but were products of a 'disciplined' reflection and embedded in his way of life.

Third, a law was bad if patently partisan in its intent or outcome. Gandhi had come across many laws in South Africa and India that were 'general' in form but 'particular' in content. The imperial British Government legislated in 1894 that no person coming from a country that had hitherto lacked 'representative institutions based on the parliamentary franchise' should be placed on the voters' role in Natal. Although the law did not specifically mention Asians, it was designed to and did in fact exclude them. And it neither clearly defined representative institutions and parliamentary franchise nor explained why citizens of the countries lacking them were unequipped to vote. In Gandhi's view it represented 'class legislation' and had no moral claim on Asians. He thought that the laws blatantly supporting an exploitative system and bearing heavily on the poor also fell within this category.

Finally, a law was bad if it was 'repugnant' to the vast majority of citizens and opposition to it was 'universal'. Its intrinsic merits, if any, were unimportant. The fact that it was passed in the teeth of widespread opposition implied that it treated its subjects with contempt. Such a law, further, involved a great deal of violence in the sense that either most people disobeyed it and had to be punished, or obeyed it out of fear of violence. It also brought the state into disrepute and weakened respect for the law.

For Gandhi the fact that a law was bad did not mean that it *must* be disobeyed, only that it *deserved* to be disobeyed. Whether it should be disobeyed depended on the likely consequences of doing so, how strongly a citizen felt about it and especially on the general character of the state in question.

Gandhi devoted considerable attention to the question of when a state could be said to be badly or unjustly constituted. He stated his views most clearly in a series of articles in 1921 and in his statement at his trial for sedition the following year. Gandhi said he had long been a supporter of the British Empire, including British rule in India. He was fully aware that the British had done grave economic and cultural damage to India. They had fought unnecessary wars at its expense, maintained a ruinously costly civil and military administration, destroyed indigenous industries and de-industrialised India, ignored its agricultural development, caused massive unemployment and famine, and in general merci-lessly exploited it. They had also sapped the foundations of Indian civilisation, de-nationalised the Indians, ridiculed their society and religion, and foisted their values on them. In spite of all this, which Gandhi had described at length in *Hind Swaraj*, he had remained loyal to the British Empire, assisted it during the Boer War and helped recruit soldiers during the First World War. He said he had done so because he admired and shared many of Britain's political ideals, had himself enjoyed the rights of an imperial citizen, including the freedom to live in South Africa, and had thought that on balance British rule had not been too oppres-sive. From about 1919 onwards the character of British rule had in his view changed for the worse and reached a point in 1921 when it forfeited all claim to his allegiance.

First, the government had become 'intoxicated with power' and shown utter contempt for the rights and liberties of its subjects as was evident in the introduction of the Rowlatt Bills in the teeth of fierce public opposition. It had also 'humiliated' the Indians and trampled on their self-respect and dignity by imposing the notor-ious crawling orders and public floggings in the aftermath of the Jallianwalla Bagh massacre. It had not even hesitated to use sol-diers as 'hired assassins' and to pervert the institution of the army.

Second, the government had systematically corrupted the sys-tem of justice and demonstrated beyond a shadow of a doubt its inability to be fair and just in its treatment of its subjects. Many of the officers responsible for the massacre and subsequent inhuman deeds had not only gone unpunished but been rewarded, whereas the innocent citizens had been summarily tried and wrongly con-victed. 'My unbiased examination of the Punjab Martial Law cases had led me to believe that at least ninety-five per cent of convic-tions were wholly bad', Gandhi argued. This was equally true of the convictions under the ordinary laws. In nine out of ten cases the condemned men were totally innocent, and in the cases involv-ing Europeans the accused Indians were denied justice in almost all cases. The courts had ceased to dispense justice and were 'prostituted' in the interests of the government.

Third, British rule had increasingly come to rest on a 'subtle but effective system of terrorism'. True, it was not blatantly dependent on force, and public life appeared calm and civilised. However, violence and terror were just below the surface, and there were periodic displays of massive force to frighten away potential critics. The government had systematically 'emasculated' its subjects, deprived them of the powers of retaliation and self-defence, built up an extensive network of informers and spies, encouraged the 'habit of simulation' and sycophancy and corrupted their relations with one another. Finally, the government had brazenly broken its solemn pledge to the people of India, especially the Muslims, and forfeited their trust. Gandhi had in mind the British government's refusal to honour its commitment to preserve the Turkish Khali-fate.

Gandhi concluded that for these and other related reasons the colonial government in India was 'evil'. Its subjects had an 'inhe-rent right' and a 'sacred duty' to withdraw their loyalty and support. Co-operation with it was a 'sin' and non-cooperation a 'virtue'. They had a *right* to disobey it because they had a right to their self-respect and dignity, and a *duty* to do so because as moral beings they had a duty to fight for the self-respect and dignity of their fellow-citizens. Gandhi contended that they also had the derivative duty to warn those helping it, including the police and the army, that they were engaged in 'sinful' activities and ought to desist from doing so. As he put it:

> You assist an administration most effectively by obeying its orders and decrees. An evil administration never deserves such allegiance. Allegiance to it means partaking of the evil. A good man will therefore resist evil system of administration with his whole soul. Disobedience of the laws of an evil state is therefore a duty.[23]

Although Gandhi discussed a badly constituted state within the colonial context, he appealed to several general principles. When abstracted from their historical context, his view seems to have been that a state failing to satisfy most or all of the following criteria was bad. First, man's self-respect and dignity were integral to his sense of humanity and should never be violated. Second, his integrity, his truth as Gandhi called it, was his supreme posses-sion. A state should make as much room for it as possible and violate it only in the rarest of circumstances. Third, since no human institution was perfect, every state must have a 'capacity for self-improvement' and provide adequate avenues for the citizens to criticise and expose its limitations. Fourth, since every state had a tendency to abuse its power, its citizens must be able to secure judicial redress. For Gandhi the judiciary was the bastion of their rights and liberties, and its independence should never be compromised. Finally, human relationships were poisoned and moral life rendered impossible under a climate of terror. Any state that relied on an organised system of subtle or crude terror and created a suffocating atmosphere of fear and distrust struck at the very roots of moral life and was 'evil'.

As we saw earlier , Gandhi was deeply troubled by the pervasive violence of the modern state. He was particularly exercised about three areas in which its violence was massive but widely accepted as inevitable, namely wars, the punishment of crime, and the exploitative economic system. In his view wars were generally born out of the desire for wealth, power and ideological domination. Although these desires were not absent in earlier societies and epochs, they were intensified, spread throughout society and morally legitimised by modern civilisation. Since we have already discussed Gandhi's critique of modern civilisation and his proposed alternative, we shall concentrate on his analysis of the other two forms of violence.

Gandhi was disturbed by the 'silent' and largely invisible but extensive violence daily committed by the state without a murmur of protest, namely the prisons. His views on the subject were derived not only from his theory of non-violence but also from his reflections on what imprisonment had done to him, to his political colleagues and the ordinary criminals who sometimes shared prisons with him during his nearly six years of incarceration in India and seven months in South Africa.

For Gandhi there were only crimes, not criminals.[24] To describe a man as a criminal was to imply that criminality was inherent in his nature and that he was nothing more than a criminal. A man committing a crime did not necessarily have a criminal disposition, both because an isolated act did not signify a pattern, and also because a crime was often the result of a number of factors only marginally related to the agent's character. Even if he was in the habit of committing crimes, he did not cease to be a human being endowed with a moral and spiritual nature. He was always more than and must be separated from his actions and tendencies. While his crimes should be condemned and punished, he deserved to be treated with the respect and love due to a fellow human being. Rather than brutalise and degrade him, punishment should help him reclaim his humanity. Men were responsible for one another, and if one of them turned delinquent, the rest could not disown their equal responsibility for his behaviour. Even as he must search his conscience, they must probe theirs.

Gandhi detected a deep contradiction between modern society's attitudes to disease and crime.[25] It viewed disease with a solicitous concern bordering on indulgence and devoted vast resources to inventing new drugs, instruments, more effective forms of treatment and acquiring greater knowledge of the human body. Diseases owed their origins to such causes as overeating, unbalanced diet, smoking, bad habits, consumption of alcohol, excessive stress and strain and an undisciplined life, all of which were moral lapses showing weak will-power and bad judgement. Society, however, attached no opprobrium to and imposed no punishment on them, and took no steps to strengthen the intellectual and moral fibre of those involved. By contrast it treated crime with the greatest of severity. Even when petty and inadvertent, it condemned it in the strongest terms and punished it in a demeaning and degrading manner. Society devoted little attention to exploring effective ways of eradicating it, and continued with the same old method of imprisonment which not only did not reduce but even increased the incidence of crime.

For Gandhi there was no real difference betweeen crime and disease. Both, alike, displayed poor self-discipline and a lack of social responsibility and concern for others, both were avoidable and both cost society a good deal of money. There was no reason to tolerate one and condemn the other or to treat one with indulgence and the other with severity. Indeed, to call one and not the other a crime was itself unjustified and reflected an ideologically biased system of values. Gandhi contended that since society adopted a wrong approach to them it ended up encouraging both, albeit for opposite reasons. Even as modern medical science pampered the body, encouraged self-indulgence, weakened self-control and allowed disease to continue unabated, the modern prison brutalised its inmates, weakened their self-respect and encouraged the recurrence of crime. Medical science rested on the fallacy of forgiveness, criminology on the opposite fallacy of revenge. As Gandhi put it, 'both institutions flourish because of wrong treatment'.

For Gandhi crime was a moral lapse, a 'disease', not the normal condition of a healthy human soul.[26] Most men never committed crimes, and those who did generally refrained from doing so when treated with love and understanding. In his view man committed crimes for one of three reasons: first, to secure the basic needs of life; second, a weak will and the inability to resist temptation; and third, in rare cases ill-will or malevolence. In the first case crime was a product of poverty, and in the other two bad social and economic conditions and poor upbringing. For Gandhi will-power and self-discipline were not natural endowments but products of upbringing and the dominant social ethos. As for malevolence it too was not natural to man, for even the most hardened and vicious criminals loved someone, at least their parents, wives, husbands, children or animals, and the question was one of widening the range of their capacity for love and goodwill. Since crime was basically a 'product of social organisation', it could be very considerably minimised by appropriately changing the latter.[27]

As long as the present social structure remained unchanged, crime would continue and had to be dealt with.[28] In Gandhi's view imprisonment was not the answer. It was generally inspired by the spirit of retribution which was morally unworthy of and reduced the state to the level of its temporarily deviant member. It provoked the spirit of vengeance in the prisoner and perpetuated the vicious cycle of violence. Above all it never solved the basic problem of reducing the incidence of crime in the long term. Once behind bars a man was generally 'lost to society for ever'.[29] He rarely came out reformed but often worse. In locking him up the state did violence to and even killed the human being in him, a crime often worse than the one committed by him. Gandhi pleaded that a state calling itself civilised must put an end to the system of daily dehumanising and brutalising its members and find less violent and inhuman ways of coping with crime, even if that involved taking calculated risks and making bold experiments. He observed:

Quite a few people say and believe that many children have been reformed through beating. It is this belief which is responsible for the increasing burden of sin in the world at present. The use of force is soul-destroying and it affects not only the person who uses it but also his descendants and the environment as a whole.

We should examine the total effect of the use of force, and that over a long period of time. The use of force has continued over a long period of time, but we do not find that those things against which force has been employed have been destroyed. Formerly there used to be heavy punishments for theft. It is the opinion of all expert observers that heavy punishments have not stopped thefts. As the punishments began to be tempered with mercy, the number of thefts declined.[30]

Until such time as an alternative to prisons was found – and Gandhi confessed that he had not yet been able to come up with one – much could be done to improve them.[31] The most important change should be at the level of attitude. We should see them as places for reforming, not punishing people. Since they could not be reformed unless kept under constant supervision, their movements had to be restricted. Even as keeping patients in hospitals or quarantining those suffering from infectious diseases was not imprisonment, keeping those guilty of crime in reformative institutions for the required period was not so either. Once society adopted a humane approach to crime and created a new moral climate, Gandhi thought that no social stigma would be attached to the stay in a prison and its inmates would themselves welcome the opportunity for self-reform.[32] In his view much could be achieved if 'prisons' were to become workshops-cum-educational institutions engaging their inmates in constructive and socially useful activities, providing for their moral education and building up their self-respect, sense of social responsibility and character. He thought that they were more likely to be reformed if trusted and provided with privacy, a decent environment, healthy diet, proper rest and civilised relations with each other and their wardens. Every social order successfully moulded the character of its members along the desired lines. There was no reason why the 'prisons' could not learn from its methods and achieve the same results.

As we saw, Gandhi was convinced that much of the individual and state violence in modern society had economic roots. The economic system silently perpetrated daily violence against the employed as well as the unemployed, and depended on the institutionalised violence of the state to protect its domestic and international interests. In this respect he did not see much difference between

capitalism and communism, the two dominant modes of organising the modern economy. His critique of them was essentially
moral and grounded in his theory of man discussed earlier.

Gandhi criticised capitalism on two grounds.[33] First, the concept
of private property lying at its base was logically incoherent and
subversive of the social order. Second, it had profoundly inhuman
consequences.

The concept of private property was logically incoherent for two
reasons. First, there was no logical basis on which a man could
claim exclusive ownership of the products of his labour. Born a
debtor, he remained one all his life. His powers, capacities, character and energies were all socially derived, and hence not his private
property but a social trust to be responsibly used for the well-being
of his fellow-men. Second, the efforts of countless men and
women flowed into one another to produce even a simple object,
rendering it impossible to demarcate the distinctive contribution of
each. Their efforts further occurred within the context of the
established social order whose silent and unnoticed but vital contribution could not be ignored either. Even as an event was caused
by a number of factors operating against the background of a given
set of conditions such that none of them could be arbitrarily
abstracted and called its cause, so no direct relationship could ever
be established between the specific activity of an individual and a
specific result. There was thus no logical basis on which the
individual could claim a specific reward. Many an Indian philosopher had used similar arguments to reject the concept of causal-
ity. Gandhi extended them to the idea of private property as well.

For Gandhi private property was subversive of the social order
because it conflicted with the fundamental principles underlying
and sustaining it. The customs, values, traditions, ways of life and
thought, habits, language and educational, political and other
institutions constituting a social order were created by the quiet
co-operation and the anonymous sacrifices of countless men and
women over several generations, none of whom asked for or could
ever receive rewards for all their efforts. And their integrity was
preserved by every citizen using them in a morally responsible
manner. Every social order was thus of necessity a co-operative
enterprise created and sustained by the spirit of sharing, mutual
concern, self-sacrifice and *yajna*. And its moral and cultural capital,
available by its very nature to all its members as freely as the air
they breathed, constituted their collective and common heritage to

be lovingly cherished and enriched. The institution of private property rested on the opposite principles and breathed a very different spirit. It stressed selfishness, aggression, exclusive ownership, narrow individualism, a reward for every effort made, possessiveness and a right to do what one liked with one's property. It was hardly surprising, Gandhi argued, that its domination in the modern age should have atomised and culturally impoverished society and undermined the basic conditions of human development.

In Gandhi's view capitalism profoundly dehumanised both workers and capitalists and lowered the level of human existence. The workers worked under inhuman conditions, found neither joy nor fulfilment in their jobs, were constantly haunted by the fear of unemployment and poverty, and led poor, superficial and empty lives. Even as the prisons brutalised their inmates, the factories brutalised the workers. Since they were treated and referred to as commodities, the workers lived as if they were and did not care how they behaved, whether it was worthy of them or what others thought of it. Thanks to their exploitation and degradation, their psyche too bore the scars of anger and hatred, and their relations with one another and their employers were deeply distorted by envy, suspicion and cynicism.

No man in Gandhi's view could degrade another without degrading himself, and the capitalists were no exception. They could not lead comfortable lives in the midst of so much poverty, suffering, insecurity and degradation without somehow justifying it at least to themselves. They generally did so by convincing themselves that the poor and the underprivileged belonged to a different, inferior or congenitally flawed species to which they were in no way related and bore no obligations. For Gandhi the central moral defect of the class-divided society was its inescapable tendency to divide mankind into two different species and deny the fundamental fact of human interdependence and unity. He thought that without some such belief and the consequent debasement and coarsening of moral sensibility, no human being could engage in wasteful consumption and mindless pleasures while his fellow-men starved, suffered from curable diseases, died premature deaths and lacked basic opportunities for growth. Like those of the workers, the minds and hearts of the capitalists too had become deeply distorted by hatred and morbid fear, and their lives were just as empty and banal.

Gandhi did not think much of communism either. Like capitalism it was based on the materialist view of man and did not
represent a new and higher civilisation.[34] It was really capitalism's
twin and only claimed to offer more of the same. It represented a
statist approach to social problems, deified the state, impoverished
the individual and dried up local sources of initiative and energy.
By combining both economic and political power in the hands of
the state, it posed a grave danger to human self-respect and
dignity. It needed a violent revolution to establish it, and all such
revolutions had in history led to greater evils than those they were
designed to eradicate. Communism, further, was based on the
belief that anyone or anything that stood in the way of the desired
goal could be justifiably eliminated. It was addicted to instant
solutions and had a profoundly anti-human thrust. Since it relied
on the state to achieve reforms, it dried up man's nobler impulses
and institutionalised the 'rule of violence'. Gandhi acknowledged
that communism eliminated poverty, discouraged greed and ensured every citizen a right to work, but he was convinced that its
moral deficiencies far outweighed its strengths.[35]

Gandhi thought that in addition to being inherently unacceptable, both capitalism and communism and indeed all such want-
based and self-centred Western ideologies were incompatible with
India's essentially spiritual civilisation. Rather than copy the West
or indigenise imported ideologies, India should evolve a distinctively humane and spiritual economy both expressing and sustaining man's moral being. As he imagined it, the spiritual economy
was based on the following principles.[36]

First, every man had a right to work. For Gandhi not material
sustenance as such but the right to secure it by working for it
constituted man's basic need. He took this view for two reasons.
First, it was by means of work that a man acquired such basic
human qualities as a sense of self-respect, dignity, self-discipline,
self-confidence, initiative and the capacity to organise his energies
and structure his personality. Welfare payments by the state sustained his body but impoverished his soul. Second, since the social
order was sustained by the spirit of *yajna*, an individual lacking the
opportunity to work was denied the privilege of participating in it,
and was thus both cut off from the moral and spiritual life of his
community and involuntarily reduced to the demeaning status of a
social parasite.

Second, economic life should be subordinated to and regulated by man's moral and spiritual needs. For reasons discussed earlier Gandhi thought that men could only gain their full moral stature in small, relaxed and interdependent communities. Since the latter lacked vitality without an autonomous economic basis of their own, he argued that production should be decentralised and each community become relatively self-sufficient in its basic needs. As Gandhi imagined it, the village land was to be owned in common, farming done on a co-operative basis, the produce equitably divided, and only the surplus land used for cash crops. The villages were to encourage locally based industries and crafts, to take pride in using local products and to import only what they could not themselves produce. Full employment or the right to work was the necessary requirement of man's spiritual nature, and Gandhi could not see how it could be ensured except in such self-sufficient communities.

Third, since the village communities were to form the basis of the Indian economy, the nature, pace and scale of industrialisation was to be determined by and subordinated to their requirements. Gandhi argued that although large-scale industries were necessary, they should be restricted to the minimum, located in the cities and only allowed to produce what the self-sufficient communities themselves could not. Since competition between them could easily lead to the present situation of unlimited production and consumerism, it was to be strictly regulated. As he was opposed to extensive state control of the economy, it is not clear how he proposed to do this. He was also worried about the competition between the large urban-based industries and the village industries, which he thought would necessarily result in the latter's destruction. A national plan was to be prepared based on a detailed survey of what could be produced locally, how it could be made efficient and helped by the large industries and what share of the market was to be reserved for each. This was the only way he thought urban exploitation of the villages could be avoided and the latter made the basis of a new economic order and a new civilisation.

Fourth, the means of production of the basic necessities of life should be collectively owned. They affected man's very survival and could easily become instruments of the most dangerous forms of exploitation. Gandhi therefore proposed that industries of vital national importance should be owned by the state. It should either set them up itself or nationalise them 'without compensation' for 'if you want the government to pay compensation it will have to rob Peter to pay Paul and that would be impossible'.[37] Fifth, since all socially useful activities were equally important, their wage-differentials should be reduced to a minimum. Finally, since a healthy moral community was impossible in a grossly unequal society, the state should embark on a programme of levelling up the poor and the oppressed and levelling down the rich. The resources needed to help the poor should be obtained by levying taxes on the rich amounting to a 'much higher figure' than the 70 per cent then obtaining in Britain.

Concerning the form of ownership, Gandhi proposed his well-known theory of trusteeship,[38] an economic extension of his philosophical concept of man as a trustee of all he had, including his powers, capacities, energy and time. The theory was intended to avoid the evils and combine the advantages of both capitalism and communism, and to socialise property without nationalising it. As he imagined it, every industrialist employing more than a certain number of workers was to look upon his industry not as his property but as a social trust. He was to work along with his employees, take no more than what he needed for a moderately comfortable life, look on them as 'members of his family' and jointly responsible with him for the management of industry, and to provide healthy working conditions and welfare schemes for them and their families. Both he and the workers were to regard themselves as trustees of the consumers, and to take care not to produce shoddy goods or charge exorbitant prices. Part of the moderate profit they made was to be devoted to the welfare of the community, and the rest to the improvement of industry. The owner was free to bequeath his industry to his children or whomever he liked only if **they** agreed to run it in the spirit of trusteeship.

Asked if any of his capitalist friends had become a trustee, Gandhi admitted that none had, the only exception being Jamanal-al Bajaj who 'came near, but only near it'. Asked what should be done to get them to become such, he replied that the sustained pressure of educated and organised public opinion, including a *satyāgraha*, was the best way. If that did not work, he was reluctantly prepared for the state to impose trusteeship by law. It would prescribe the remuneration to be paid to the trustee 'commensurate with the service rendered and its value to society'.[39] He was free to choose his heir, but the choice had to be 'finalised' by the state. Gandhi thought that such a co-operative decision checked both. The trustee retained formal ownership of his property; his use of the profit, his income and choice of heir were subject to state control. As Gandhi put it, 'I desire to end capitalism almost if not quite as much as the most advanced socialist and even communist. But our methods differ, our languages differ'.[40]

Professor Dantwala and other socialists had a long discussion with Gandhi regarding the nature and implications of his theory of trusteeship. They summed up his views in a draft, to which he made a few changes all designed to strengthen its egalitarian thrust. The final version read as follows:

1. Trusteeship provides a means of tranforming the present capitalist order of society into an egalitarian one. It gives no quarter to capitalism, but gives the present owning class a chance of reforming itself. It is based on the faith that human nature is never beyond redemption.
2. It does not recognise any right of private ownership of property except in so far as it may be permitted by society for its own welfare.
3. It does not exclude legislative regulation of the ownership and use of wealth.
4. Thus under state-regulated trusteeship an individual will not be free to hold or use wealth for selfish satisfaction or in disregard of the interests of society.
5. Just as it is proposed to fix a decent minimum living wage, even so a limit should be fixed for the maximum income that would be allowed to any person in society. The difference between such minimum incomes should be reasonable and equitable and variable from time to time, so much so that the tendency would be towards obliteration of the difference.
6. Under the Gandhian economic order the character of production will be determined by social necessity and not by personal whim or greed.[41]

The draft was a fairly accurate statement of Gandhi's mature economic views. As we saw earlier, since the early 1930s he had increasingly begun to turn radical, partly in response to the political pressures of the discontented groups and partly because he was beginning to see more clearly than before the economic implications of his moral and political thought.

Gandhi, of course, had to be most careful lest he should alienate his capitalist friends, whose moral and especially financial support he badly needed, or heighten the expectations of the poor and provoke violence, or accentuate the deep ideological divisions within the Congress and endanger its precarious unity. From time to time he therefore moderated his utterances. Since he was committed to non-violence, which had its obvious limits, and since he was averse to an interventionist state, there was also some doubt about how far he would have pressed his economic radicalism in practice. Furthermore, he was far more sympathetic to the demands of the land-hungry peasants than the industrial workers, because the former provided the bulk of his supporters and had a crucial role to play in his conception of the regenerated India.

All this has led some of his Marxist commentators to cast doubt on the sincerity of his radical pronouncements and to call him a 'mascot' or 'spokesman' of the capitalist class.[42] The criticism is misconceived and fails to take account of the evolution of his economic thought. As we saw, he not only approved of but strengthened the Dantwala draft. He was also prepared to impose trusteeship by law, considerably increase the level of taxation and nationalise vital industries. He offered a powerful moral critique of capitalism and repeatedly warned the Indian bourgeoisie of the 'inevitable' violence of the workers and the peasants. He also urged the latter to stand up for their rights and, if necessary, launch *satyāgrahas*. Even as late as 1944 he told Louis Fischer that he was prepared to condone the use of minimal violence in the cause of economic, especially agrarian, justice. He himself announced that once India became independent, he might have to lead *satyāgrahas* against the vested interests which were likely to be 'more bitter' and protracted than those against the British. And although generally hostile to an interventionist state, he had increasingly begun to realise that it had a major regulative and redistributive role. Gandhi was neither a socialist nor an apologist of capitalism for the simple reason that these and other cognate categories did not apply to him. They are conceived within the framework of European theories of the state, the economy and the range of their possible relationships. Gandhi's world of thought was radically different.

In this connection his attitude to Birla, whose relations with him have rightly aroused Marxist suspicion and hostility, is most instructive. In spite of their close freindship and all the financial help he secured from him, Gandhi remained deeply suspicious of him and said so both in private and public. He had no hesitation in saying in public that Birla had taken no steps to become a trustee of his property. When Birla set up a mill in the Gwalior state, the government acquired the land for him without paying adequate compensation to its owner. Gandhi pursued the matter in a series of letters, and told him to drop the project rather than harm the 'just and legitimate interests of the poor'.[43] When Birla blamed local 'agitators' for stirring up trouble, Gandhi wrote, 'The dispossessed class is today full of rancour. There is no denying the fact that they have been sinned against and as a class we have a lot to expiate for, not necessarily our sins but of the system with which we are identified'. The attempt to exonerate Birla as an individual but inculpate him as a member of his class was typical of Gandhi. He asked him to show understanding and generosity 'not in a spirit of virtue but as a simple discharge of a debt overdue'.

When Tata, Birla and Kasturbhai Lalbhai led an industrial delegation to Britain just before independence, Gandhi feared that they might compromise India's vital interests and establish unacceptable links with their British counterparts.[44] He issued a public statement warning them against a 'shameful deal'. Birla was most upset and cabled Gandhi from Cairo expressing sadness that the latter did not trust him. Gandhi reiterated his view in a telegram and, to rub salt in the wound, blessed him in the name of 'famishing and naked India'. He followed it up with a letter saying that Birla and his associates had no reason to be upset 'provided they are sincere in their protestations of injured innocence' and pouring scorn on Tata's concern for the poor.[45] The distraught Birla assured him that Tata was a 'genuine article' and asked to know once again why he had suspected him of a lack of patriotism.[46] Gandhi's reply is not traceable. When asked by Louis Fischer if Birla's generous financial contributions to the Congress did not compromise it, Gandhi replied, 'It creates a silent debt. . . . It does not pervert our policy'.[47] That elusive and typically Gandhian remark must remain the best short summary of his relations with the Indian bourgeoisie.

6

Satyāgraha and a Non-rationalist Theory of Rationality

For Gandhi to be moral was to lead the life of truth, that is, constantly to examine and be true to one's sincerely held beliefs in thought, word and deed. Such an integrated life involved not only eliminating all traces of hypocrisy and incoherence from one's way of life but also fighting against untruth when one felt strongly and was in a position to do something about it. This raised two important questions. First, since different men perceived truth differently, it was not only possible but an inescapable feature of human life that 'what appeared to be truth to the one may appear false to the other'. Even as a moral agent did not wish to live with untruth himself, he could not consistently ask others to do so either. The question therefore arises as to how they should resolve their differences or, as Gandhi perferred to put it, co-operatively search for truth. Second, a moral agent had no alternative but to take a stand and fight when his opponent either refused to talk or to do what they both agreed to be the right or 'true' thing to do in a given situation. The method of fighting for an objective was not external to it but an integral part of it. Every step towards a desired goal determined its character and had to cohere and be congruous with it lest it should end up distorting or damaging it in the very process of attaining it. The goal did not exist at the *end* of a series of actions designed to achieve it; it shadowed them from the very beginning. For Gandhi the distinction between means and ends ignored this fundamental fact and was untenable. The so-called means were ends in an embryonic stage and represented the seeds of which the so-called ends were a natural flowering. Since this was so, the fight for truth had to be conducted by truthful means, raising the obvious question as to what mode of action was truthful.

Gandhi's theory of *satyāgraha* was intended to answer these two questions. The term itself was suggestive. *Satya* means truth, and *agraha* which, contrary to what almost all his commentators have said, Gandhi used in its ordinary Gujarati and not the classical Sanskrit sense, means insisting on something without becoming obstinate or uncompromising. When the two terms are combined there is a beautiful duality of meaning, implying both insistence *on* and *for* truth. A moral agent insists *on* truth as he sees it, but acknowledges that he might be wrong or only partially right and invites his opponent to join him in a co-operative search *for* truth. When the invitation is declined, he *insists* on it in a truthful manner and continues to do so until his opponent is ready to talk. Insofar as it is concerned to *discover* truth, Gandhi's theory of *satyāgraha* is an integral part of his theory of truth; insofar as it is an attempt to insist on and *realise* truth, it is an inseparable part of his theory of non-violence. Gandhi's theory of *satyāgraha* is at once both epistemological and political, a theory of both knowledge and action, and much misunderstood when seen as either alone.[1]

For Gandhi rational discussion and persuasion were the best ways to deal with a situation of conflict. Since each individual was uniquely constituted, his perception of truth necessarily differed from and even conflicted with those of others. The point of rational discussion was to step into each other's shoes, look at the subject in question from each other's point of view, appreciate the force of each other's arguments and arrive at a view based on the insights of both and acceptable to both. For Gandhi it was necessarily based on three assumptions. First, since neither party was in possession of the Absolute Truth, each should enter the discussion in a spirit of *humility* and with an open mind.[2] Second, since each saw truth differently, he should make a *sincere* effort to enter into the other's world of thought and appreciate why he saw the matter differently. He might ultimately disagree with another, but only after making every possible effort to understand his position in its own terms. For Gandhi rational discussion entailed the duty of sincerity, and its purpose was defeated if each party could not count on or trust the other to make a genuine attempt to look at the dispute from his point of view. Third, rational discussion was of no avail if the parties concerned were selfish and ill-disposed towards or hated each other. Selfishness, hatred and ill-will led to emotional and moral rigidity and blocked the processes of sympathetic understanding and critical self-reflection indispensable for all rational discussion. Objectivity required an open mind, and an open mind presupposed an 'open heart'. When the heart rejected someone, that is, when he did not come within one's range of sympathy and form part of one's emotional and moral universe, reason tended to reject him too and did not take due account of his feelings and interests. Sympathy, love or good-will was a necessary precondition of rationality, and only universal love guaranteed total objectivity.

Gandhi argued that when these three basic and interrelated preconditions of rational discussion were met, it was likely to resolve differences between the parties involved. And if sometimes it did not, at least it served the vital purpose of deepening their mutual understanding and reducing their hostility and suspicions. In such a climate they could be reasonably expected to work out a tentative and mutually acceptable way of coping with the conflict.

In Gandhi's view the basic preconditions of rational discussion did not generally obtain in practice. Self-righteousness, dogmatism, insincerity, prejudice, ill-will, self-interest, limited sympathies, moral inertia and sheer obstinacy often distorted and blocked the operations of reason. He claimed to have 'discovered' this 'painful truth' after a series of unpleasant experiences in South Africa. He had led there several movements against the laws subjecting Asians to the most offensive forms of racial discrimination. For years he wrote open letters, circulars, leaflets, letters to newspapers and editorials in his weekly paper refuting the arguments and correcting the misinformation on which white racism was based. The Whites said that Asians were an 'uncivilised and aboriginal people', the litany of whose defects included low intelligence, lack of morality, bad habits, want of personal hygiene, mendacity, sharp business practices, miserliness, the practices of untouchability, lack of family loyalty and the tendency to live in overcrowded and ugly surroundings. In two remarkable documents Gandhi assumed the role of a judge, distanced himself from his own people and 'impartially' analysed the 'charges' against 'those men'. He agreed that they lived in insanitary and overcrowded houses, used their shops as bedrooms, lacked personal hygiene and practised untouchability. He admitted some of the other criticisms, but insisted that these applied to the whites as well. His countrymen did engage in sharp business practices, have a habit of telling lies, and were miserly. However, 'I would only say without meaning in the least to defend them, let those that are without sin cast the first stone'. Finally, Gandhi rejected the rest of the criticisms altogether. The Indians did not neglect their children, nor the latter their parents. And they did not have a low sense of mutual loyalty. Indeed, 'in all social matters the English are far more fitted to sit at the feet of the Hindus and learn as disciples', said Gandhi, quoting Frederick Pincott. Gandhi found that his white audience rarely entered into a dialogue with him and that when it did, it repeated old stereotypes, relied on anecdotal evidence, gave credence to unchecked stories and displayed utter lack of objectivity. 'To men steeped in prejudice an appeal to reason is worse than useless', he painfully concluded.[3]

He noticed too that on many occasions he was confronted not so much with traditional and deeply entrenched prejudices as crude self-interest dressed up in the meretricious disguise of a philosophical and moral theory. The whites had for decades been in the habit of recruiting indentured Indian labourers. When Indian traders began to arrive, the whites felt threatened by their competition and demanded immigration control. Rather than admit their real reasons, they argued that the presence of the Indians posed a threat to the integrity of Western civilisation. Some said that the Indians had no or an inferior civilisation; others argued that it was wholly different and that the two suffered from close contact. Gandhi produced testimonials from such 'authorities' on the subject as Maine, Andrew Carnegie, Munro, Charles Trevelyan, William Hunter and Max Muller to prove that ancient India had developed a great civilisation and chalked up remarkable achievements in mathematics, the natural sciences, political science, philosophy, comparative religion, psychology and the science of grammar.[4] He even assured his audience that Indians were descended not from an 'inferior stock' but one that had produced the Greeks, the Romans and the English themselves. For Gandhi this point was particularly important, as 'one-half or even three-fourths' of the indignities inflicted on them were 'justified' in terms of their alleged racial inferiority.[5] Gandhi also reeled off the names of S.N. Banerjee, Pherozeshah Mehta, Mutuswami Aiyer and Christodas Paul to prove that modern India too had thrown up men of great eminence. He even tried to sell the Indians as a hard-working, pliable, profitable, desirable and educable lot who had helped increase South Africa's wealth and who deserved well of their civilised and fair-minded white masters. While India had a dark side, Gandhi concluded, it also had a bright side. However, if judged with the 'impartiality of a Daniel', there were enough positive points to 'induce you to believe that India . . . is a civilised country in the truest sense of the term'.

Gandhi was saddened to find that his white opponents were not at all interested in the debate and only used the language of civilisation to legitimise their self-interest. He concluded:

> Hypocrisy pressed political theory into service in order to make out a plausible case. A bare-faced selfish or mercantile argument would not satisfy the intelligent Europeans of South Africa. The human intellect delights in inventing specious arguments in order to support injustice itself, and the South African Europeans were no exception to this general rule.[6]

Gandhi concluded that the head and the heart, reason and morality, were inseparable. Men found it almost impossible to be objective about those they loathed or found strange and alien. If they were reflective and self-critical, they might to some extent rise above their hostility and consider others' interests with some degree of impartiality. However, their recognition of those their hearts rejected was bound to remain abstract, tentative, fragile, partial and lacking the power to 'move' them. The rationalists did not appreciate this fundamental fact and made a 'fetish' of reason. Despite all evidence to the contrary they insisted that all disputes were amenable to rational resolution, that men could always be convinced by arguments and that, if they were not, the fault lay with the quality of the arguments. In Gandhi's view their 'attribution of omnipotence' to reason was a 'piece of idolatory', an act of 'blind faith' and fundamentally irrational. He observed:

> I have come to the fundamental conclusion that if you want something really important to be done, you must not merely satisfy the reason, you must move the heart also. The appeal of reason is more to the head.[7]

Gandhi argued that the obvious limitations of rationality had led many to advocate violence as the only effective method of fighting untruth or injustice. They agreed that violence was evil but insisted that it was fully justified when used to eliminate a greater evil. Although Gandhi had some sympathy for this view, he was totally opposed to violence as a method of social change. Spontaneous violence under unbearable conditions or grave provocation was one thing; to use it as a matter of deliberate policy was wholly different.[8] First, violence was based on untruth and could never be a means of attaining truth. It denied the fundamental ontological fact that all men were essentially one and that love and goodwill, not hatred and ill-will, were the only valid bases of human relationships. It also assumed that some men were so degenerate that they had lost the *ātman* and could not be won over by appealing to their fellow-feeling and moral impulse. Gandhi found the assumption arrogant and preposterous.

Second, unlike many other critics of violence Gandhi advanced a novel espistemological argument against it. In his view it was a fundamental fact of human life that men perceived truth differently, that 'we see truth in fragment and from different angles of vision', and that all knowledge was fallible and corrigible. In Gandhi's view the use of violence denied this basic epistemological fact. In order to be justified in taking the extreme step of harming or killing someone, one must assume that one is *absolutely* right, the opponent *totally* wrong and that violence would *definitely* achieve the desired result. The consequences of violence were irreversible in the sense that a life once terminated or damaged could never be revived or easily put together. And irreversible deeds required infallible knowledge to justify them, which was obviously beyond human reach. Gandhi acknowledged that, taken to its logical extreme, his theory of 'relative truth' undermined the very basis of action, for no man could ever act if he constantly entertained the nagging doubt that he might be wholly mistaken. However, he thought that one must at least acknowledge one's fallibility and leave room for reflection and reconsideration. Violence did not allow this. It generated feelings of anger, hatred and insecurity, none of which was conducive to critical self-reflection. It also required an investment of enormous emotional energy and commitment, and made acknowledgement of mistakes and graceful retracing of steps exceedingly difficult. Violence was doubly flawed: it assumed infallibility and ruled out corrigibility.

Third, Gandhi rejected violence on moral grounds. Morality consisted in doing what was right *because* one believed it to be right, and required unity of belief and behaviour. Since the use of

violence did not change the opponent's perception of truth, it
compelled him to behave in a manner contrary to his sincerely held
beliefs. By disjoining his belief and conduct, it created an untruth
at the very heart of his being, violated his integrity and diminished
his status as a moral being.

Finally, Gandhi argued that violence could never achieve lasting
results. An act of violence was deemed to be successful when it
achieved its intended immediate objectives. However, if it were to
be judged in terms of its long-term consequences and the kind of
society it created, our conclusion would have to be very different.
Every apparently successful act of violence encouraged the belief
that it was the only effective way to achieve the desired goal, and
developed the habit of using it every time one ran into resistance.
Society thus became used to it and never felt compelled to explore
an alternative. Gandhi thought that violence also had the habit of
generating an inflationary spiral. Every successful use of it blunted
the community's moral sensibility and raised its threshold of
violence, so that over time an increasingly larger amount became
necessary to achieve the same results. Initially throwing a stone
might be enough to draw the government's attention to a griev-
ance; soon the assassination of an officer and later that of several
of them became necessary. Every act of violence led to a vicious
circle of mutual fears from which neither party was able to extricate
himself. Each armed himself to the teeth, and not truth but
superior force carried the trophy.

For Gandhi then rational discussion was the only truthful way to
deal with untruth. However, reason was often ineffective in practice. To insist that all matters should be resolved by rational
discussion alone was therefore to confront a moral being with the
equally unacceptable alternatives of either acquiescing in untruth
or resorting to violence. One violated his own integrity, the other
that of his opponent; both alike were immoral.

Gandhi thought that his method of *satyāgraha* offered a way out.
It combined the patience and persuasive power of reason with the
urgency and energy of violence. It respected and reconciled the
integrity of the parties involved, tapped and mobilised their moral
and spiritual energies, and paved the way for a better mutual
understanding.[9] It also had the further advantage that unlike
violence, it did not replace but complemented reason. It saved it
from becoming irrational by locating it within a wider hospitable
framework and creating the three basic conditions of rational

discussion mentioned earlier. Although often presented as a simple-minded moral method relying on the power of the soul, Gandhi's *satyāgraha* involved an ingenious and complex tripartite strategy based on a fascinating blend of rational discussion, self-imposed suffering and political pressure. The first appealed to the head, the second to the heart, and the third activated both by influencing the structure of power sustaining the relationship between the parties involved.

For Gandhi *satyāgraha* was a 'surgery of the soul' made necessary by the opponent's refusal to talk or to do so in the spirit of humility, sincerity and good-will. Since his psyche had been distorted by hatred, narrow self-interest and such other extra-rational factors, and since his heart had become 'narrow and hard', he was unable to recognise the other person as a fellow-human being whose interests had a moral claim on him. The purpose of *satyāgraha* was to touch his heart, awaken his sense of humanity and activate his moral impulse. He saw the *satyāgrahi* as an enemy or a trouble-maker to be resisted, outwitted or forcibly put down. The *satyāgrahi* refused to reduce himself to that level and accept his misguided definition of their relationship. He saw him instead as a fellow-human being, a moral being, whose sense of their common humanity was temporarily eclipsed and which could and must eventually be restored if they were to live together as members of a community. He knew that moral opacity was in no way unique to his opponent. Inhumanity was a shared human predicament, not the monopoly of a few, and eliminating the opponent did not reduce but only compounded and intensified it.

Even as every community required a widespread sense of justice to hold it together, it presupposed a deeper sense of shared humanity to give meaning and energy to its sense of justice. The sense of humanity consisted in the recognition of the fundamental ontological fact that humanity was indivisible, that men grew and fell together and that in degrading and brutalising others, they degraded and brutalised themselves.[10] This sense constituted a community's vital moral capital without which it had no defence against and no resources to fight injustices, exploitation, oppression and the consequent collective degradation. The slow and painful task of cultivating and consolidating the sense of humanity and thereby laying the foundations of a truly moral community was an essential collective responsibility, which the *satyāgrahi* took it on himself to discharge. He assumed the burden of the common evil, suffered for it, sought to liberate both himself and his opponent from its tyrannical automatism and helped reduce the prevailing level of inhumanity. He overcame his opponent by refusing to see him as such and by appealing instead to his sense of decency and their common humanity. As Gandhi put it, the old sages 'returned good for evil and killed it'.[11] The *satyāgrahi* took his stand on this 'fundamental moral truth'.

For Gandhi a *satyāgrahi* relied on the power of suffering love. Confronted with untruth he sought a dialogue with his opponent. When this was denied or reduced to an insincere exercise in public relations, he took a stand and accepted whatever punishment was meted out to him. Since his sole concern was to evoke a moral response in his opponent, he did everything to put him at ease and nothing to harass, embarrass, anger or frighten him. In the meantime he suffered the punishment without hatred or ill-will in the hope of triggering off in him a slow, intensely personal and highly complex process of self-examination. The moment his opponent showed the slightest willingness to talk in a spirit of genuine goodwill, he suspended his struggle and gave reason a chance to work in a more hospitable climate.

In all his *satyāgrahas* Gandhi observed several basic principles. Before it was launched almost every one of them passed through three stages: a clear and reasoned defence of its objectives, a popular agitation to convince the government of the intensity of popular feeling, and an ultimatum to give it the last chance for negotiation. Throughout the *satyāgraha*, the channels of communication with the government were kept open, the attitudes on either side were not allowed to harden, and intermediaries were encouraged. Gandhi insisted that since a *satyāgraha* was a deeply moral act, only those with the highest moral character and generally in the habit of obeying the law had the *adhikār* or moral right to participate in it. Violence was never encouraged and every *satyāgrahi* was required to take a pledge to eschew it. He was also required never to complain about his punishment or to hit back, or resist arrest or the confiscation of his property, to impede, harass or spread gossips and innuendos against government officials or to insult the Union Jack. Similar rules were laid down for the *satyāgrahi* prisoner who was expected to be courteous, ask for no special privileges, do as ordered and never to agitate for conveniences 'whose deprivation does not involve any injury to his self-respect'.

Gandhi nowhere clearly explained how and why the suffering love worked. Although a couple of his remarks lend credence to it, he would have been totally unsympathetic to a widely canvassed explanation, of which the following remark by Sir Vitthalbhai Patel, one-time speaker of the Indian Central Legislative Assembly, is a good example:

> I am going to make you beat me so outrageously that after a while you will begin to feel ashamed of yourself. Even your own family will be horrified at you. And after you have stood this scandal long enough, you will come to me and say, 'Look here, this sort of business cannot go on any longer. Now why cannot we two get together and settle something? And then we will begin to talk . . . cold turkey. Otherwise you will have to go on beating me till I go crazy'.[12]

Gandhi seems to offer three related but different explanations. First, he sometimes referred to the *psychological* impact of *suffering*. In his view it was most difficult for a human being to continue to inflict suffering on another. Sooner or later he became emotionally exhausted and morally worn out, especially when the victim offered no resistance.[13] Richard Gregg, of whom he thought well, compared *satyāgraha* to the Japanese Jiu-Jitsu style of wrestling in which a wrestler used the weight of his opponent to throw him off balance and subdue him.[14] Violence confirmed the opponent's expectations and paradoxically sustained his morale and self-confidence. Since the *satyāgrahi* played the game by wholly different rules, he confused and unhinged him, undermined his moral self-confidence and created in him a psychological space for critical self-reflection. The greater his opponent's anger and violence, the greater was the psychological energy available to him to create a sense of guilt and subtly transform him.

Second, sometimes Gandhi stressed the *spiritual* power of *love*.[15] Like the natural world, the spiritual realm had its laws and a unique mode of operation. Even as electricity and gravitation worked in ways only a scientist could comprehend, one spirit acted on another in mysterious and hitherto unexplored ways, of which the continuing influence of Christ on the Cross was an obvious example. The *satyāgrahi's* love, sustained even in the midst of most brutal treatment, released a 'silent' and 'unseen force' that touched the innermost spiritual being of his opponent, activated his sense of their shared identity and broke through the barriers of ill-will.

Third, and this seems to be Gandhi's well-considered view, he stressed the complex interaction between the spiritual impact of love and the psychological impact of suffering.[16] The *satyāgrahi's love* and moral nobility weakened his opponent's feelings of anger and hatred, awakened his sense of decency and humanity and morally transformed him; his uncomplaining *suffering* generated a sense of shame in him, denied him the pleasure of victory, mobilised public opinion and created a mood conducive to calm introspection. The two together triggered off the complex process of critical self-examination on which a *satyāgraha* relied for its success. Love by itself was not enough as otherwise the *satyāgrahi* could quietly expostulate with his opponent without launching a campaign. Self-imposed suffering by itself was not enough either, for it had little value and was even counterproductive if accompanied by hatred and anger. Self-imposed suffering was effective and indeed acceptable only when born out of and sustained by love, and love was effective only when expressed and articulated through such suffering. Love spiritualised suffering, which in itself had only a psychological value; suffering gave love a worldly and visible manifestation as well as psychological energy and power.

Gandhi realised early in his political career that suffering love had its limits.[17] His *satyāgraha* against the 1907 Registration Act of the Transvaal Legislative Assembly went on for months and yielded little. The one against the Natal immigration bills was even more painful and protracted. The provisional settlement he reached with the government included no major concession, and even then the government tried to wriggle out of it by putting dubious glosses on its important clauses. As the *satyāgraha* dragged on, the government resorted to the familiar tactic of harassing, dividing and tiring out its opponents, misrepresenting their case and misguiding public opinion. Predictably they became demoralised, and their numbers began to decline drastically. If suffering love was all-powerful, numbers would not have mattered. Gandhi realised that they did, for he could not exert any pressure on the government without mass support. After a few months he decided to draw in the indentured labourers whom he had hitherto ignored by including their demand for a repeal of the three pound tax in his programme. He called them out on strike in 1913 and travelled around the mining districts bringing out the workers and discouraging those showing signs of returning to work. This put pressure on the coal owners and eventually on the government.

The strike also spread to the coastal sugar districts and had a considerable economic impact. Gandhi now acquired the bargaining power he desperately needed to negotiate with the government on more or less equal terms.

Although Gandhi continued to maintain that suffering love was omnipotent and, when pure, was capable of 'melting even the stoniest hearts', he knew that the reality was very different. Most *satyāgrahis* were ordinary human beings whose tolerance, love, determination and ability to suffer had obvious limits and who could not 'act beyond their capacity'. When confronted with a deeply prejudiced and obstinate government that paid no heed to and anaesthetised itself and its subjects against their suffering, they had little chance of success. Their suffering love had then to be reinforced by other forms of pressure. As Gandhi put it in the course of his South African struggle: 'I do not believe in making appeals when there is no *force* behind them, whether moral or material. Moral force comes from the determination of the appellants to do something, to sacrifice something for the sake of making their appeals *effective*. Even children instinctively know this principle.'[18]

Gandhi saw this even more clearly on his return to India where he was fighting not a weak provincial government but a powerful empire determined at all costs to protect its vital interests. The Jallianwala Bagh massacre convinced him how ruthless the government was prepared to be and how little it was influenced by the 'innocent suffering' of hundreds of women and children. Not surprisingly he felt it necessary to redefine *satyāgraha* and to add to its 'armoury' the novel and highly effective 'weapons' of social, economic and political boycott, civil disobedience, non-payment of taxes, non-violent raids, strikes and other forms of non-cooperation, none of which relied on suffering love alone and which were all designed to 'compel' and 'force' the government to listen and negotiate. Even his description of *satyāgraha* underwent a radical change, and he began to call it 'non-violent warfare', 'peaceful rebellion', a 'civilised form of warfare' and a 'war bereft of every trace of violence'. With all these changes in his manner of action and language of discourse, the very concept of *satyāgraha* came under strain, and it is doubtful if the social and economic boycott, strike and non-payment of taxes could be called *satyāgraha* in the moral sense in which he had used the term so far. As usual Gandhi's praxis outpaced his theory.

As Gandhi realised that the *satyāgraha* against the government was very different from that against a private individual, and as he saw the need to put economic and political pressure on the government, he began to analyse the nature and basis of political power and the way it sustained oppressive and unjust systems. His reflections on his South African experiences led him to several interrelated 'discoveries'. First, all power was ultimately derived from the victims. It was because they thought and behaved *as if* they were powerless that their masters acquired power over them. Second, all systems of oppression ultimately depended on and were maintained by the co-operation of their victims. Third, the oppressed were a party to and responsible for their oppression and never wholly innocent. Fourth, no system of oppression could come into being let alone last unless it was rooted in the minds and hearts of its victims.

When the Natal government passed discriminatory laws against the Asians, the latter either accepted or resorted to devious ways of circumventing them. When Gandhi urged them to protest none was ready and they expected him to do their fighting for them. Not surprisingly the government became bolder and passed increasingly vicious laws. Again, when it passed the Asian Licensing Act, making it extremely difficult for the Asians to obtain trading licenses, rather than unite and fight they went about bribing the officials and procuring the licenses. In sheer frustration Gandhi remarked, 'Shall we blame the Whites alone for these things? We at any rate cannot. If we behave like worms, we are bound to be trampled upon.'[19] The white South Africans were not angels and were naturally tempted to pursue their interests at the expense of the Asians. However, they would not have dared put their intentions into practice if they had feared fierce resistance. Since the Indians behaved like worms, they encouraged, even invited, the whites to trample on them with impunity. Whenever there was a coward, argued Gandhi, there was bound to be a bully. Indeed it was the coward's fault that he had allowed someone to become a bully. He was thus doubly guilty, for his own dehumanisation as well as that of the bully. By freeing himself from his cowardice, he also liberated the bully from his bullying tendencies. Sometimes Gandhi got carried away and advanced the untenable thesis that the oppressed were themselves to be blamed for their condition. For the most part, however, he was content to argue that while the oppressors were not blameless, their victims were not innocent either, and that the latter should devote their energies to organising themselves and fighting against the oppressive system rather than blame and hate their masters.

As Gandhi vividly realised in the course of the Natal *satyāgraha* of 1910, the entire economic system of South Africa was sustained by the labour of its workers. If they were to stop working, it would not last a day. They were thus not its helpless victims, and had the power to overthrow it. It continued because and as long as they co-operated with it; they were therefore accomplices in their own exploitation. Similarly British rule in India owed its existence to the fact that the Indians co-operated with it, supplied the necessary manpower, and above all accepted its legitimising ideology. If they stopped co-operating with it in all areas of life including the ideological, it would not last a day. The government had no power of its own; it derived it from their co-operation. Gandhi's continued emphasis on non-cooperation from the time he assumed leadership of the Indian National Congress was based on this theory of power. Since co-operation was the source of the government's power and its people's powerlessness, non-cooperation was the only way to reverse the situation.

For Gandhi then power was a complex relationship. Both the oppressor and the oppressed believed that all power lay with the former. While the belief gave the oppressor self-confidence and the courage to act decisively, it demoralised the oppressed and reduced them to supplicants begging for concessions. Each concession both intensified their collaboration in their exploitation and reinforced their master's power and prestige. The belief that the oppressor had all the power was, of course, totally mistaken. However, insofar as it was taken to be true by both the parties and formed the basis of their expectations and mutual responses, it became self-fulfilling. This was broadly the Hindu doctrine of *māyā*, on which Gandhi drew heavily. Every system of oppression rested on *māyā* which veiled the underlying *satya* that the oppressor had no power save what his victims chose to give him. Their salvation lay in their own hands.

For Gandhi a system of oppression derived its strength and durability from two interrelated sources: first, the victim's illusion that his oppressor was all-powerful and he himself powerless; and second, his incapacity for action. Since the victim believed himself to be powerless, he fell into the habit of looking after himself at the expense of others and lacked the courage or capacity to organise himself. The oppressor took advantage of the resulting vacuum and built up a formidable apparatus of coercion that further strengthened the power of the illusion. Those wishing to change the system must therefore act at two levels; they should help the victim see through the illusion of powerlessness and build up his self-confidence and capacity for concerted action. Political education and political praxis were inseparable and neither had a chance of success in the absence of the other. They were also dialectically related in the sense that each was both a precondition and a consequence of the other.

This was precisely what Gandhi's *satyāgraha* aimed to do. It educated the people and *de-mystified* the system. It also organised them, built up their political power and *threatened* the system. It sought popular 'awakening', an evocative term with a strong religious resonance, by means of and as a prelude to political action. Each of his *satyāgrahas* was a well-calculated step towards and a necessary moment in the dialectic of national regeneration. Remedying a specific injustice was its immediate goal through which it aimed to realise its far more important long-term objectives. Each *satyāgraha* carefully selected a target that met the three crucial criteria of dramatically highlighting the evil character of the system, mobilising popular attention and energy and standing a good chance of success. Its success partially lifted the veil of *māyā*, gave people both a better insight into the nature of the system and a sense of power, weakened the government's self-confidence and morale and slightly shifted the overall balance of power in favour of the people. More *satyāgrahas* followed, each progressively giving a further nudge to the shifting balance of power, until a point was reached when the 'awakened' masses had seen through the ingenious mechanism of colonial rule and were no longer prepared to put up with it.

Gandhi's *satyāgraha* then was an ingenious combination of reason, morality and politics; it relied on the powers of argument, suffering love and organised pressure, and appealed to the opponent's head, heart and interests. Although each *satyāgraha* brought in all three elements which it combined differently to suit different conditions, they were not all equally important. Reason or rational discussion remained its ultimate goal. It was because reason had failed that the *satyāgraha* had become necessary. The constant aim of the *satyāgrahi*, of which he was never to lose sight, was to get the dialogue going in the spirit of goodwill. Self-imposed suffering was not important in itself, but accepted only in order to facilitate and unblock the exercise of reason. As for organised political pressure it contained the element of coercion and did not appeal to the opponent's moral nature. Strictly speaking it was therefore not moral and was only intended to activate the head and the heart.

Each of the three elements constituting the *satyāgraha* had its own distinct requirements. Reason was only effective when the *satyāgrahis* carefully prepared their case, collected all the relevant facts, marshalled powerful arguments, exposed the weaknesses of their opponent's case and convincingly demonstrated that what they called untruth was really so. This meant that their goals had to be concrete, limited and clearly stated. The more abstract and general their goals, the greater the room for honest disagreement, and the more difficult it was to demonstrate their truth. Like reason, suffering love too had its distinct requirements and was only effective when the *satyāgrahis* were men of high moral calibre, guided by love, accepted their suffering with calm dignity and did not provoke their opponent into acts of brutality in the hope of subsequently blackmailing him. As for organised political pressure, it required a skilful identification of the opponent's weak points, a careful co-ordination of efforts, strong discipline and a well-planned strategy of mass action.

The *satyāgraha* as Gandhi understood it, then, had both moral and political dimensions, and relied on the moral power of self-imposed suffering as well as the political pressure exerted by social, economic and other kinds of action. Since political pressure was only designed to facilitate and intensify the moral, Gandhi underplayed its role and saw the *satyāgraha* as essentially a moral method. His opponents viewed it very differently. They felt and responded to the impact of political pressure and regarded it as basically a political method like any other, whose moral component was incidental, marginal or even a mere smokescreen. While he interpreted its political dimension in moral terms, they saw its moral dimension in political terms. The results were often fascinating.

When Gandhi called a *hartāl*, he said that it was not so much a strike as an expression of collective sorrow and grief at the untruth committed by the government. That it also involved cessation of work was only its incidental consequence. When he launched a social and economic boycott, he said that it was meant not so much to put pressure on the government as to express his countrymen's moral determination to withdraw co-operation from an unjust government which they had every right and duty to do. When a *satyāgraha* led to a settlement, he claimed that it had 'touched' the government's 'heart' and 'converted' it. The British saw the whole thing in opposite terms. A *hartāl* involved a strike, and the fact that the strikers subjectively saw it as a *hartāl* did not alter the objective fact that it was and had all the consequences of a strike. This was equally true of the economic boycott which was not merely an assertion of the moral right to non-cooperate but also and primarily a refusal to buy British goods and cause considerable hardship to the workers in British textile mills and put pressure on the government. When a *satyāgraha* resulted in a compromise, the government saw it as no more than a response to public pressure.

Their conflicting conceptualisations of *satyāgraha* also led to differences in the way each approached the other. Gandhi was always anxious to establish some kind of moral relationship with the government and lift their discussions to a new level. He often addressed the Viceroy as a 'friend', articulated his demands in moral terms, appealed to his 'conscience' and 'sense of justice' and wondered how a man of his moral sensitivity could wish to live with untruth. For his part the Viceroy studiously stuck to the conventional language of politics where he had an advantage over his spiritual opponent. He addressed him as 'Mr Gandhi', used the formal language of official communication, asked him for a 'clear statement' of his 'demands' and warned him of the 'illegality' of his contemplated course of action. Each skilfully resisted entering an unfamiliar territory and talking in a language of which he had an insecure grasp. During a series of such encounters involving fascinating manoeuvres, each scored limited victories. Gandhi did on occasions manage to evoke a moral response from and establish a friendly and at times even warm and trustful relationship with his antagonist. For his part the latter from time to time forced Gandhi to speak in conventional political idioms, descend from his high moral pedestal and negotiate as an ordinary politician.

Gandhi's *satyāgraha* also led to a distinct style of negotiation.[20] He was primarily concerned to evoke in his opponent a spirit of goodwill and deepen their mutual understanding. During the course of the *satyāgraha* he therefore probed him in his characteristic ways to reassure himself that his opponent was better disposed than before, meant well and could be trusted. Once he was satisfied, he treated the detailed negotiations as a relatively minor matter. Establishing a basis of goodwill, one of the essential conditions of a meaningful rational discussion, and paving the way for a better future relationship represented a vital long-term gain and mattered most to him. As for the specific issue in question Gandhi felt sure that since his opponent was well-disposed and knew the strength of popular feeling, he was bound to concede at least some of his demands. Since, however, he could not wholly transcend his point of view and the considerations of self-interest, he obviously could not concede them all. The practical outcome of the negotiations was therefore more or less certain, the only question being whether he should hold out for more than he was likely to get. He knew that he could increase the pressure and insist on more. However, if that was likely to spoil the atmosphere of good will, Gandhi did not consider the price worth paying and preferred to wait for a more opportune moment. It would seem that almost as a matter of policy he left some ambiguity in the final settlement. This was his way of testing, even tempting, his opponent. If he later took advantage of it and went back on the agreement, Gandhi knew how to shame and deal with him the next time round. Since his *satyāgraphic* style of negotiation did not often yield much and caused considerable frustration among his followers, who felt that their suffering and sacrifices had been sold cheaply, Gandhi also needed the ambiguity to put a different and reassuring gloss on the settlement.

In addition to such methods as economic and social boycott, non-cooperation, refusal to subscribe to government loans, strike, civil disobedience and non-payment of taxes which he tried out on different occasions with varying degrees of success, Gandhi also introduced the highly controversial method of fasting. It is not entirely clear whether he classified it as *satyāgraha*. He rarely referred to it as one, although it probably satisfied all the relevant criteria. He fasted on 17 different occasions, none of his fasts lasting more than a week unless he had set himself a longer duration. Of these three were against untouchability, three for Hindu-Muslim unity, four against violence, one to encourage the Ahmedabad striking workers to stick to their pledge, three for self-purification, and only three against a government. Of these last, one was against the Thakore of Rajkot, one against the colonial government's refusal to allow him to continue Harijan work in the prison, and one as a protest against the Viceroy holding him responsible for the violence of his followers. He never fasted against the colonial government to extract political concessions or to exert political pressure. There is only one recorded occasion when a group of people fasted against him, but he was able to dissuade them from it within a couple of days.

Gandhi knew that his fasts caused considerable unease among his critics and followers, and went to great lengths to defend them.[21] He argued that over the years he had thoroughly identified himself with his countrymen and devoted his entire adult life to their service. They had reciprocated his love for them, trusted him and given him their unstinting support and loyalty. He had thus become a 'vehicle of their longings' and a universally accepted custodian of their conscience. As a truly representative being who had become one with his people, he thought that he had both acquired the *adhikāra* to rebuke and reproach them and incurred a *dharma* to accept responsibility and atone for their misdeeds. He was not fasting against strangers, for that would be coercion, nor for personal gain and glory, for that would be moral and emotional blackmail, but on behalf of those to whom he was bound by the mutually acknowledged bonds of love in order to wean them away from what they themselves accepted as grave moral lapses. His fast was really a 'voluntary crucifixion' of his flesh for their moral uplift, which he had both a right and a duty to undertake. It is worth noting how Gandhi took over the Christian concept of vicarious atonement and Hinduised it. Like Jesus on the Cross he sought to atone for his countrymen, but thought that he could only do so because and after he had earned the *adhikār* by virtue of his *karma*.

Gandhi argued that his fast had three objectives. First, it was his way of expressing his sense of sorrow and hurt. He could not bear to see those he loved degrade themselves and wanted them to know how much they had hurt and disappointed him. Second, as their leader he felt responsible for them, and his fast was his way of atoning and accepting responsibility for their misdeeds. And third, it was his last desperate attempt to stir their 'sluggish conscience', 'sting them into action' and awaken and mobilise their 'moral energies'. It was an 'intense spiritual effort', a *penance*, intended to 'burn up' the dross of their ill-will and hatred. For a variety of reasons his countrymen had temporarily lost their senses as in the case of communal violence, or become insensitive to injustice and suffering as in the case of untouchability, or shown utter lack of self-discipline as when a *satyāgraha* became violent. By suffering himself and inducing sympathetic suffering in them, he intended to activate the process of moral self-examination in them. Gandhi conceded that a fast could easily become a form of moral blackmail, and imposed four limiting conditions. It should only be undertaken against those to whom one was bound by the mutually acknowledged bonds of love, only when their conduct was outrageous and admitted by them to be such; it should aim at their reform, and should be undertaken only after all other methods had failed.

Gandhi agreed that his fast exerted pressure, even perhaps coercion, on his intended targets, but insisted that the coercion was purely moral, 'the same kind of coercion which Jesus exercises upon you from the Cross'. Human life was necessarily interdependent and men could not avoid exerting pressure on one another. Furthermore, every man had a right to preserve his integrity and stop co-operating with those he considered misguided or evil. If he was a political leader he had a duty to exert pressure on his followers to wean them away from what they themselves knew to be evil. And when the evil was egregious and widespread, a votary of non-violence had no other remedy available to him save that of a fast. Gandhi asked what he was to do when his countrymen were busy murdering one another or treating some of them as worse than animals. Either he remained a helpless spectator, in which case he was a party to the evil, or he acted, and the only effective form of action open to him was the fast. Since it was only intended to get them to reflect on their behaviour and observe the values they themselves claimed to hold, Gandhi contended that the coercion it exerted was really the coercion of conscience and inherent in all moral conduct.

Although this could not be said of all of them, some of his fasts exercised a profound and essentially moral influence. Take, for example, his Calcutta fast against one of the most horrendous waves of communal carnage India had known. When communal passions were running incredibly high in 1946 the interim government, paralysed by the conflict between the Congress and the Muslim League, was able to do little to contain the violence in Calcutta that had killed and maimed thousands. At the age of 78, in poor health and shattered by the thought of the impending partition, Gandhi undertook the arduous journey to Calcutta and, when all his appeals failed, decided to fast. The impact was dramatic and peace returned not only to Calcutta but throughout India. He succeeded in achieving single-handed what the boundary force of 50 000 men could not achieve in the Punjab. His fast triggered off an immensely complex moral process in every Indian, both Hindu and Muslim, shook him up and compelled him to examine his conscience and give his most urgent attention to his own direct and indirect responsibility for the communal violence. It became a kind of national *yajna* in which the entire country participated and underwent a partial but profound moral transformation or rebirth, made an oblation of its violent impulse and emerged chastened and purified. There is no better description of the psychological and moral mechanism on which his fast relied than the following moving account by Dr Amiya Chakravarty. It deserves to be quoted in full.

To most Indians, as to people outside, Gandhi's decision to fast as a means of changing an acute situation of social or political impasse, seemed remote, irrelevant and based on individual habit and unreason. And yet the challenge was clear; right in the heart of a brutal communal upheaval in Calcutta, resting in a broken house exposed to streets where fighting was going on. Gandhiji had chosen to impose self-suffering and penance upon his aged body, as well as on his mind, which he had put to the test of fire. Everyone knew that within a day or two the sheer physical agony mounted to an hourly and momently torture which nothing could relieve; the toxic processes and tissue destruction would begin, not only bringing death nearer but setting up an intolerable psycho-physical sequence. His face and eyes, made luminous by suffering and controlled suffering, would show little trace of the agony that his will had mastered, but the nature of his ordeal was unmistakable to the millions. Even while repudiating his method and its efficacy, the one question in people's minds would be, 'How is Gandhiji?' People would begin to feel uncomfortable; the grocer's boy, the rickshaw-puller, the office clerk, the school and college students would scan the news columns early in the morning and listen to the radio throughout the day and feel more and more personally *involved* in the situation. I remember how University students would come up to us and ask to be excused from attending their classes because they felt disturbed and did not know what to do. But why feel disturbed? They would say that though they did not believe in such methods and in the philosophy behind it all, one thing struck them as curious; after all, if anybody had to suffer for the continued killing and betrayal in the city, it was not Gandhiji. He had taken no part in it. So, while others were engaged in crime, it was he who had to suffer like this. They felt awkward and some wanted to stop his suffering, and even gathered together weapons from streets and homes at great personal risk; they wanted to return them to Gandhiji.

As we know, Gandhiji would look at groups who came with steel guns and knives and now offered these in return for his promise to break the fast and ask them, 'why'? Why should it matter to them whether one more man, a man of seventy-eight, suffered or died when they had easily allowed hundreds of innocents to suffer and die? If all the agony and shame had not mattered, why should one more individual signify at all in a situation of retaliation, vengeance and crime that they had accepted as being moral and courageous? So it was to save him, Gandhiji, that they had come; but the saving of Gandhiji or not saving him, was not the point at all.

So the fast would continue. Men would come back from their offices in the evening and find food prepared by their family, ready for them; but soon it would be revealed that the women of the home had not eaten during the whole day. They had not felt hungry. Pressed further, the wife or mother would admit that they could not understand how they could go on when Gandhiji was dying for their own crimes. Restaurants and amusement centres did little business; some of them were voluntarily closed by their proprietors. Why this total and pervasive suffering for a whole city? Why did it all begin to matter? The nerve of feeling had been restored, the pain began to be felt; the pain of the whole society, because of the pain of its members, whether Hindu, Muslim or others. Gandhiji knew when to start the redemptive process. Involvement did not merely mean pain: it was fundamentally the joy of union, and the acceptance of new responsibility which such glad assurance of united strength makes possible. An immense release filled the atmosphere when Gandhiji declared that now we had all suffered and shared, his fast would be broken. Release turned into rejoicing, the fast actually led up to feasts in which the warring communities joined heartily, while Gandhiji sipped his small glass of orange juice.

One would like to carry the story further; but the meaning of his fast was clear. Suffering was happening in a social and moral vacuum, with no response from peoples whose minds had lost all human sensitiveness. It could only be reciprocated and then redeemed by the process of suffering. Then, out of sharing and involvement would arise a new situation; it would not be merely change but transformation.[22]

Gandhi's theory of *satyāgraha* makes a great contribution not only to political praxis but also to political theory. It provides a mode of action which recognises the importance of rational persuasion but takes full account of and finds ways of overcoming the processes that block and distort it. Rational discussion implies that the parties to it are prepared to advance and be influenced by arguments. Since all arguments are made from within a larger framework of beliefs and values, they cannot be fully understood nor their force appreciated without the parties involved making a genuine attempt to interchange positions, exchange arguments and look at the world from each other's point of view. Rational discussion is only possible under certain conditions including those listed by Gandhi; in their absence it is either not rational but mere rationalisation, or not discussion but alternate and mutually opaque monologues. It presupposes a specific attitude of mind and, since attitudes are socially structured and reinforced, a specific kind of society. Most rationalists ignore the moral and social context in which reason functions, and treat it as if it were a transcendental faculty operating in a psychological and social vacuum and in no way influenced by values, interests and prejudices. Indeed, insofar as they make reason the final arbiter of social and political disputes but pay scant attention to the basic conditions of its existence and success, they are open to the charge of insincerity. Gandhi's great contribution consisted in exploring and finding ways of creating these conditions and saving reason from losing its credibility or turning into its opposite. Nearly 50 years before the Critical Theory put it at the top of the philosophical agenda, Gandhi diagnosed the crisis of modern rationalism and pleaded for a richer concept of rationality. His doctrine of the unity of head and heart, reason and morality, logos and eros, intellect and emotion, points to the direction in which such a concept might be found.

In much of the traditional understanding of political life all political praxis is reduced to a choice between the mutually exclusive methods of rational discussion and violence, the former alone being worthy of man. This simple-minded approach proves bankrupt before the intractable and complex political reality. As all historical evidence including Gandhi's struggle in South Africa and India confirms, rational discussion is often unable to deal with deeply entrenched prejudices and vested interests. To believe that all human conflicts can and should be resolved by rational discussion alone is therefore really an act of blind faith. Much of traditional rationalism thus rests on an irrational foundation, a paradox of which it is little aware and which it is unable to resolve within its narrow framework. Not all discussion is rational; therefore we need a theory of what constitutes rationality. Rational discussion has its obvious limits, and therefore we also need a meta-theory of the conditions under which rational discussion represents a *rational* course of action.

Traditional rationalism runs into difficulties at a different level as well. Since rational discussion has its obvious limits, a moral being is confronted with a painful dilemma. Either he reposes all his faith in rational discussion and acquiesces in injustices, or he resorts to violence, the only available alternative within the traditional framework. In one case he adheres to reason but abandons morality; in the other he does the opposite. While rightly insisting that man is both a rational and a moral being, traditional rationalism cannot avoid creating a conflict between rationality and morality which it cannot resolve within its framework. Contrary to its intention it also ends up making violence respectable and morally legitimate. Since not all injustices can be endured, and since reason is at times unable to do much about them, a moral agent thinking within the traditional rationalist framework remains at liberty to resort to violence. By continuing to insist on the efficacy of rational discussion when evidence calls for caution, the rationalists also make the advocates of violence look for comparatively more truthful, honest and realistic.

With all its limitations to be explored presently, Gandhi's theory of *satyāgraha* addressed itself to and sought to come to grips with these and other long-neglected questions. Like the rationalists he was committed to rational discussion, but unlike some of them he realised that what often passed as rational discussion was in fact not such and that making a fetish of it was an act of irrationality. Accordingly he explored the criteria and conditions of rational discussion and offered a theory specifying what constituted rational discussion, what its limits were and how these could be overcome. Even as he was aware of the limitations of rationality, he was acutely conscious of the dangers of violence. He knew that narrow rationalism and violence tended to feed off each other, and that the obvious inadequacy of rationality rendered violence morally respectable. He therefore sought to break through the narrow straitjacket of the reason-violence dichotomy lying at the basis of traditional rationalism. He imaginatively explored the uncharted terrain between reason and violence and arrived at new forms of political praxis designed to supplement, strengthen and save the former and to undercut the moral basis of the latter. His *satyāgraha* was basically a new kind of dialogue, a form of discussion which, although not rational in the narrow sense, was not irrational either. It involved trying hard both to persuade others of one's point of view and to understand theirs, and relied on each opening himself up to others by both sharing with them his thoughts and feelings and letting theirs flow into and inform his own. The method of *satyāgraha* was ultimately a way of enabling men to realise their full potential for rationality and goodness and creating a new and tentative consensual truth.

Although invented and practised in a colonial context, Gandhi's *satyāgraha* is capable of wider application and is particularly relevant in modern Western society which has rendered most of the traditional forms of radical action either irrelevant or obsolete. The regnant ideology has so rigidly defined the terms of political debate and so skilfully predetermined the political agenda that new interests, values and ideas lack adequate means of rational articulation and stand little chance of a fair hearing. At the same time Western society is ideologically and politically too well-defended to be challenged by revolutionary violence. Gandhi's *satyāgraha* offers one possible mode of action. It patiently probes and exposes the society's moral defences, asks disturbing questions and unsettles settled convictions without frightening those involved. It also cuts across ideological and party lines, builds up communities of concerned citizens, cultivates and mobilises new constituencies, gives hope to those paralysed into inaction by an externally engineered feeling of powerlessness and releases a new moral energy.

While the moral and political significance of Gandhi's *satyāgraha* is beyond doubt, it suffers from several limitations, of which we might mention a few. First, while he was right to stress the unity of reason and morality or the head and the heart as he called it, he was wrong to think that all or even most social conflicts could be resolved by touching the opponent's heart. Although self-interest, prejudices and moral inertia do play a part, many conflicts occur because 'men of good-will' take very different views of what human well-being consists in. On the basis of the principle of the sanctity of human life, one man finds abortion outrageous while another reaches the opposite conclusion. And, again, both Christians and communists stress the unity of mankind, yet arrive at wholly different social theories. Moral and political preferences ultimately spring from specific conceptions of man and, although the latter can be rationally discussed, there are no objective criteria for conclusively resolving their differences. A *satyāgraha* does in some cases loosen up the moral and emotional rigidity of the participants and creates a climate conducive to a relaxed and sympathetic dialogue. Sometimes, however, the differences run so deep and are so sincerely held that no *satyāgraha* could hope to resolve them. Gandhi's own life bears eloquent testimony to the insolubility of fundamental conflicts of interests and values. He and Jinnah strongly disagreed about the desirability of the Partition of India. Their disagreements centred on such questions as the nature of the state, the relation between it and religion, the mode of articulation of the collective identity of a community and the interpretation of Indian history. Since disagreements on these matters could not be resolved, the negotiations between the two men failed and Gandhi was reduced to the most noble but ultimately inconsequential professions of love and gestures of self-sacrifice.

Second, although *satyāgraha* has a strong moral core, Gandhi was wrong to overlook its non-moral dimensions and to confuse the ideal with the actual. As we saw, he initially intended it to rely on the moral power of uncomplaining suffering alone. The reality of political life convinced him that this was not always possible and that it must either remain impotent or incorporate other forms of pressure. Accordingly he kept inventing new modes of action or 'weapons' as he sometimes called them so as to 'compel' the government to negotiate in good faith. As he well knew, non-cooperation, boycott and civil disobedience were not wholly or even substantially non-coercive and moral. Non-cooperation involved social ostracism of the British and exerted social pressure on them; it involved the boycott of British cloth and exerted considerable economic pressure as well; it also exercised enormous political and administrative pressure by denying the civil service, the judiciary, the police and the universities the required manpower. R. C. Majumdar was hardly exaggerating when he observed that there was 'no real *satyāgraha* campaign in India, in the sense that there was no campaign in which moral pressure was the only pressure relied upon'.[23] While Gandhi's rhetoric remained moralistic, his practice was different. Since his method exerted non-moral pressure as well, his claim that it genuinely *converted* his opponents is untenable. In some cases, such as Judge Broomfield's remarks at Gandhi's trial in 1922, it did 'convert' them in the sense that they came to realise that they were unjust and insensitive. In some other cases, however, the government gave in largely because it realised that its policies had run into such fierce opposition that it was far more prudent to accept a compromise than provoke a rebellion. In yet other cases the fear of violence played an important part.

Third, Gandhi was not so much wrong as one-sided in seeing suffering in exclusively moral terms. In the salt *Satyāgraha* of 1930 a white sergeant, having to hit a tall and undefending Sikh, held back his arm in horror saying, 'It is no use, you can't hit a bugger when he stands up to you like that'. He 'gave the Sikh a mock salute and walked off'.[24] Again, the 'crack troops' of the Indian army, posted in the North-West Frontier provinces to suppress non-violent agitation, chose to be court-martialled rather than open fire on an unarmed mass meeting. There were many similar occasions when the police felt morally degraded by their use of force. There were also, however, other cases where their reaction was more complex. They simply felt disgusted, exasperated and degraded at having to beat people up. It was not the suffering of their victims that 'touched their heart'; rather not being used to this kind of brutality they simply gave up.

Consider, for example, another incident. Following the Salt Act of 1930, the Congress decided to raid the government-owned saltworks in Dharsana. About 2500 people participated. The police lashed out, hitting the unprotected heads of the 'raiders' with steel-spiked clubs. The latter continued to march undaunted. The police hit them yet more until most of them fell to the ground. They then squeezed the testicles of the wounded, thrust sticks up their anuses and kicked them in the abdomen. Webb Miller, an American journalist who saw and reported the event, remarked: 'In eighteen years of reporting in twenty-two countries, during which I have witnessed innumerable civil disobediences, riots, street fights and rebellions, I have never witnessed such harrowing scenes as at Dharsana'.[25] The pain and agony of the raiders had virtually no impact on the police. The Viceroy in his letter to George V found the whole thing rather 'amusing', and expressed his perverse happiness at the fact that his policemen had 'obliged' the resisters with a few 'honorable' bruises they had begged for'.[26] The point of this example is that the suffering of Gandhi and his followers did not always have the desired effect on the government. Sometimes it had the opposite effect to that intended in the sense that instead of converting and uplifting them, it either brutalised the police and provoked them into savage acts of fury or produced disgust and exasperation rather than genuine moral conversion. Gandhi's assertion that his own and his followers' suffering penetrated the moral defences of the government and awakened their sense of common humanity was an exaggeration.

Fourth, Gandhi is probably right to argue that a human being is generally affected by the suffering of another and regrets it even if he personally does not and cannot do anything about it. However, he overlooked the fact that if he thought the suffering deserved, his reaction would be different. For example, one slaps a child when he steals and regards his suffering as merited, fails a weak student in the examination and does not shed tears over his unhappiness, regrets the tragedy of a woman but puts her murderer husband safely behind bars. In short, not the suffering *per se* but the agent's judgement of it determines his response to it. And here a genuine problem arises which Gandhi with his optimistic view of man overlooked. Men differ in their standards of judgement and disagree as to whether a specific form of behaviour is right or wrong, an action good or bad, a punishment deserved or undeserved. It is not difficult to imagine ideologically blinded or morally self-righteous men who are not in the least affected by their victims' suffering. The Sharpville massacre left many a White South African unmoved; the pictures of the Vietnamese victims of American napalm bombs did not move many Americans either; and despite Gandhi's optimism, the patient suffering of the Jews or the Kulaks would never have converted Hitler or Stalin. Gandhi's belief that non-violence *never* fails and 'melts even the stoniest heart' has no basis in fact, and is a dangerous article of faith. As Martin Buber put it in a letter to him, '*Satyagraha* is testimony. Testimony without acknowledgement is martyrdom'.

At a more general level his emphasis on suffering as a means of political change contains a danger. Like violence, suffering too can easily generate an inflationary spiral and become a ritual or a cult. This was evident in the case of Gandhi and some of his followers who sometimes almost idealised suffering as a test of their spiritual strength. As Nehru put it, it then became 'morbid' and 'even a little degrading'.[27] When suffering is glorified and made an integral part of a community's moral culture, it might even produce the opposite results to those intended. The amount of suffering required of a *satyāgrahi* to eradicate or even highlight an injustice might be so great and incompatible with elementary self-respect that a community might reject non-violence as a practicable moral doctrine. The experience of India since independence points in that direction.[28]

7

Partition and the Non-nationalist Discourse

Let posterity know what agony this old man went
through thinking of it. Let not the coming generations
curse Gandhi for being a party to India's vivisection.

(Gandhi, 1947)

Ever since the British decided to introduce representative institutions in India, their nature and basis became a subject of acute controversy. Most Indian leaders of both the conservative and liberal political persuasions subscribed to what some of them called the liberal theory of representation and pleaded for representative institutions along the same lines as in Britain. For them the state was a secular institution, castes, creeds and religions were politically irrelevant, decisions should be taken on the basis of the majority principle and the rights of minorities should be fully protected by appropriate constitutional safeguards.

Many a Muslim leader strongly disagreed and advocated a community-based theory of representation. Sir Syed Ahmad, one of its earliest and ablest advocates, argued on the basis of a 'close study of John Stuart Mill's views in support of representative government' that the liberal theory presupposed an ethnically and religiously homogeneous society in which there was a basic harmony of interests and it did not therefore matter if some citizens sometimes found themselves in a minority.[1] The situation was 'totally' different in such a society as the Indian where the majority and minority were 'permanently' divided and their interests in constant conflict. Some citizens were not just *in* a minority but *were* a minority and needed more than constitutional safeguards to protect them against the domination of the majority community. Sir Syed contended that not individuals but 'nationalities and creeds' should form the basis of the Indian state. Its citizens should acquire and exercise their right to vote not as individuals but as

171

members of specific communities, and enjoy legislative representation not in proportion to their numerical strength but their 'importance' to the wider community. Sir Syed never explained what he
meant by nationality and creed, how their importance was to be
assessed or why he thought that the religious divisions were the
most important. Sir Syed Amir Ali went further and contended
that Hindus and Muslims must enjoy 'equal consideration', and
that no political arrangement was acceptable to Muslims that
'subordinated' their interests to those of the nearly three times
larger Hindu community. Like Sir Syed Ahmad, he never explained why Muslim interests could not be protected by consitu-
tional safeguards, why they must enjoy parity with Hindus, and
how the interests of the other minorities were to be protected
under his scheme.

The Indian National Congress at its first session in 1885 threw its
weight behind the liberal theory of representation. The Executive
Committee of the Central Mohammedan Association criticised its
decision on the ground that although it had 'much sympathy' with
'some' of the objectives of the Congress, it was 'firmly convinced'
that the adoption of the liberal theory would lead to 'the political
extinction' of the Muslims.[2] In order to reassure and win over the
Muslims, the Congress elected Baddruddin Tyabji as its President
in 1887. Within a few months Tyabji urged that in order to give it
time to reconcile its differences with them, the Congress should be
'prorogued, say at least for five years', and then it should either
'renew' itself or 'retire with dignity'. The vast majority of Congress
members considered the suggestion preposterous and rejected it.

For its part the British government opted for community-based
representation and decided to grant the Muslims a separate electorate. Their reasons were varied and complex, the desire to placate
the Muslims and build them up as, what Lord Minto in 1906 called,
'a counterpoise' to the Hindus being among the most important.
As an official wrote to Lord Minto, the latter's move to concede the
Muslim demand was a 'work of statesmanship' and amounted to
'nothing less than the pulling back of sixty two millions of people
from joining the ranks of the seditious opposition'.[3] Lord Olivier,
the Secretary of State for India in the first MacDonald Government,
admitted in a letter to *The Times*:

No-one with a close acquaintance with Indian affairs will be
prepared to deny that on the whole there is a predominant bias
in British officialdom in favour of the Moslem communtiy, partly

on the ground of closer sympathy but more largely as a make-weight against Hindu nationalism.[4]

Liberal opinion in India and even Britain was most unhappy with the separate electorates. The Congress, which had long agreed to a greater representation for Muslims than was warranted by their numbers, objected to it in the stongest terms. It argued that under the system of separate electorates the state reproduced the divisions of society and, rather than impartially arbitrate between them, became an arena of their conflicts. By basing citizenship on religion, it mixed up religion and politics to the detriment of both. And by entrenching the religious divisions into the very structure of the state, it was bound to make Indians abnormally conscious of their differences and prevent them from developing a sense of common citizenship.

After duly reassuring the Congress that they were only an 'exceptional form of representation' and intended to be temporary, the Indian Councils Act of 1902 reserved seats for which only Muslims could vote. The Montagu Chelmsford Report of 1918 'unhesitatingly' condemned the separate electorates as 'unnecessarily' divisive and a 'very serious hindrance' to common citizenship, but recommended their continuation on the grounds that they were 'settled facts' and that tampering with them was likely to 'strain' Muslim loyalty to the Raj.[5] Seeing Muslims reap the political and other advantages of a separate electorate, the other communities began to put in demands for it. The British government was happy to oblige. The Government of India Act of 1919 extended communal representation to the Sikhs, the Anglo-Indians, the Europeans and the Indian Christians. The Communal Award of 1932 extended it to the Scheduled Castes who had until then voted with the Hindus in joint electorates. This was vigorously opposed by Gandhi and eventually dropped. The separate electorates, which were promised to be temporary, became a permanent feature of the colonial state. As a result throughout the half century of subsequent British rule, Indians were never able to vote and interact as citizens of a common state. They knew that they were citizens by virtue of their religion, and that their political strength depended on organising themselves along religious lines. The British brought liberal political culture to India but, thanks to the inherent logic of colonialism, corrupted it by embodying it in non-liberal representative institutions.

Under the system of separate electorates only a Muslim could represent the Muslims, but he was not tied to a specific political party. The Congress took full advantage of this and successfully fielded Muslim candidates in Muslim constituencies. The provincial elections of 1937 were crucial, especially as the 1935 Act had granted considerable autonomy to the provinces and was generally seen as paving the way for independence. The Congress did very well in the general constituencies and, although it performed badly in the Muslim constituencies, so did the League. The Congress formed ministries in all but four provinces.

The period that followed was of critical importance. Although the Congress had hitherto recognised the Muslims as a separate political unit, it now refused to countenance any proposal that might appear to do so.[6] It declined to include them in its ministries even in those provinces where they formed a significant minority. In Uttar Pradesh there was an informal working arrangement between the two parties before the election, and it was hoped that the Congress would form a coalition with the League.[7] It agreed to take 'one or two' of its members into the Cabinet provided the League Assembly Party was dissolved and its members signed the Congress pledge. In Bombay the Congress High Command rejected B. G. Kher's proposal to allow the League to join his government.

The Congress requirement was not improper, for no government could function if its members pulled in different directions and had divided loyalties. However, it was a grave error of judgement. It allowed the Muslim leaders to exaggerate their real and imaginary grievances, especially as this was the first time in Indian history that the Muslims had come under Hindu rule. Lacking the responsibility of power they equated the Congress Raj with a 'Hindu Raj', blamed it for largely non-existent atrocities and frightened the Muslim masses about the dangers of becoming the 'slaves of our slaves'. Furthermore, the Congress ministries were caught up in a paradoxical situation. The increasing Congress use of socialist rhetoric since the mid-1930s tended to alienate the Muslim landlords and upper classes. Since, however, its ministries did little to put their socialism into practice and introduce measures to help the peasantry and the industrial workers, many of whom were Muslims, it alienated the latter as well.

The 1937 election results presented the Congress with both a challenge and an opportunity. It knew that the Muslims were not behind it and *had* to be won over. It knew too that they were not behind the League either and *could* be won over. Accordingly it launched a programme of 'mass contact' with a view to reassuring them that it was non-communal and posed no threat to their religious and other interests. The League read the situation in more or less the same way, and launched a similar campaign of its own. Its campaign was rather vicious and concentrated on arousing their fears and sense of insecurity. Realising how much and how quickly the Muslim masses were becoming 'communalised', the Congress called off its mass contact programme and made tentative approaches to the League for a reciprocal gesture. Jinnah not only refused to call off but intensified the campaign.

Jinnah obviously could not mobilise the vast and illiterate Muslim masses without simplifying the political reality and offering them a simple-minded and rather distorted conception of themselves and their place in India. In a brilliant stroke of political imagination, he introduced the language of nationalism and dramatically changed the character of the political debate. Hitherto he and the League had argued that the Muslims were a minority *community* entitled to a separate electorate and constitutional safeguards; they now began to argue that they were a *nation*, a distinct cultural and political unit entitled to full equality of status with the Hindus.[8] To be sure, Jinnah's thesis was not wholly new, for Syed Ahmad, Syed Amir Ali and other Muslim leaders had expressed similar sentiments several decades earlier. However, they had been vague and tentative. Although they were convinced that the Muslims were not a 'mere community', they were not sure what else they were. And although they insisted that the Muslims were 'quite different' from the other minorities, they were not clear as to where the difference lay and what it entailed. Even Iqbal was confused on this point, and appealed to *both* their separate identity and Indian roots. Jinnah's great contribution lay in defining the Muslims as a nation, articulating Muslim nationalism in easily intelligible idioms and mobilising the masses behind it. He insisted in a way no other Muslim leader had done before that India was and had always been a binational state consisting of the two equal and unassimilable nations of Hindus and Muslims. Although he was initially content to plead for their equality within a single state, he knew that the logic of his position pointed towards two separate states, a view both he and millions of his followers initially found so absurd that they dared not espouse it until a few years before it became a historical reality.

Jinnah pursued his 'two-nation theory' with relentless logic. In order to show that the Muslims were a nation, he had to argue that India itself was not a nation. He wrote to Gandhi, 'I have no illusions in the matter and let me say again that India is not a nation, not a country. It is a sub-continent composed of nationalities, Hindus and Muslims being the two major ones'. In his view what was called India was an artificial creation of the British and was bound to disappear with their departure. He would not speak of Hindus or Muslims *in* India, but only of Hindu and Muslim India. The Congress appeal to 'national interest' provoked from him the reply, 'Whose national interest? Which nation? Hindu or Muslim?'[9]

For Jinnah the Muslims were a nation on 'any definition of the term:

> We maintain that Muslims and Hindus are two major nations by any definition or test of a nation. We are a nation of a hundred million, and what is more, we are a nation with our distinctive culture and civilization, language and literature, art and architecture, names and nomenclature, sense of value and proportion, legal laws and moral codes, customs and calendar, history and traditions, aptitudes and ambitions. In short, we have our distinctive outlook on life and of life. By all canons of international law, we are a nation.[10]

In his view Hindus and Muslims had nothing in common. Hinduism and Islam

> . . . are not religions in the strict sense of the word, but are in fact different and distinct social orders, and it is a dream that the Hindus and Muslims can ever evolve a common nationality. This misconception of one Indian nation has gone far beyond the limits and is the cause of most of our troubles and will lead India to destruction if we fail to revise our notions in time. The Hindus and Muslims belong to two different religious philosophies, social customs, literature. They neither intermarry, nor interdine together and, indeed they belong to two different civilisations which are based mainly on conflicting ideas and conceptions. Their views on life and of life are different. It is quite clear that Hindus and Mussalmans derive their inspirations from different sources of history. They have different epics, their heroes are

different, and different episodes. Very often, the Hero of one is a foe of the other and likewise their victories and defeats overlap.[11]

Since the Muslims were a nation, Jinnah argued that three important conclusions followed. The first was what I might call the concept of exclusive and indivisible representation. Since the Muslims were a distinct nation, only a 'Muslim party' consisting of and deriving its support exclusively from the Muslims had a 'right' to represent them. This undermined the Congress claim to speak for them or put up Muslim candidates in Muslim constituencies. Further, since the Muslims were a nation, their interests were identical and could only be represented by one party. This meant that the other Muslim parties were really 'factions' of the League, the only authentic Muslim party. Their independent existence not only divided and betrayed the Muslim nation but was inherently illegitimate.

Second, Jinnah argued that since both the Hindus and Muslims were nations, they were equal in status and entitled to equality of representation in all branches of government. The fact that Hindus vastly outnumbered Muslims was 'totally irrelevant'. The Muslims were a nation not a minority, and hence the individualistic and 'merely' numerical liberal concepts of majority and minority were wholly inapplicable to the Indian context. Jinnah frequently called the liberal theory of representation a 'disease', an 'alien' notion, and repeated the criticisms levelled against it by Sir Syed Ahmad Khan and others.[12]

Third, Jinnah argued that even as the Muslims were a nation, so were the Hindus; and like the Muslim League the Congress was their sole and exclusive representative. It was not a national party as it claimed to be, but a Hindu party only entitled to speak for Hindus. He ruled out all claims to cross-communal representation as 'inherently' illegitimate.[13]

The Congress rejected the assumptions underlying Jinnah's arguments. Its case was ably presented by Gandhi. He argued that the language of nationalism was both inapplicable to India and inherently absurd. Unlike the European countries India was not a nation but a civilisation which had over the centuries benefited from the contributions of different races and religions and was distinguished by its plurality, diversity and tolerance. It was a community of communities, each enjoying considerable autonomy within a larger and shared framework. As for Hindus and Muslims, they had lived side by side in the villages and cities for centuries without ever feeling that they were enemies or oppressed one by the other. India was a united country long before the Muslims came, and it was absurd to argue that it had ceased to be so afterwards. What was more, most Muslims were converted Hindus and their claim to nationhood was no more valid than that of a section of English citizens converted to Islam to a separate state in England. As Gandhi wrote to Jinnah, 'I find no parallel in history for a body of converts and their descendants claiming to be a nation apart from the parent stock. If India was one nation before the advent of Islam, it must remain one in spite of a change of the faith of a very large body of her children.'[14]

Gandhi's and the other Congress leaders' description of the Muslims as 'ex-Hindus', 'converts' and 'basically Hindus' caused much misunderstanding and resentment. The Muslims construed it as an implicit denial of their separate cultural identity and a sign of Hindu imperialism. They were both right and wrong, for Gandhi and the Congress used these terms in two very different senses which they did not clearly distinguish. First, they used it in a *religious* sense implying that Muslims had once been Hindus who had later converted to Islam out of fear or hope of reward. In this sense the terms implied that they had betrayed their ancestral religion and were inauthentic Muslims, and carried derogatory overtones. The second sense of the term was *cultural* or civilisational and had quite different associations. It grew out of a search for the deeper bonds binding the two communities. Since the vast majority of Muslims had once been Hindus, they shared in common with them their beliefs, customs, social practices, values and ways of life and thought, in a word a civilisation. Their conversion to Islam changed their religious identity but could not and did not affect the deeper cultural continuity between the two communities. Indeed, they carried their old culture with them to their new religion and profoundly Indianised it. They were therefore not just Muslims but Indian Muslims, Indians not merely in a territorial but cultural sense, and co-heirs with the Hindus to Indian civilisation. It is this that Gandhi intended to emphasise in describing them rather clumsily as 'ex-Hindus' or 'basically Hindus'.[15] Since he did not clearly distinguish the two senses, and since many of his followers generally used the terms in their accusatory sense, their use was a source of irritation to Muslims.

Having challenged Jinnah's conception of Indian civilisation and history, Gandhi went on to question his criteria of nationhood. He rejected religion on the grounds that Islam in India was heavily influenced by Indian civilisation, was quite different from its counterparts elsewhere and had much in common with Hinduism. He rejected language on the grounds that Muslims spoke the languages of the regions where they lived and that Urdu, their allegedly common language, was shared by a large number of Hindus as well. He rejected such criteria as a shared way of life and a common conception of man and society on the grounds that these were too abstract to be helpful and substantially overlapped with those of the other Indian communities. Gandhi conceded that indeed Muslims did have several distinct customs and social practices, but he insisted that this was equally true of every other community and could not prevent them from living peacefully within a single state.

Jinnah had considerable difficulty answering Gandhi's criticisms. He stressed religion as a criterion of nationhood, yet refused to consider the Parsis and the Indian Christians as nations. When pressed by the Sikhs, he drew an untenable distinction between a nation and a sub-nation. He said that the Scheduled Castes were a community, neither a nation nor a sub-nation, and was unclear about the tribals. He was not sure either whether the Muslims had always been a nation or had become one at some specific period in Indian history. He did not say what he meant by Islamic civilisation and ways of life and thought, precisely how they differed from the Hindu and whether his abstract statements about Islam applied to the Indian variety of it. When Gandhi asked him how a separate state would benefit the Muslims, Jinnah dismissed the question as irrelevant. Gandhi asked him if it was economically viable, and again he avoided it.

Seeing that Jinnah was adamant, Gandhi argued that respect for feelings and opinions of those involved demanded that at least a plebiscite should be held in the Muslim majority areas. In the Punjab, for example, non-Muslims made up nearly 47 per cent of the population and, as the 1937 elections had shown, not all Muslims shared Jinnah's views. Jinnah summarily dismissed Gandhi's proposal on the grounds that it presupposed the liberal-individualist view of democracy he had already rejected. Only Muslims were entitled to decide their future, and the rest must either stay on as a minority or emigrate. Self-determination as he understood it was a 'national' not a 'territorial' concept. He observed:

> . . . can you not appreciate our point of view that we claim the right of self-determination as a nation and not as a territorial unit, and that we are entitled to exercise our inherent right as a Muslim nation, which is our birth right? . . . The right of self-determination, which we claim, postulates that we are a nation, and as such it would be the self-determination of the Muslims, and they alone are entitled to exercise that right.[16]

But as the Congress rejected Jinnah's basic premises, it came to very different conclusions. It insisted that unlike the League which only aimed to represent Muslims, it aspired to and did, to a considerable extent, represent all the citizens of India irrespective of their castes, creeds and religions, and was therefore a qualitatively different political party. While the League was a 'communalist organisation' consisting of 'Muslim nationalists', it was a 'nationalist' organisation whose Muslim members were 'nationalist Muslims'. Not the Congress but the Hindu Mahasabha, an avowedly communal body, was the Hindu counterpart of the League. Recognising the Muslim League as a representative of the Muslims, the Congress rejected its claim to be their *sole* representative.

As the debate went on, Jinnah was willing to concede that the Congress was not an exclusively Hindu party and that it spoke for the non-Muslim minorities as well. He observed,

> All the other minorities such as the Scheduled Castes, Sikhs and Christians have the same goal as the Congress. They have their grievances as minorities, but their goal and ideology is and cannot be different from or otherwise than that of a United India. Ethnically and culturally they are very closely knitted to Hindu society.[17]

However, he remained adamant in his view that the Congress could not represent the Muslims. Unlike the others the Muslims did not have their roots in India, shared little in common with the rest and represented a wholly different civilisation.

The Congress felt that Jinnah's claim to be the sole representative of the Muslims challenged 'all it stood for', diminished its national character and foisted on it a political identity totally opposed to its self-image and aspirations. It was prepared to give way on all other questions but not this. Although it had rejected Jinnah's demand for equality of representation, it eventually gave in. It accepted the Cabinet Mission plan according to which the Executive Council was to consist of 14 members, five belonging to the League, six to the Congress, of which one was to be a member of the Scheduled Castes, and three belonging to three smaller minorities. It also agreed that government portfolios should be equitably divided, the political structure of the country organised along federal lines, and the provinces should enjoy the greatest possible autonomy. However, since it looked on itself as the representative of all the communities in India including the Muslims, it insisted on appointing a Muslim as one of its representatives on the Executive Council. Jinnah strongly objected to this. To allow the Congress to appoint a Muslim implied that a non-Muslim body could represent Muslim interests and that a Muslim spokesman could belong to a non-Muslim organisation. As he put it, to agree to the Congress nomination of a Muslim amounted to 'an abject surrender on our part of *all* we stand for' and strikes 'at the very *root* and the very existence of the Muslim League'.[18] He was not even prepared to sit at the same table with the Muslim Congress President. While the Hindus were his enemies, the Congress Muslims were 'traitors'. As he wrote to Maulana Azad:

I refuse to discuss with you by correspondence or otherwise as you have completely forfeited the confidence of Muslim India. Cannot you realise you are made a Muslim show boy Congress President to give it colour that it is national and deceive foreign countries? If you have self-respect, resign at once.[19]

For his part, Gandhi was not prepared to budge an inch from his basic position that the Congress represented the Muslims as well. Lord Wavell told him in a personal interview that the 'only stumbling block' to the settlement was the inclusion of a nationalist Muslim in the interim government. He conceded that the Congress had the 'undoubted right to nominate a nationalist Muslim', but suggested that since Jinnah was obstinate, there was perhaps no harm in waiving it. Gandhi replied, 'One may waive a right, one cannot waive a duty'. The following day in a letter summarising their conversation of the previous day, Gandhi wrote to Wavell,

You recognised fully the reasonableness of the Congress position, but you held that it would be an act of high statesmanship if the

Congress waive the right for the sake of peace. I urged that if it was a question of waiving a right it would be a simple thing. It was a question of non-performance of a duty which the Congress owed to non-League Muslims.

Negotiation after negotiation broke down, the delicately and skilfully contrived arrangements collapsed, and an egregious amount of ill-will was generated as a result of the conflict about the representative claims of the two major parties. The conflict was not trivial, at least as far as the Congress was concerned, for it affected its secular character and values as well as its ability to run independent India where a large number of Muslims were bound to remain.[20] After the 1946 elections it was in little doubt that the League represented the 'overwhelming mass' of Muslims, although not all of them. It acknowledged the fact, but continued to insist that it could not compromise its moral right to speak for all the communities. While the controversy lingered on, the country witnessed unprecedented inter-communal violence and was moving fast towards Partition. In a curious about-turn Jinnah appointed a Hindu as a League representative to the interim government of 1946, partly to snub the Congress and partly perhaps to prepare for the new state of Pakistan where a sizeable Hindu minority seemed likely to remain. He even radically changed his tune and began to speak the secular language of the modern state. In his address to the League members of the Constituent Assembly two weeks before Partition and to the first session of the Pakistan Constituent Assembly four days before it, he urged the two communities to 'cease to be Hindus and Muslims' and to regard themselves as 'common citizens of the state'. He even argued that religion had 'nothing to do with the business of the state' and that Muslim interests were 'perfectly safe' in India.[21] He had evidently used the ideological language of nationalism to legitimise and realise his political objectives. Once they were secured and the arduous task of running the state began, the ideological baggage became a grave liability and had to be abandoned at the first opportunity.

Like all great events the Partition of India was full of intriguing paradoxes. The Muslims in the Hindu-majority provinces were its most vociferous supporters, yet many of them refused to emigrate to Pakistan. It was expected to put an end to communal carnage; in fact it resulted in the migration under most tragic conditions of several million people, thousands of deaths and the abduction and rape of over 50 000 women. Jinnah, the most vigorous champion of Pakistan, was its least likely founder. He came from Gujarat which had a long tradition of communal amity, was only a second generation convert to Islam, not at all a practising Muslim, married to a much younger and highly Westernised Parsi girl, a fact for which he was heavily criticised by his fellow-religionists, had little Urdu and addressed most of his mass meetings in English which barely a few in his audience understood. He had begun his political career under Gokhale, a leader of impeccable secular credentials, had the ambition to become a 'Muslim Gokhale' and cherished the title of 'ambassador of Hindu-Muslim unity'. He strongly disapproved of the religious approach to politics and had retired to England when it became dominant in the 1920s. The life of Gandhi, Jinnah's principal antagonist, contained strange paradoxes too. Like Jinnah he was a Gujarati, his close boyhood friend and hero was a Muslim, his mother belonged to the Pranami sect which was influenced by Islam, he owed his first worthwhile job to a Muslim firm, was deeply indebted to Muslims for fighting in his *satyāgrahas* in South Africa and for helping him acquire a national and international reputation that stood him in good stead on his return to India, and he was eventually killed by a Hindu for being pro-Muslim.

The Partition was obviously a result of the interplay of many complex factors. The fact that the Muslims had ruled over India for several centuries made it difficult for them to accept the rule of the Hindu majority. The knowledge that their rule had from time to time led to grave injustices and violence to the Hindus aroused fears of reprisal. Their inability to separate religion and politics and the consequent incapacity to come to terms with life under a non-Islamic state added to their difficulty. The economic conflicts between Hindus and Muslims, the introduction of the separate electorates, the mistakes of the Congress ministries during their period of office, Jinnah's unscrupulous exploitation of Muslim fears, his sheer intransigence and unprincipled call for violence, Mountbatten's vanity and impatience and Hindu intolerance also played their part. Our concern here, however, is not to assess the comparative importance of these and other factors, nor to examine Gandhi's role in the Partition, but to explore the theoretical roots of both his desperate anxiety to avert it and his inability to do so.

Gandhi was passionately concerned to avoid Partition and was shattered when it occurred. He was not particularly worried about the loss of territory. Like most Hindus he defined India in civilisational not territorial terms and was far more concerned about the integrity of its civilisation than its territorial boundary. Partition deeply disturbed him because it shattered his conception of Indian civilisation. As we discussed earlier, Indian civilisation was for him plural and synthetic and not only tolerated and respected but positively cherished diversity and differences. It had provided a hospitable framework within which different communities, cultures and religions had lived side by side and made their distinctive contributions. With all its limitations and occasional quarrels, India had been a 'happy family' to which all its 'children' were privileged to belong. Since for Gandhi this was the 'truth' about India, Partition was a 'lie'. It denied the deepest truths about Indian civilisation and history including Muslim rule, and contained a profound 'untruth'.[22]

Furthermore Gandhi had fought for India's independence because, among other things, it represented a distinct civilisation that was being eroded by British rule and needed an independent state to protect it. Partition implied that the grounds on which he had fought for India's independence were false. The contradiction between the basis of Indian independence and that of Partition haunted him. When India was about to be divided, he plaintively appealed to the Muslims in the rest of the country not to emigrate to the new state of Pakistan. Even after Partition had become a reality, he kept urging his countrymen to 'disprove' Jinnah's two-nation theory by providing complete security to the Muslims, if necessary at the risk of their lives. He spent his last few months urging the intensely bitter Hindu refugees not to harm the Muslims or take over their property. He chided Sardar Patel for not doing enough to protect them. And his last act, which probably cost him his life, was to pressure the government of India to give to Pakistan its agreed share of the collective assets and 'affirm' the 'honour' and 'spirit' of India.

Although Gandhi was desperately anxious to avoid Partition, his capacity to do much about it was severely limited. He was handicapped by the complex legacy of history and the potentially explosive patterns of social and economic inequalities between the two communities. He had to function within a colonial context which exacerbated his difficulties. He also had his fair share of human limitations and made errors of judgement. I suggest that some of the reasons for his failure are to be found in his theoretical perspective on politics in general and on Indian politics in particular.

Although Gandhi's political theory had considerable merits, it also had its limitations, the most relevant to our discussion being its essentially moralist and individualist orientation. For him human conflicts owed their origins to the fact that men had 'narrow hearts' and failed to take account of each other's interests. Accordingly he sought to unite the hearts of the parties concerned by means of moral appeals and voluntary self-imposed suffering. He was convinced that no human being was morally so opaque that he could not be won over and that if someone remained recalcitrant, that was only because the moral pressure was not strong or the party exerting it not 'pure' enough.

Gandhi's political theory created three difficulties for him. First, since he himself did not much care about material interests, he could not fully appreciate why others did. Second, when confronted with ideological, economic and other conflicts, he felt uneasy and impatient. Rather than accept them and work towards a compromise, he rebuked the parties involved for their pettiness and urged the stronger of the two to give in. Sometimes they yielded, sometimes they did not; and when they did, they did so largely to please Gandhi or under pressure from his colleagues, although he attributed it to their change of heart. Third, for Gandhi the individual was the sole social reality, and groups were mere collections of individuals. The conflicts between them were ultimately like and reducible to those between individuals, and capable of being resolved in the same way as those between friends or members of a family. His approach prevented him from appreciating their autonomous dynamics.

Thanks to the basic limitations of his approach, Gandhi was unable adequately to conceptualise, let alone resolve, the Hindu-Muslim conflict. He could not see why men should quarrel at all, especially members of the same national family. He could not appreciate the deeper economic and historical roots of the conflict either, and attributed it to narrow hearts and emotional insensitivity. He thought that if Muslims stopped killing cows and Hindus ceased playing music outside mosques, most of their quarrels would disappear. He could not see that his sincere attempts to establish cordial and even friendly relations with individual Muslims made no impact on the relations between the two groups. Nor did he have much insight either into the deepest fears and suspicions Muslims had entertained about Hindus since 1857, or the painful historical memories of Muslim persecution nursed by the latter. Every time a conflict occurred he turned to the Hindus and asked for heroic sacrifices. Since they were in a majority, better educated and more advantaged, he asked them to 'yield up to the Mohammedans what the latter desire and . . . rejoice in so doing'. Their sacrifices, he insisted, must not be 'cheap and tawdry' and based on 'mere reciprocation', but should spring from 'love' and 'generosity'. When they resisted, he felt hurt and sought to 'purify' their consciences by means of fasts and plaintive appeals. This inherently precarious method worked for a while, but soon began to provoke strong feelings of resentment and bitterness among them. Some of them accused him of being anti-Hindu and even suggested that he was *using* them to raise his political stature and was being moral *at their expense*. The fanatics among them made repeated attempts on his life until one finally succeeded.

Another reason why Gandhi had difficulty appreciating the nature and basis of the Hindu-Muslim conflict had to do with his South African experiences, which distorted his understanding of the Indian situation and whose irrelevance he took years to recognise. He had gone there as an employee of a Muslim firm and had led and established excellent relations with the Muslim migrants. Most of them came from Gujarat and spoke his language, shared his culture and followed a way of life very similar to his own. They all faced the common problems of a minority settled in a foreign country and were too deeply involved in making money and fighting racist laws to worry much about their internal differences. As Gandhi wrote to Gokhale in 1907, the 'struggle we are undergoing here has resulted in making us feel that we are Indians first and Hindus, Mohammedans, Tamils, Parsis, etc. afterwards'. Three years later he wrote on the basis of his South African experience that to 'create among the inhabitants of India the consciousness of their being one nation, no Herculean efforts are necessary. We are of course a single nation and brothers as among ourselves'. He argued that nationality had nothing to do with religion or language and was entirely a matter of culture, which Muslims, being 'simply converts from Hinduism', shared in common with Hindus.

When Gandhi returned to India he made two assumptions, both based on illicit generalisations of his South African experience.

First, Indian Muslims were all like Gujarati Muslims he had met in South Africa, and second, Muslims and Hindus primarily thought of themselves as Indians. It took him nearly ten years to realise that the assumptions on which he had hitherto based his action were profoundly mistaken. Muslims in north India were acutely conscious of their ethnic and cultural identity. It was true that the two communities had evolved a common culture as they had done in Gujarat. However, in Gujarat Muslims had largely fitted into the Hindu culture, whereas the opposite was generally the case in the north. Again the two communities, especially the Muslims, defined themselves in religious not political terms, and unlike South Africa all the power of the colonial government in India was used to perpetuate this state of affairs.

Around 1926 Gandhi's views began to undergo a decisive change. In that year he wrote to Nehru that the two communities were going 'more and more away from each other'. He told a meeting in Bengal a year later that the 'Hindu-Muslim problem had passed out of human hands into God's hands'. He told Jinnah a few months later that he wished he could do something, but was 'utterly hopeless'. He kept striving for unity, but increasingly felt that the British policy of 'divide and rule' stood in the way and that nothing much could be done until after independence. He told Ansari in 1930 that 'the third party, the evil British power' was creating the difficulties. Over a year later he wrote that 'the moment the alien wedge is removed, the divided communities are bound to unite'. He repeated the view as late as 1942 and thought that 'unity will not precede but succeed freedom'. This was why he kept urging Jinnah to delay Partition until after independence and assured him that if things did not work out, he would have his Pakistan. Gandhi remained convinced until the end of his life that since the two communities shared common civilisational, ethnic and other bonds, nothing substantial divided them save the British policy of 'divide and rule' and 'small' misunderstandings. It was not until he saw the outcome of Jinnah's mass contact campaign that he appreciated how very differently the Muslims perceived their place in India. And it was only when he went to Noakhali and N. K. Bose explained to him its social geography that he realised how deep the economic and social divisions between the two communities ran.

Gandhi was also handicapped by the fact that like many of his predecessors he could not come to terms with the centuries of

Muslim presence in India. Most leaders of the earlier generations including the liberals held Muslim rule responsible for their degeneration. For some it represented the 'dark ages' marked by the sustained persecution and forcible conversion of the Hindus and contributed little if anything of value to the enrichment of Indian civilisation. The others were less contemptuous but no better informed. Although, as we saw, Gandhi did not denigrate Muslim rule, he too had great difficulty integrating it in his interpretation of Indian history. With the exception of Akbar he saw little to admire in Muslim rule, and he could only think of the idea of equality as Islam's great contribution to India. His writings and speeches contained scant references to Muslim poets, administrators, architects, musicians, craftsmen or even saints. And if his reading of the Koran were to be excluded it was difficult to infer from his way of life, dress, courage, manner of conversation and environment that he was and saw himself as an heir to the centuries of Muslim presence in India. The rich Muslim culture that meant so much to Nehru and many others in north India evoked no sympathetic echo in him. Of the three great civilisations that have shaped the cultural physiognomy of India and left it with a trifurcated psyche expressing itself in their characteristic idioms in the relevant areas of life, Gandhi knew well the Hindu and the British but remained ignorant of the Islamic. Not surprisingly he remained an incomplete Indian unable to represent the full range of Indian self-consciousness and to evoke and mobilise the total conspectus of historical memories.

Although Gandhi himself did not put it this way, Indian history for him began with the arrival of the Aryans and continued for several thousand years during which it developed a rich Hindu culture. The Muslim and British periods were largely aberrations made possible by Hindu decadence, and significant because of their revitalising influence on Hinduism. The Muslims were basically converted Hindus whose religion was but an icing on their essentially Hindu cultural cake. And as for British rule, it imported an alien civilisation unsuited to the Indian genius of which the culturally revitalised India was only to assimilate a few elements. The Muslim perception of Indian history and identity was diametrically opposite to Gandhi's. In their view they were outsiders in both their historical origins and cultural sympathies and of a different stock from the Hindus. While some had inter-married with Hindus, many had for centuries retained their ethnic 'purity'.

It was true that a significant number of them were Hindu converts. However, the conversion was not a mere credal change but a process of profound transformation that de-Hinduised them, gave them a wholly new identity and marked a drastic rupture with their past. For the Muslims their history had begun outside India and was continued and flourished in it for several centuries before it was interrupted by British rule. They were not sure where their future lay. Some thought that like their past, it too lay outside India in a separate state; others hoped for a suitable autonomous space within India.

A large number of Hindus felt nervous and uneasy about their Muslim past which dredged up many a traumatic and historical memory. For their part a large number of Muslims felt equally nervous about their Hindu past as it drew attention to their Hindu origins and both stirred up a deep sense of insecurity and impugned their claim to a separate national identity. Since it did not accord an adequate recognition of the millenium of Muslim presence, the Hindu definition of India marginalised the Muslims and had an anti-Muslim bias. Since it wholly obnubilated its Indian roots and the way Hindu India had deeply shaped and structured its identity, the Muslim definition of India exorcised pre-Muslim India and had a deep anti-Hindu thrust. Their mutually exclusive conceptions of the past meant that the India beloved of one was odious to the other. Deeply divided about their past, their present became a shaggy terrain on which they jousted for their divided future. They needed a balanced view of Indian history capable of recognising the rich contributions each had made to the development of Indian civilisation. Gandhi was obviously not in a position to provide it.

It is true that unlike Tilak, Aurobindo, Savarkar and others for whom Hinduism was to be the basis of Indian unity, Gandhi took a genuinely plural view of India. His India was a creative synthesis of many civilisations and a happy home of different religious, linguistic and ethnic groups. However, when it came to articulating the nature of the synthesis and the manner of their co-existence, he unwittingly fell back on Hinduism. The cultural synthesis was for him a uniquely *Hindu* achievement and a tribute to the *Hindu* spirit of tolerance. Furthermore, since Gandhi's approach to life was essentially moral and spiritual, the differences in culture, customs, habits of thought, literature and forms of art between the two communities disappeared at that highly abstract level and never really entered his perceptual universe. Rather than recognise and reconcile the historically generated differences, he took his stand on a trans-historical plane and simply ignored them. A view of history that left out history itself could hardly be expected to unite those haunted by it. To be sure unlike Tilak and Aurobindo, Gandhi's India did leave a large and autonomous cultural space for Muslims. However, it was a space *within* a basically Hindu framework. They were given the fullest freedom to preserve their identity and grow, but not integrated into and seen as a vital and indispensable *component* of the larger Indian identity. Unlike the Hindu fundamentalists who Hinduised India, Gandhi genuinely tried to Indianise Hinduism and opened it up to Muslim and other influences. While this was a momentous step in the right direction, his India continued to rest on a Hindu foundation.

Gandhi could have avoided this if he had done two things. First, rather than equate pre-Muslim India with Hinduism he should have seen it as a home of many different cultures, of which the dominant Hindu culture was but one. While recognising the great Hindu contribution to the development of India, this would have allowed him to separate the two, challenge Hindu possessiveness about India and to provide a broad framework within which the non-Hindus could claim to be just as authentically Indian as the Hindus. Secondly, he should have appreciated more fully than he did that 'Hinduism' was not an undifferentiated whole but a loose and complex structure of beliefs, values, rituals and practices evolved out of the sediments left behind by many an indigenous and foreign civilisation. It was a continually evolving and an incredibly diverse and open tradition so that one could be a Hindu in several different and sometimes incompatible ways. The *Vaishnavites*, the *Saivites*, the *Tantric* schools of the 'left' and the 'right' and the others, who shared little in common, not even belief in the *Vedas*, rebirth and the *varnāshramadharma*, were all Hindus. The orthodox, or *sanatani*, Hindu is therefore a contradiction in terms. Indeed, insofar as it imposes an unwarranted credal unity, the term Hinduism itself is inaccurate and does injustice to Hindus.

Of the two essential steps Gandhi needed to take in order to arrive at a historically accurate view of India, he did not take the first and took the second only to a limited degree. This was not at all because he shared the Hindus' possessiveness about India or took a parochial view of Hinduism. On the contrary, his views of both India and Hinduism were remarkably catholic and open.

What got in the way were his limited knowledge of Indian history, inadequate historical imagination and the failure of the earlier generations of leaders to do the necessary spadework. Gandhi could hardly be blamed for not doing what none before had done and none since either.

Before concluding this chapter it would be helpful to highlight one important feature of the Indian independence movement under Gandhi. Much of the literature on the Asian and African independence movements is vitiated by the attempt to conceptualise them in terms of largely irrelevant and ethnocentric Western categories.[23] The use of the term nation and its derivatives is one example of this. There is no obvious reason why every independence movement should be called *national*, for not every country wishing to be free of foreign rule conceives itself as a nation in the conventional sense of a more or less homogeneous and self-conscious ethnic, cultural or ethno-cultural unit. There is even less reason for calling it *nationalist* for where there is no consciousness of a nation, there can be no nationalism either. What is more, nationalism refers to a specific way of justifying a nation's demand for independence, usually in terms of such beliefs as that mankind is 'naturally' divided into nations, that each nation has an unambiguous and homogeneous identity, that it shapes the consciousness and character of its members and that it has a natural or historical right to self-determination. Since Europe has been divided into long-established, internally cohesive and self-conscious communities for centuries, such arguments have come easily to it. The historical experiences, modes of social organisation and ways of self-conceptualisation of the other parts of the world were often very different, and not surprisingly they articulated their demand for independence differently. They generally argued that they wished to be free in order to preserve the integrity of their culture, civilisation or traditional way of life, to avoid being exploited and impoverished by foreign rulers, as a matter of familial loyalty to their ancestors, because they had long lived without external interference and saw no reason why they should not continue to do so, or simply that their right to independence needed no more justification than a man's right not to be a slave.

It is, of course, true that most of the independence movements outside Europe did borrow some of its nationalist rhetoric. However, they did so largely because their masters only understood and responded to demands articulated in the language of European nationalism. When the colonial leaders spoke to their own people, they generally used a very different rhetoric for the simple reason that the illiterate masses could not be mobilised in European idioms! By its very nature every independence movement had two targets, the colonial rulers and the masses, and had to speak in at least two languages. This is sometimes denied on the dubious grounds that the desire for collective or political independence is distinctively European in origin and that the non-European societies do not have the requisite vocabulary for articulating a demand for it. The idea of political independence was very much present in India and China where scores of principalities and kingdoms fought wars in its name, and even in Africa where politically motivated wars between empires and large tribal kingdoms were not uncommon either. It is true that the idea of *Indian* independence was relatively recent, but that was because the consciousness of the whole of India as a single political entity was recent, not because the concept of political independence was new. Even if it were conceded that the concept of political independence was a uniquely European export, obviously the colonial leaders could not make sense of it, let alone popularise it, without translating and redefining it in the far more familiar local idioms.

Not every independence movement in the colonies then was national; not every movement for national independence was nationalist; not every nationalist movement was articulated and legitimised in terms of the European doctrines of nationalism; and not every movement that did so opted for the French and especially the German variety on which so many writers on nationalism tend to concentrate. As a matter of historical fact the German nationalist doctrine has had very little influence on Asia, Africa and Latin America for the obvious reason that the writings of the German philosophers were often not translated into English, were not easily comprehensible and failed to connect with the experiences of the countries concerned. If they were to be intelligible, the colonial leaders had to address their rulers in the latter's own language. As B. C. Pal and Aurobindo discovered, their heavily Hegelian nationalist vocabulary made not the slightest sense to the British rulers. Nationalism was a response to colonialism, and the way it articulated itself was necessarily conditioned by the ideology in which the latter justified itself. Unless the writers on nationalism learn the indigenous languages and appreciate the nuances and highly complex modes of discourse of the Asian and African countries, they are likely to be misled by their Eurocentric bias and the unreliable translations of the writings and speeches of (and the false polemical trails left behind by) the leaders of the independence movement.

The point we are making would become clearer if we examined the internal logic of the independence movement under Gandhi. Like the other Indian leaders he knew that India was radically different from every European country. It was vast in size, highly uncentralised, deeply divided, had a long and chequered history and consisted of different and not fully-integrated ethnic, religious, linguistic and cultural groups. Since it was not united in terms of religion, language, race, ways of life, common historical memories of oppression and struggle or any of the several other factors stressed by the European nationalist leaders, they either did not apply without a great deal of casuistry or united one group only by alienating the rest. Gandhi instinctively knew that the language of nationalism not only did not make sense in India but was bound to have fatal consequences. He was acutely aware of the fact that when Hindus flirted with nationalism during the first two decades of the 20th century, they frightened away not only the Muslims and the other minorities but also some of the lower castes. And he hardly needed to be reminded of the confusion and mischief caused by Jinnah's introduction of nationalist language into Indian politics. That Gandhi and most other Indian leaders preferred the relaxed, even chaotic, plurality of Indian life to the homogeneity of the modern European state was a further factor pulling them away from European nationalism.

Accordingly Gandhi turned to the vaguer but politically more relevant and, to him, morally more acceptable concept of civilisation. Not race, ethnicity, language, religion or customs but the plural and evolving civilisation of the kind described earlier united the Indians. As we saw earlier, foreign rule was unacceptable because it choked and distorted India's growth and imposed a way of life incompatible with its basic character. India needed independence in order to undertake the long and painful task of revitalising its civilisation and regenerating its people. Its independence was desirable only insofar as it created the conditions for its autonomous moral growth, and it signified not a millennium but an invitation to decades of hard work. Since the civilisation Gandhi wanted the Indian state to nurture was synthetic, tolerant, spiritual and open, his vision of India had little in common with the collectivist, monolithic, aggressive and xenophobic nationalism of some of the Western and central European countries.

Gandhi's political thought thus more or less completely bypassed the characteristic nature and vocabulary of European nationalism, and conceptualised the Indian struggle for independence in a non-nationalist and non-national language. He rarely used the term 'nation' except when forced to do so by such antagonists as Jinnah, and then largely to refer to the fact that India was not a motley collection of groups but consisted of people sharing common aspirations and interests and a vague but nonetheless real commitment to the kind of spiritual civilisation discussed earlier. When he occasionally used the term 'nationalism' he largely meant 'love of one's country'. For the most part he preferred to speak of *swadeshi* spirit which captured the interrelated ideas of collective pride, ancestral loyalty, mutual responsibility and intellectual and moral openness. It is true that his conception of Indian civilisation was narrow and limited and, although not anti-Muslim, it had a strong Hindu orientation. However, it had nothing in common with the ethnic or even cultural nationalism of Tilak and Aurobindo, let alone such Hindu fundamentalists as Savarkar. Thanks to the non-nationalist philsophical framework within which he conceptualised the independence movement, the latter did not throw up a Hindu nationalism to match that of the League, but guaranteed full protection to Muslims even under the greatest provocation, laid the foundations of a secular state, bore no hostility to the British, and gave the country the confidence to invite Mountbatten to stay on as Governor-General of independent India and use him as an instrument of the new state. All this was truly remarkable in a people enjoying independence after hundreds of years of foreign rule and intensely bitter about both the fact and the manner of their country's Partition. While Gandhi's spiritual approach to politics must be held partly responsible for the Partition, it must also be given most of the credit for containing the nationalist virus and giving the independence movement a rare measure of breadth and depth.

8

Critical Appreciation

In the earlier chapters we outlined and commented on specific aspects of Gandhi's theory of spiritual politics. In the concluding chapter we shall look at it as a whole and examine it both philosophically and in terms of its impact on India.

Gandhi's political theory cuts across several moral, religious and philosophical traditions and rests on an unusually broad philosophical foundation, showing both the rich harvest that can be garnered from and the problems involved in a cross-cultural dialogue. Enjoying access to several cultures, he is overwhelmed by none of them and is able to chisel out an autonomous space from which to evaluate them. Like a multilingual novelist skilfully playing with words and images drawn from different languages, he borrows ideas from different traditions, all of which he regards as part of his common human heritage, and produces ingenious combinations, some unstable, some beautifully integrated, but all fascinating.

He takes over the Hindu concept of *ahimsā*, finds it passive and negative and turns to the cognate Christian concept of love to help him understand and redefine it. He realises that love is an emotion, compromises the agent's autonomy and builds up attachments to the world, and so he redefines it in the light of the Hindu concept of *anāsakti* or detachment. Gandhi's double conversion, his Hinduisation of the Christianised Hindu concept, yields the fascinating concepts of a non-emotive, serene and detached but positive and active love, and a non-activist life of action. Although the concepts contain tensions, they are highly suggestive and beyond the reach of either tradition alone. Again, he takes over the Christian concept of vicarious atonement, combines it with the Hindu practice of fasting as a penance and a form of moral pressure, and arrives at the profound notion of fasting as a form of voluntary crucifixion undertaken by a moral leader to atone for, redeem and uplift his temporarily deviant followers. Neither the Christian nor the Hindu tradition had or could by itself have developed such a concept. Gandhi does similar things with such concepts as the state, law, freedom, morality, action, property, nation, religion and rights. In each case he sets up a creative dialogue and sometimes an imaginative confrontation between the relevant traditions and not only combines what strikes him as their valuable insights but also occasionally generates wholly new concepts. Even when his 'discoveries' are unconvincing, his intellectual and moral 'experiments' are invariably stimulating.

Every historical epoch articulates and centres on a specific vision of man. Although the vision is never monolithic, except in the case of a total historical amnesia, and permits a wide variation, the variations revolve around and their perimeter is circumscribed by its central principles and assumptions. It highlights and gives pride of place to specific human capacities, emotions, aspirations, activities, areas of life and ways of understanding the human condition, and ignores, suppresses, trivialises, distorts and assigns a subordinate status to the others. No vision of man is ever without its legitimate and pampered as well as ill-treated step-children and its systematically harassed victims. As a creative thinker intensely sensitive to the political victims of the currently dominant view of man, Gandhi's great contribution consists in taking up the cudgels on behalf of the victimised human faculties and emotions, restoring the suppressed sensibilities and breathing new meanings into the ideals and aspirations it has systematically stifled, scorned, ridiculed or misinterpreted.

As we saw, he challenges the anthropocentric view that man enjoys absolute ontological superiority to and the consequent right of unrestrained domination over the non-human world. He rightly argues that the grounds on which such claims rest are philosophically suspect and that the havoc they cause ultimately rebounds on man himself. By radically recreating the non-human world in his own image and subordinating it to his interests, he indiscriminately alters the basic conditions of his earthly existence, denies himself the regulating presence of the 'other' and perpetrates massive and often wholly unjustified violence on other living beings. He also renders himself rootless and falls prey both to anthropomorphic narcissism and species imperialism. Gandhi's cosmocentric anthropology restores his ontological roots, establishes a more balanced and respectful relationship between him and the natural world, assigns the animals their due place and provides the basis of a more satisfactory and ecologically conscious philosophical anthropology.

Even as he locates man in the cosmos, he locates him in a historically grounded social order and gives a new and deeper meaning to the much debated concept of man's social nature. He rightly argues that every man owes his humanity to others, that he is a recipient of unsolicited but indispensable and non-repayable gifts from countless anonymous individuals, and that his inherently unspecifiable moral duties and obligations extend far beyond those based on consent, promise, contract and the membership of a specific community. Indeed, only a small cluster of moral relationships subsist between identifiable individuals and are deliberately incurred. And even these are embedded in and shadowed by a large range of invisible and conveniently unnoticed relations with others. The vast bulk of moral relationship stretches out to men and women in the community's remotest past and the most obscure corners of the globe to whom one is bound by invisible bonds and whose legitimate claims deserve a sensitive response.

Gandhi's profound analysis of morality places many new and important questions on the agenda of moral and political philosophy. He asks how a moral being should respond to involuntarily incurred and inherited debts and give moral articulation to the profound sense of gratitude they inspire, whether and to what extent morality is a matter of choice at all, and whether it is ever a relationship between two individuals unmediated by the silent and invisible presence of others. He asks too whether the currently dominant individualistic conception of man has the necessary philosophical resources to give an adequate account of morality and to resist the attempts to reduce it to reciprocal egoism and enlightened self-interest. At a different level Gandhi asks what new concepts should replace the traditional litany of rights, duties, claims, interests and obligations which are all too superficial and atomic to conceptualise and probe the depth and complexity of moral life, and whether moral relationship is autonomous enough to be analysed in terms of moral categories. Although Gandhi's theory of *yajna* is not free from difficulties, it offers one interesting way of answering these and other related questions.

Like his analysis of moral life Gandhi's concept of indivisible humanity contains important insights and gives a new meaning to the elusive and much discussed idea of human unity. In the course of their attempts to understand the nature of man's relations with his fellow-men, philosophers have argued that they are all similar, members of a common species, species-beings, equal, brothers or members of a community. Gandhi advances the highly original thesis that they are all one. By this he means that whatever a man does to others he does to himself as well, that his relation to them is only the obverse of his relation to himself, that men can only be human together and that their humanity is indivisible. Although he exaggerates the point, he is right to argue that in degrading and brutalising their respective victims, the white South Africans, the metropolitan powers, the capitalists and the high-caste Hindus degraded and brutalised themselves as well. Debilitated and distorted by their abnormal fears, anxieties, obsessions and hatreds, they could barely hold themselves together without elaborate self-deception and maintain their moral balance without the crutches of a flimsy ideology. Their enormous wealth and power not only did not make them better men and their lives richer and more fulfilling, but in fact so crippled them psychologically and morally that they were only capable of pursuing and enjoying pleasures just as infantile, banal and self-defeating as their victims. As Gandhi concludes, when all the relevant factors are taken into account, oppressive and exploitative systems do not admit of winners. He is therefore able to attack them from the standpoint of their victims as well as their alleged beneficiaries. He takes a stand on their *shared* humanity and *common* interests and shows why it is in the interests of *all* to fight against inequalities and injustices, and why the fight should be so conducted that the future victors do not brutalise themselves and forget their shared humanity with their erstwhile masters. Unlike the crude versions of the Marxist and other theories of liberation, Gandhi's has a built-in theoretical protection against misuse and perversion. The Gandhian revolution cannot devour its own children.

On the basis of his theory of man Gandhi proposes that a well-considered philosophy of politics must find ways of reconciling the claims of the individual, the political community and mankind, the three fundamental axes of moral life for him. Every human being is necessarily an individual, a uniquely constituted, self-determining agent coming to terms with himself and the world in his own way and at his own pace. He is the architect and centre of a unique world of relationships structuring and organising it in his own distinct manner. To take over his life and run it for him is to violate his integrity, destroy his wholeness and perpetrate a most unacceptable form of moral violence. Gandhi grounded human uniqueness in his theory of rebirth. The theory is suspect, but the thesis stands.

As Gandhi rightly argues, an individual is not an abstract atom but a member of a specific community which profoundly shapes and moulds his deepest instincts, aspirations, unconscious memories, habits and ways of life and thought. Since it constitutes and structures him as a self-determining agent, it is the necessary basis and presupposition of his existence. It is his spiritual home; he belongs to and feels at ease in it and becomes rootless and dries up outside it. His self-respect and love of himself are inseparable from his respect and love of it. As Gandhi argues, the deepest ties of affection, love and loyalty by which he is bound to it are by definition not a matter of conscious choice. They are pre-rational and pre-moral and set the limits of his moral choices. Since he derives so much benefit from his community, knows it better than any other and is bound to its members by ties of mutual expectations, rational reflection confirms and reinforces the pre-moral ties.

For Gandhi mankind is the third fundamental unit of moral life. Since all men are moral beings, they enjoy ontological equality and make both negative and positive claims on one another whose strength and urgency cannot be diminished by the contingent factor of physical distance. If a man claimed that as a moral agent his integrity should be considered inviolate and his freedom and self-determination not be interfered with, he could not consistently refuse to acknowledge the similar claims of others, let alone interfere with them himself. Unlike many an egalitarian thinker Gandhi grounds moral equality in the unity of all human beings, thereby giving it a philosophical and moral depth. Since humanity is indivisible, men are responsible to and for one another, and it ought to matter to each how others live.

Since the individual, his political community and mankind are ontologically and morally inseparable, they are all equally important and none can be ignored or treated as a mere means to the other two. As Gandhi observes, a community that treats its members as mere 'resources' or means to its so-called collective well-being is guilty of the deepest form of violence and not a moral community at all. And similarly an individual who treats his community as a mere means to his self-interest contradicts the basic conditions of his existence and does violence both to it and

himself. While this is generally appreciated by most political philosophers, a similar relationship between the community and mankind that Gandhi establishes is not. He rightly maintains that no
political community can ignore the claims of those 'outside' its
boundaries and still call itself moral. Although territorially outside
it, they are very much inside it by virtue of a shared moral nature
and ontological and cultural interdependence. As a member of a
subject country and race Gandhi was unusually sensitive to this,
and knew well that equating the territorial with moral boundaries
led to some of the worst and most insidious forms of violence. He
rightly insists that every community must recognise the equally
legitimate moral claims of others and define and pursue its national
interests accordingly. Not to do so is to forfeit the claim to be a
moral community.

Gandhi's spiritual perspective also enables him to notice and
highlight some of the morally problematic aspects of the modern
state. If man's integrity is inviolate, then the prisons, the domestic
use of terror and wars obviously raise disturbing questions. It
would not do to say that some men are 'really' brutes and deserve
to be locked away, for to give up on them, to put them outside the
moral pale and even positively to brutalise them is hardly a form of
behaviour consistent with belief in human dignity. A similar problem arises with respect to the poor, the weak and the underprivileged both in other communities and especially in one's own.
They are often caught up in a vicious cycle not of their own making
and their degradation is often the product of a social order upheld
and protected by the state. As Gandhi argues, the modern state is a
highly complex institution. Much of its violence is institutionalised, structured, exported abroad, perpetrated behind the backs of
its members and cleverly rationalised. It does not cease to exist
simply because one does not see it on the streets; indeed what
occurs there may be only a reaction to it. Gandhi rightly remarks
that it is morally arbitrary to be exercised about one form of
violence but turn a blind eye to the others. All forms of violence,
those of the state as well as the rioters on the streets, raise
questions of justification. The former cannot be justified in terms of
the inherently vague ideas of law and order or public interest, for
one needs to ask why the maintenance of order and the public
interest requires such violence and whether a social order that can
only be preserved by massive violence does not need to be radically reconstituted.

Gandhi also raises the important question of the citizen's responsibility for the actions of his government. As he points out, the state is ultimately nothing more than a system of compulsory and institutionalised co-operation, and each of its citizens is a party to its actions and partly responsible for their consequences. Unless he opts out of it altogether, which obviously he cannot, he is implicated in its decisions. Whether he acknowledges it or not, everything he does has a political dimension. He can never be apolitical, and apathy is really a form of moral irresponsibility. A citizen cannot hide behind the façade of collective responsibility for it is composed of and does not replace individual responsibility. As a moral being he has a duty to be concerned about what is done in his name to this fellow-men both inside and outside his community. As Gandhi points out, the government has a tendency to use the sheer complexity of political life and its monopoly of information to morally overwhelm and paralyse its citizens and foster a culture of moral inertia. Since the entire weight of the state is used to put their consciences to sleep, they have a duty to remain especially alert lest they should be morally seduced or blackmailed into unacceptable compromises.

While enabling him to notice aspects of political life ignored by many a political thinker, Gandhi's vision of man also blinds him to several others. For him the good is real whereas the evil is not. Evil is essentially negative, parasitic upon good, contingent and the product of a temporary failure to perceive or live up to the good. In his view there is no man whose basic sense of decency cannot be evoked and who cannot be made to see the error of his ways. However wicked he might be, his evil is basically a *māyā* behind whose veil lies the source of his essential goodness. Not surprisingly Gandhi had great difficulty coping with evil, especially one of great intensity and magnitude. His theory had not prepared him for it and lacked the capacity to help him make sense of it. Although he was right to reject the manichean postulate of evil as an independent principle, he was wrong to see it solely in negative and passive terms and only as a temporary lapse that could soon be rectified. When confronted with the incredible intensity and sheer mindlessness of the inter-communal hatred and violence both before and after Partition, he was unhinged and kept wondering how human beings could fall 'so low' and fail to rise up to the minimum expected of 'decent' men and women. Although Gandhi pitted all his immense goodness against the evil and single-handed managed to contain it, a feat beyond the power of several thousand thoroughly armed soldiers, his success in each case was short-lived and over time it sapped his will to live. Gandhi had a similar difficulty making sense of Hitler whom he thought misguided, and not all the eloquence of Martin Buber could convince that he was evil and beyond all moral appeal.

At a different level Gandhi had considerable difficulty coming to terms with social conflicts. For him harmony, a form of good, was real whereas conflict, a form of evil, was essentially negative, contingent, temporary and the product of a misguided head or a narrow heart. His moral theory prevented him from appreciating that conflict was an integral part of social life, had deep and intractable roots and was not amenable to easy resolution. As a lifelong fighter against all manner of injustices, he knew that they were pervasive and tenacious and had to be vigorously fought. At the same time, since conflict challenged his basic assumptions about man he was never at ease with and even felt morally threatened by it. He therefore initiated campaigns against injustices but refused to press them beyond a certain point and settled for whatever was possible under the circumstances. Since the deeper roots of conflicts were often left untouched, they not only continued to recur but sometimes grew worse. Racial discrimination in South Africa was only mildly abated by his efforts, grew more vicious after he left the country and continues to persist some 40 years after his death. He had only moderate success in tackling the three great evils of untouchability, inter-communal violence and poverty he had placed high on his political agenda, and left the deeper roots of the last two more or less untouched.

Gandhi's analysis of the nature of oppression, too, suffers from the limitations of his theory of man. While he is right to argue that the victims of oppression are not necessarily innocent and sometimes only too willing to collaborate, he fails to appreciate that this is not always so. They might merely acquiesce in their predicament rather than actively assist their masters, render the required services most grudgingly, co-operate at one level but quietly subvert the system at another, or bide their time until the ripe moment. To subsume all these and other acts under the capacious category of co-operation is to deprive the term of all meaning. We also need to ask *how* their 'co-operation' is secured. They might 'co-operate' because they are terrorised by a brutal use of force as in the case of slaves, denied education or brainwashed into believing that the existing system is divinely ordained as with the untouchables in India, manipulated and divided as the British did with Hindus and Muslims, or be starved, tortured and demoralised, as in the case of Jews in the Nazi concentration camps. The victims are often too fragmented, confused, busy eking out a miserable livelihood for their families and devoid of energy and organisation to have the ability, strength or courage to see through and challenge the subtle and complex mechanisms on which all oppressive systems rely. They *are* therefore often innocent, and to accuse them of silent collaboration is to misunderstand their predicament. To say that it is the coward who creates the bully is too simple-minded and psychologistic an explanation to account for the complex patterns of interaction between social groups.

Although Gandhi's moral theory as we observed earlier contains important insights, it is handicapped by his epistemology. His theory of relative truth represents an interesting, if a little mystical, way of defending individual freedom. However, it cannot explain the existence of a moral community. If each individual perceives truth differently, it is difficult to see how they can arrive at a body of common values lying at the basis of every community and, if they somehow do, agree on their interpretation. As we saw, Gandhi's theory of *satyāgraha* is predicated on the existence of common values and relies on them for its success. Insofar as he cannot account for them, it lacks an epistemological basis. His theory of relative truth, further, renders his concept of integrity morally problematic. For him every man sees truth in his own way and is entitled to live by it. It would seem that there is no-one, not even a slave-owner or a Hitler of whom he would say that he does not live by his truth and whose integrity should not be respected. Gandhi called Hitler mad but disallowed personal violence against him and had either to tolerate him or, as he himself preferred, allow hundreds of lives to be sacrificed in order to 'melt' his stony heart. He is forced to take this extraordinary position because his epistemology confers moral dignity on *whatever* a man *sincerely* happens to believe. As a man who had to deal with many an insincere racist, imperialist and capitalist foe, Gandhi did not, of course, need to be reminded of the fact that men might not sincerely believe what they say or fail to discharge their fundamental moral obligation constantly to re-examine their sincerely held beliefs. But he has no objective principles with which to regulate their sincerity and decide what they may not believe. As a result almost every interest and prejudice acquires the status of a personal truth and commands not only respect but a heavy price in human suffering. Contrary to his intention Gandhi's theory of relative truth could easily lead to the perpetuation of grave injustices. By entitling a dominant group to claim moral legitimacy for its beliefs and practices, it imposes such severe constraints on its victims' mode of action, including the choice of means, that the latter might not think it worth their while to fight.

Gandhi's moral theory also makes it difficult for him to come to terms with and adequately conceptualise the modern state. He is obsessed with its coercive character and remains deeply hostile to it. It took him a long time to appreciate its moral, regenerative and redistributive role and even then his acceptance of it remained half-hearted and unintegrated into his general perspective. Furthermore, the good life as Gandhi defines it is austere and simple and largely moral in nature. It has only a limited place for the intellectual, aesthetic and other dimensions of life and does not need constant access to the rich world of art, literature, philosophy and culture. Since his local communities meet the conditions of good life, they are not only economically but also morally self-sufficient and self-contained. Gandhi is therefore unable to establish inner and moral connections between them and the state and, at a different level, between the latter and mankind. He does see the need to connect the two and talks about concentric circles. However, he only shows that the transition from the narrow to the wider circle is economically necessary, not that it is required by man's well-rounded development and the realisation of his full human potential.

Even when Gandhi's local communities are federally united into a larger polity, their consciousness does not rise above the local level. There is no area of life in which they are collectively engaged in the pursuit of a common enterprise. They debate local, not national, issues and do not take part in direct elections to the national assembly. The polity is not a moral presence and enjoys only a limited political presence in their daily lives. Not only does it therefore remain deeply fragmented and fragile, it is also difficult to see how its members can be morally concerned about their fellow-citizens elsewhere with whom their contacts are minimal and who do not materially and morally impinge on their consciousness.

The same problem occurs at the international level. Since their contacts with men and women in distant parts of the world are severely limited, it is difficult to see why Gandhi's citizens should at all feel morally concerned about them. They would certainly not be aggressive and might even feel positively well-disposed towards them. However, Gandhi cannot show why and how they would develop active love for them, and how the love of those with whom one is in daily contact can by itself lead to the love of those whom one has never seen and about whom one knows nothing. Unless the indivisibility of humanity is a tangible presence in their daily lives, it cannot be the basis of their moral consciousness. And it can only be a tangible presence in a technologically advanced and interdependent world, which Gandhi rules out. This is not to say that small communities cannot develop universal love, only that Gandhi's cannot. Small communities enjoying and requiring constant contacts with the other parts of the world in a technologically advanced society are very different from Gandhi's, which are relatively isolated, largely use local products and lack knowledge and sensitive understanding of the rest of the world.

As organising principles of social life, the ideas of active universal love and indivisible humanity are essentially modern and reflect the consciousness of an interdependent world. Gandhi appropriates the intellectual and moral achievements of modern civilisation but rejects the very science and technology that both generate and sustain them. Since this cannot be done, a deep contradiction lies at the centre of his system. His heart seeks identification with every human being on earth, but his head cannot rise above small and intimate groups. Gandhi's spiritual vision so alienated him from modern civilisation that he was unable to grasp its complex moral dialectic.

In the Indian context Gandhi's contribution was immense and at various levels. He successfully persuaded his countrymen to concentrate their energies on the urgent task of national regeneration. Like the other Indian leaders he was deeply disturbed by the ease with which India had for centuries fallen prey to foreign rule. Unlike many of them he realised that this could not be explained in terms of the foreigners' guile and superior force or India's moral innocence, alleged other-worldliness and the caste system. The roots of its weakness lay deep and required a comprehensive and carefully planned reform of its character, culture, social structure and religion. Gandhi was one of the first to realise that, largely thanks to their unfortunate history and the British policy of divide and rule, the Hindus and Muslims had begun to move apart, and that unless their relations were improved India could not become a viable polity. He was also one of the first to notice the deepening hiatus between the Westernised intellectuals and the Indian masses, and the sharpening conflict between the rich and the poor, the landlords and the peasants, the capitalists and the workers, the high caste Hindus and the untouchables and between the urban and rural India. He realised too that the old moral and social order was crumbling and that only a new *yugadharma* could form the basis of Indian unity.

Not only Gandhi's diagnosis but also his authority, style and remedy were new. He was the only Indian leader so thoroughly to identify himself with his countrymen that he acquired a rare and unchallenged moral authority over them. His authority was not religious or even spiritual but essentially moral. Apart from a few illiterate people, hardly any Indian saw him as an *avatār*, both because he was all too human to conform to the traditional conception of it and because Hindu India had more or less stopped believing in it. Nor did many see him as a *saint*, for sainthood is not a category of classical Hinduism and Gandhi displayed none of the features associated with a *sant* in popular Hinduism. Nor did they see him as a *rishi* or even a *muni* as he was essentially a man of action and not spiritual in the traditional sense. The Hindus dug deep into their collective unconscious and described him as a *yugapurusha* or a *mahātmā*, a title he had conferred on Gokhale and which was in turn conferred on him by Tagore.[1] The term had a long lineage and a chequered history. Tagore, and the millions of Indians who adopted it, used it not in the strict philosophical sense of a realised soul, but in the popular sense of a man who had 'absorbed all selves into his own' and become the unique expression of both the aspirations of his people and the 'truth' of his time and place.[2] It captured the vital insight that Gandhi's authority over his countrymen was not religious or spiritual but moral and derived from the way he cared for, loved, served and became one with them and represented what Nehru called the 'ancient and proud spirit of India'.

Gandhi sublimated his love of India into love of the Indians, a feat unmatched by any other leader. Every Indian, however small, poor, illiterate or insignificant, mattered deeply to him. He not only fought for their collective interests but cared for each of them individually and answered their letters, advised them on their personal problems, spoke frankly about his failings and limitations, sought their guidance and attended to their grievances, with the result that his whole life became one continuous and largely silent dialogue with them. Each instinctively understood the other and said much while speaking little. The Indian practice of *darshan*, meaningless in the case of most other leaders, acquired its true significance in his. The masses who came to 'see' him saw something of themselves in his lambent eyes and went away charged with the scintilla of his spirit and strength, even as he glimpsed the spirit of India in their plaintive but uncomplaining eyes. Not surprisingly he was the least noisy of the Indian leaders. As he often said his life was his message, and it did speak volumes.

Gandhi dug deep into Indian culture and evolved a highly evocative mode of vernacular discourse. Indian sages and seers had argued over the centuries that profound moral and spiritual insights could not be stated but only hinted at, not described but only pointed to, and could only be expressed through myths, symbols, images and intensely concentrated aphorisms which each individual had to decode and interpret according to his ability. The so-called gods and goddesses with their distinctive physical and moral properties, favourite animals and the intricate myths surrounding them were really ways of conveying complex metaphysical and moral doctrines. Gandhi had mastered the indigenous style of symbolic discourse and fully exploited its obvious advantages. It was familiar to his audience, had a deep historical resonance and fitted in with his theory of the unity of head and heart. It also confused and marginalised the foreign rulers and created a private public space in which he could carry on a public conversation with his countrymen in relative privacy. He not only invented and used symbols but became one himself, and his manner of dressing, walking, talking, eating, sleeping, sitting, raising his index finger and choice of sites for his *āshram* tapped deep historical memories. The symbols were both packed with and went beyond arguments, and both explained situations and stirred people into action. They gave Gandhi's message a power no other form of discourse could have given.

Gandhi presented to his countrymen his programme of national regeneration neither as a way of becoming like the British nor as a way of reviving an ancient period of glory, but first, as a debt they owed to their forefathers, second, a means to become strong and independent and third, an opportunity to make their unique contribution to mankind.[3] They were heirs to a great civilisation and owed a deep *runa* (debt) to its founders to preserve and continually enrich their sacred legacy. They were not a weak and primitive people condemned to be exploited and ruled by foreigners but a talented nation capable of creating an energetic, vibrant and free society. As heirs to a spiritual civilisation they also had a moral duty as well as the capacity to show bewildered mankind a way out of its current mess. The first argument appealed to their sentiment of family loyalty, the second to their collective self-interest, and the third to their sense of pride. The Indians therefore *had* to reform and regenerate themselves.[4] Over time he so decisively changed the national climate that not the reformers but the conservatives were thrown on the defensive, an unparalleled achievement in modern Indian history. His moral authority over the masses was so great and his power to inspire them so considerable that he did not have to conceal his plea for reform in the revivalist language of his predecessors or support it with the religious authority of the pandits and the *sāstras*. Neither did he find it necessary to cultivate the Brahmins and keep them on his side. He simply ignored them as irrelevant to his task, and none dared challenge him. The Indians were 'his' people. He loved them passionately, cared for them deeply, had given his entire life to their service and become a vehicle of their longings. He had thus acquired the *adhikāra* to guide, rebuke and criticise them, and no one was to be allowed to stand between the two of them. Gandhi's courage, even arrogance, was simply breathtaking.

Gandhi not only made reform an integral part of the modern Indian self-consciousness but also went about reforming the Hindu religion, society and character on a massive scale. As we saw, he took a dim view of *jnānayoga* and *bhaktiyoga* as paths to *moksha* and stressed *karmayoga*. Although basically sympathetic to the *Gita's* theory of *karmayoga*, the only theory of action developed by classical Hinduism, Gandhi thought it was conservative, lacked political content and did not explain whose duty it was to fight against social and economic injustices. Accordingly he built on the legacy of earlier writers who had wrestled with the problem, especially Vivekananda and Tilak, and developed a socially and politically orientated form of *karmayoga* appropriate to the modern age. He made action the vehicle of *moksha*, gave an activist and social orientation to almost all the major Hindu concepts, equated religion with broadly defined morality, and made the removal of human suffering the very centre of moral and religious life. Hinduism had a weak social conscience; he infused into it a strong sense of social justice. It emphasised *moksha* or liberation from the world of illusion as the highest human ideal; Gandhi argued that *moksha* consisted in the active service of mankind. Hinduism took a low view of and shunned politics; Gandhi redefined it and put politics at the very centre of moral life. For centuries Hindus had lived with the practice of untouchability; Gandhi declared war on it and challenged its moral and cultural basis. Women had long occupied a low position in Hindu society; Gandhi brought thousands of them into public life, gave them high social and political visibility and made them an equal and integral part of Indian society. The upper strata of Hindu society had treated the peasant with scorn; Gandhi catapulted him into the centre of the political stage and gave him an unprecedented political and cultural presence. Some of Gandhi's reforms did not prove durable, but he at least initiated them and put them on the political agenda of independent India.

Although one of the greatest reformers in Indian history, Gandhi's reforms had important limitations derived largely from his narrow view of man and a limited understanding of Indian civilisation. His austere view of man led him to stress the moral at the expense of the intellectual, aesthetic, sexual and other dimensions of life. As a result he not only remained insufficiently sensitive to the rich and varied possibilities of human existence, but advanced an ascetic, lean and rather narrow view of morality itself. A critic once remarked that his *āshram* only grew vegetables and had no room for flowers. Although exaggerated, for Gandhi's cabbage assuaged a hungry stomach while his rose would only have delighted a well-fed and probably foreign observer, the comment highlights an important limitation of his thought.

Gandhi's austere conception of man also distorted his view of Indian civilisation. He stressed only the moralistic strand in it and ignored its sensuous, aesthetic, philosophical and other dimensions. He took only a passing interest in classical art, science, literature, music, dance, philosophy and even the *Upanishadas*, only a couple of which he seems to have read with care. Strange as it may seem in someone who spoke so much about the spiritual nature of India, he had a limited understanding and appreciation of what the ancient *rishis*, the Buddha, Mahavira, Ramkrishna

Paramhamsa, Raman Maharshi and Aurobindo were engaged in doing. Although at liberty to criticise and even reject their concerns and claims, Gandhi had a duty to make sense of and find a place for them in his view of Indian civilisation. His intense moralism, much needed in a callous society that fed ants and cows while its humans starved, tended to blot out several important achievements of Indian civilisation and led him to offer a highly one-sided account of it.

Gandhi's view of man limited his reforms at another level also. He so redefined the four *purushārthās* that they collapsed into one. He found little room for *kāma*, equated *moksha* with *dharma*, assigned a limited place to *ārtha* and only if regulated by *dharma*, and thus made *dharma* the sole basis of life. In so doing he drastically undervalued, even delegitimised, sexuality, affluence, prosperity, industrialisation and the traditional spiritual pursuits, and sought to plant in the Indian mind an unaccustomed sense of guilt at the enjoyment and celebration of life. While he was right to attack the vulgar and offensive life-styles of the rich in a country scarred by poverty and despair, he was wrong to reduce the majesty and grandeur of life to the one-dimensional pursuit of *dharma*. This had important social and political consequences. For example, his disapproval of sexuality except for procreative purposes meant that he saw and honoured women largely as mothers, never as wives or lovers. When he said that he wanted to become a woman, he had in mind nothing more than nursing the sick and raising children. He did bring women into public life in a way no-one had done before, but largely to play motherly roles; even in *satyāgrahas* they fought and suffered as mothers and sisters fiercely defending their children and brothers, but not as wives and sweethearts defending their husbands and lovers. While improving the condition of women, Gandhi also reinforced the traditional sexual stereotypes and roles.[5]

Gandhi's reform of untouchability suffered from a similar limitation. He did more than any other Indian to undermine it, yet his attack had a profound weakness. He saw it as a blot on the Hindu religion and made it the sole responsibility of the high-caste Hindus to fight against it. The untouchables themselves, reduced to passive and pathetic symbols of high-caste Hindu tyranny, were not involved in the struggle for their emancipation, a strange attitude in a man who everywhere else wanted the victims to fight for themselves. As a result they had no opportunity to work and fight alongside the Hindus, and they neither occupied important positions in the *Harijan sevak sangh* and the Congress nor set up an independent and effective organisation of their own. Not surprisingly they hardly grew under Gandhi's shadow, and a man who created so many great leaders was unable to create a single Harijan leader of equal stature. Ambedkar, one of the few exceptions, was not his favourite Harijan and grew in opposition to him.

Gandhi not only energised his countrymen to embark on a comprehensive programme of national regeneration but also fostered their cultural and moral autonomy, self-respect and pride. British rule had intellectually and morally overwhelmed the Indians and generated in them a deep sense of inferiority. They had become a nation of imitators, and their aggressive references to their great past thinly veiled their low self-esteem. Gandhi, who had himself been its victim for many years in South Africa and had managed to get rid of it only after a protracted and painful personal struggle, had little difficulty diagnosing the nature and causes of the colonial psychosis. He knew that a man who did not respect or love himself was unable to respect and love others either, and that self-contempt and self-pity often led to the contempt and hatred of those deemed responsible for them. On his return to India he saw that the Indian psyche had become profoundly distorted by the impotent hatred and morbid fear of the British, and that the relations between the two could not be placed on a healthy foundation until the Indians developed a sense of self-respect and power. Gandhi's scathing critique of British civilisation and his vigorous defence of the Indian were intended to undermine the hold of the imperialist ideology and restore his countrymen's cultural self-respect and autonomy. His *satyāgrahas* were designed to break the spell of 'official terror' and build up their sense of power. He was remarkably successful in both his objectives largely because of a fascinating blend of a simple and coherent philosophy and the force of personal example.

Gandhi's critique of Western and defence of Indian civilisation would not have restored his countrymen's cultural self-respect had he not adopted a life-style and a mode of discourse eloquently exemplifying and affirming it. Unlike nearly all other leaders who sang the glory of their civilisation but spoke, dressed, thought, behaved and debated like foreigners, Gandhi actually *lived* it. He insisted on speaking in Hindi and Gujarati, thereby reassuring his countrymen that the Indian languages were not private languages only to be used at home to express private feelings but vehicles of public communication to be used within the hearing of their masters for discussing political issues. He freely invoked Indian cultural allusions, symbols and images in his dealings with the colonial government and gave them a public status. He met the Viceroys, senior British ministers and even the emperor in his loin cloth, and talked to and behaved towards them exactly as he did to his countrymen. He had the courage to be the same in London, Marseilles and Geneva as in Delhi, Ahmedabad and Vardha and was never false to himself or to them. No other Indian leader during British rule had symbolised personal and cultural self-respect to this degree. Gandhi practised the cultural autonomy he preached, and the unity of his thought and action became a powerful source of national inspiration. Neither his personal example nor his philosophy by itself would have been enough to restore Indian pride and self-respect. The example would have been merely symbolic, and a culture used to symbols would have adored the Mahatma and discarded his message. The philosophy would have lacked the power to compel attention let alone move the vast masses, especially in a culture accustomed to dealing with abstractions by embodying them in concrete images.

Gandhi instilled courage and a sense power among the Indians by means of a similar combination of a coherent philosophy and the personal example underlying his *satyāgrahas*. The *satyāgraha* was a vernacular mode of action long familiar to them in one form or another, and its philosophical basis was reasonably clear to them. They knew its grammar and alphabet and Gandhi only had to teach them how to compose coherent sentences. The name itself evoked powerful historical memories and indicated to them that they were fighting for nothing less than *satya*, the central principle of Hindu culture. Above all it bewildered the colonial rulers who, not knowing how to cope with it, either gave in or more often resorted to brute force and discredited their claim to be a 'civilised' nation.

Gandhi not only preached but personally led many of the *satyāgrahas* and made light of his imprisonment. The sight of him and his well-chosen colleagues defiantly disobeying the law, daring the government to do its worst and no longer afraid of going to prison or worse had an electrifying effect on the Indians and generated a euphoriant climate of fearlessness. Nehru's beautiful description of this deserves to be quoted in full.

And then Gandhi came. He was like a powerful current of fresh air that made us stretch ourselves and take deep breaths; like a beam of light that pierced the darkness and removed the scales from our eyes; like a whirlwind that upset many things, but most of all the working of people's minds . . . The essence of his teaching was fearlessness and truth, and action allied to these, always keeping the welfare of the masses in view. The greatest gift for an individual or a nation, so we had been told in our ancient books, was *abhaya* (fearlessness), not merely bodily courage but the absence of fear from the mind. Janaka and Yajnavalkya had said, at the dawn of our history, that it was the function of the leaders of a people to make them fearless. But the dominant impulse of India under British rule was that of fear – pervasive, oppressing, strangling fear; fear of the army, the police, the widespread secret service; fear of the official class; fear of laws meant to suppress and of prison; fear of the landlord's agent; fear of the moneylender; fear of unemployment and starvation, which were always on the threshold. It was against this all-pervading fear that Gandhi's quiet and determined voice was raised: Be not afraid. Was it so simple as all that? Not quite. And yet fear builds its phantoms which are more fearsome than reality itself, and reality, when calmly analysed and its consequences willingly accepted, loses much of its terror.

So, suddenly, as it were, that black pall of fear was lifted from the people's shoulders, not wholly of course, but to an amazing degree. . . . It was a psychological change, almost as if some expert in psycho-analytical methods had probed deep into the patient's past, found out the origins of his complexes, exposed them to his view, and thus rid him of that burden.

There was that psychological reaction also, a feeling of shame at our long submission to an alien rule that had degraded and humiliated us, and a desire to submit no longer whatever the consequences might be.[6]

At the political level Gandhi's greatest contribution consisted both in building up a powerful national organisation of the kind India had never known and helping create a new political culture.[7] For nearly two decades after its birth the Congress was an essentially middle and upper middle class organisation functioning with the blessings of the British government and wedded to the method of constitutional pressure and the goal of creating a liberal democratic polity. Lala Lajpat Rai, Tilak, B. C. Pal and others brought in lower middle classes, introduced the politics of agitation, put dominion status on its agenda and gave it a distinctively Hindu orientation. None of them, however, had the temperament, ability or even the desire to transform the Congress into an effective national organisation capable of reaching out to and mobilising the remotest villages of India. Almost single-handed and within a remarkable short time, Gandhi metamorphosed it into a powerful national organisation, brought in the peasantry and some sections of the working classes, set up local units, established a clear chain of command stretching right down to the villages, introduced a system of public accountability and secured the necessary funds from his capitalist friends. The Nagpur session of 1921, barely six years after his arrival in India, bore a distinctively Gandhian stamp. The European clothes vanished, Hindi was widely spoken, the lower middle class delegates were present in large numbers, new issues were debated, and the Congress, hitherto seen as a debating society, was widely perceived as an instrument of action and a truly national forum commanding the unquestioned loyalty and support of the bulk of the country.

Before long the Congress had built up a remarkable structure of authority paralleling and presenting an effective challenge to the established system, and acquired all the visible and invisible features of a state within a state, of a future Indian state slowly gestated in its womb and ready at the appropriate time to replace the colonial state. Its annual sessions took on the character of a 'national parliament' debating and evolving a consensus on the large issues affecting the country as a whole. Its president was almost like the head of a state and the All India Congress Committee and especially the smaller Working Committee functioned like his Cabinet. It had its own uniform, a system of 'franchise', elections, rules, procedures, the paraphernalia of government, symbols, ginger groups, an intelligence system almost as efficient as the British, and an informal system of honouring and conferring titles paralleling and as widely valued as the official. At its annual session its president, suggestively called *rāshtrapati*, (head or protector of the nation) made a triumphal entry on the back of a decorated elephant, and the Indians were far more interested in him than in the Viceroy. The Indian mind, which had great difficulty accepting the alien institution of the modern state, learned to appropriate and make sense of it through the mediating influence of the familiar and semi-personal 'congress state'. The Congress also built up its own independent basis of authority and legitimacy which was eventually transferred to and facilitated the popular acceptance of the new state of independent India.

Since the radically reorganised and broadly based Congress brought together regions, classes, castes and political groups that had never before met, let alone worked together for a common cause, it had to develop a new way of articulating, debating and resolving their differences. Gandhi's contribution in fashioning the new political culture was considerable. The new culture which held the Congress together both before and after independence was an ingenious and highly complex construct forged out of Indian metaphysics and epistemology, the inescapable constraints imposed by the struggle for independence and Gandhi's own style of leadership. Those aspects of it that had deep roots in Indian philosophy and culture survived him, the others proved short-lived.

As we saw, for Gandhi human existence was characterised by two fundamental features. First, each individual was uniquely constituted and had a right to live by the truth as he saw it. Second, all men were one; what united them was far more important than what divided them and there were no differences that could not be resolved or lived with in the spirit of charity and good-will. Since both unity and difference, harmony and disagreement, were the necessary features of human existence, Gandhi argued that every human association must fully acknowledge and find ways of reconciling them. To insist on unity alone was to do moral violence to those who disagreed, suppress genuine disagreement and pave the way for a more acute conflict later. Differences by themselves rendered co-operation impossible and led to chaos and conflict. For Gandhi and most other leaders the Indian joint family institutionalised the *principle of the unity of unity and difference*, exemplified an unity-in-diversity, and provided a desirable model for all human associations, including the political.

Since men necessarily disagreed and their perceptions of truth were partial, a sympathetic dialogue between them was the only way to reduce their partiality, resolve their differences and arrive at a higher consensual truth. As we saw earlier the dialogue presupposed that each participant opened himself up to the others in the two-fold sense of fully sharing with them his ideas, fears and feelings and in turn sharing theirs. Obviously he could only do so if he did not feel threatened by them. Gandhi translated this doctrine in political terms and concluded that political parties hampered the relaxed flow of ideas and rendered the resolution of differences impossible. Since they competed for popular support each had a vested interest in defining its identity in opposition to others, emphasising its distance from them and insisting on doctrinal purity. Thanks to the very conditions of its survival, the party system led to ideological rigidity and undue exaggeration of differences, and the consequent reluctance and incapacity to enter into an open-minded dialogue. For Gandhi it rested on a false epistemological foundation, and wrongly assumed that opposition not dialogue, confrontation not co-operation, the adversarial combat not a relaxed and collaborative search was the only way to discover truth. Accordingly he insisted that rather than form themselves into independent and competitive political parties, different social groups and points of view should remain part of a single larger and loosely structured organisation. This created the necessary moral and psychological climate for a genuine dialogue and facilitated the discovery of consensual political truth.

Gandhi therefore insisted that the Congress should become, and ensured that it did become, a broad church permitting a wide variety of beliefs and the utmost freedom of conscience within the framework of shared political goals.[8] Its objectives were pared down to the barest minimum, stated in highly general terms and stayed clear of controversial social and economic issues. It members included atheists as well as Hindu fundamentalists, liberals and conservatives as well as socialists and even a few communists, the staunch defenders as well as the fiercest critics of the caste system, landlords as well as peasants, capitalists and their workers, Westernised and traditional intellectuals as well as the illiterate masses. They remained free to say and do what they liked as long as they did not implicate the Congress, and were not bound by its decisions in cases of conscientious objections; only the executive was subject to strict discipline. It encouraged discussions and even debates, provided they were expressions of individual 'truths' and not articulated in ideological terms backed by group alliances. It tolerated, even welcomed, disagreement, provided it did not take the form of open dissent and was punctuated by professions of loyalty to the head of the national family, the major unifying link between its disparate members. Nehru filled the bill beautifully and not only survived but flourished; Subhas Bose did not and had

to go. When a disagreement seemed unresolvable, Gandhi inter-
vened and relied on persuasion, pressure and personal appeal to
secure unity.

The Congress culture had obvious advantages. It fostered not
only tolerance of but also respect for opposing points of view. It
avoided ideological rigidity and posturing and encouraged political
realism. It accommodated different interest groups and presented
a united front to the government. It offered them a much needed
public space where they could meet, interact, get to know one
another and evolve a tentative national consensus. Above all it
facilitated the emergence of a national political language, a great
achievement in a vast country where so many different groups had
never before met and talked to one another. Gandhi skilfully
played the role of a common interpreter sensitising the peasants
and the landlords, the capitalists and the workers, the intellectuals
and the illiterate masses, the Westernised intellectuals and the
traditional elite, the Hindus and the Muslims, the old and the
young, the high-caste Hindus and the untouchables to each other's
interests, expectations, hopes and fears. Thus he openly chided
the landlords for exploiting the peasants and the latter for being
too impatient and ill-disciplined, and urged both to settle their
differences in the spirit of justice and good-will, befitting the
members of a common family. He threw his weight behind different groups at different times and ensured that none felt neglected.
Since his role was crucial, every group knew that if it could find a
soft spot in his heart, it had a good chance of finding one in the
nation's heart as well, and that if it could leave a thought in his
mind, it would eventually find a place on the national agenda.
Gandhi's mind and heart became the most important avenues to
the national public space, and every group sought access to it.

Although the Congress organisation and the culture in which it
was embedded were remarkable achievements and served India
well both before and after independence, they suffered from
important limitations. The Congress reproduced but did not transcend religious, regional, social and other identities. Its membership neither conferred a new and larger identity nor cultivated a
higher and truly national level of consciousness. Lacking a wider
principle in terms of which to formulate and resolve their differences, its constituent groups followed the only available alternative
of seeking fuzzy compromises and a vague and tentative consensus. The Congress therefore remained a loose coalition with poor

discipline and weak internal unity. During the quarter of a century of Gandhi's leadership only a handful of its members were disciplined, let alone dismissed, which is remarkable in a vast organisation with no experience of concerted action and which he repeatedly accused of corruption and indiscipline. Its largely dormant and poorly co-ordinated organisational structure only sprang into action at the time of national or local *satyāgrahas* launched at long and irregular intervals. It is striking and says a good deal about Gandhi's confidence in it that the *satyāgrahas* were generally led not by the ordinary Congress hierarchy but the specially appointed 'dictators' related to the national 'General' by a specifically established chain of command for the occasion.

The Congress culture reinforced and was in turn reinforced by its weak organisation. It smoothed over differences, accommodated but did not argue out and reconcile the conflicting points of view and failed to evolve a comprehensive social and economic programme. In Gandhi's as in the Indian epistemology in general the doctrine of relative truth largely applied to individuals, not groups. Individual differences were therefore accepted as normal, even welcomed, whereas organised group differences were frowned on. Since, further, the dividing line between difference and conflict was necessarily thin, the differences expressed in a strong language or pressed beyond a certain point were viewed with disfavour. This often resulted in an unnatural and false sense of harmony. Many Congress leaders had grave reservations about some of Gandhi's ideas and policies, but rarely dared express them. They needed Gandhi and went along with him hoping that once independence was achieved, they would in Nehru's words 'go their own way'. This encouraged 'untruth' in their behaviour and paved the way for Gandhi's eventual disillusionment.

At the philosophical level Gandhi was right to maintain that different points of view had a better chance of influencing each other when not cast in a hostile or competitive relationship, and that the European party system born within a specific political culture could not be mechanically transplated into India. However, he overlooked the critically important fact that a point of view could be fully developed only if first it was allowed a secure *space* for growth and enjoyed a conceptual and often physical *distance* from others; second, it had a clear conception of what it was *not* and hence the presence of the 'other'; and third, a climate in which it was encouraged to give itself a *clear* form and shape. The

Congress culture did not provide the last two, and provided the first only to a limited degree. The Indian joint family on which the Congress was modelled has great strengths, but it does not provide adequate space for the autonomous growth of its members and discourages a strong sense of identity or ego. The Congress culture had similar disadvantages at the political level and hampered the development of a strong ideological and organisational ego. It put so much emphasis on discovering the common ground between the different points of view that none of them ever came into its own, with the result that they had little to talk about and the dialogue it encouraged was largely formal. Gandhi was rightly dissatisfied with the European party system, but his alternative was no more satisfactory.

As a result of a weak organisation and an excessively tolerant culture, the Congress under Gandhi's leadership was neither a political party of the European kind, nor a people's movement, but a mass movement. The European political party is ideologically self-conscious, knows what it stands for and how it differs from its rivals, and has a well-structured language of debate, a clear programme, organisational unity and a sense of institutional obligation. The Congress had none of these. A people's movement such as Mao's has a carefully worked out social and economic programme, a strategy for capturing power, selective membership, a disciplined and committed cadre and a clearly defined manner of mobilising the masses. Gandhi's Congress was wholly different in almost all these respects. Its programme had a vague and minimal content, and avoided almost all contentious issues. It had a weak discipline and made minimal demands on its members. Unlike a political party and a people's movement, it did not have an independent identity and an autonomous principle of unity and remained heavily dependent on his charisma. It is striking that every time there was a national *satyāgraha* or a fear of confrontation with the government, it had to call Gandhi back from his temporary retirement; and once he and the prominent national leaders were arrested it became thoroughly demoralised and the government had little difficulty dealing with it.

Given Gandhi's views and style of leadership the relations between him and the Congress contained a deep tension. He treated the transformed Congress as his creation and felt possessive about it. It had, however, its own corporate interests and included men and women of strong and independent views, and could not become a pliant instrument of his will. Since Gandhi's political theory made it difficult for him to appreciate the nature and importance of the state, he could not see the point of 'entering' the state and running its institutions. The Congress perspective was very different. Many of its members did not accept his views on the state, nor share his confidence that the Constructive Programme would regenerate India. Unlike him it was therefore well-disposed to the colonial state and constantly pressed for participation in it. The Congress also had an additional reason for doing so. Since from time to time it found itself in strong disagreement with him, it knew that it could not resist and defy him without an independent power base of its own. Obviously it could not appeal to the masses over whom Gandhi's hold was unshakable. It had therefore little alternative but to turn to the colonial state. It needed the latter to give it political legitimacy and power, even as the colonial state needed its support to acquire moral legitimacy and authority. Although the two struck up a relationship of mutual dependency, it contained a paradox. The colonial state had no use for the Congress unless it was able to carry the masses with it, and that it could not do without Gandhi. It could become independent of him only by depending on him! It knew that it could never dispense with Gandhi. For his part he could not do without it either. His programme of national regeneration could not be implemented without its active support, and his personal authority over the masses remained fragile and diffused without its organisational base.

As independence drew nearer, the tension between the two came to a head. Now that power was being transferred to it, the Congress had no political use for Gandhi. And since it decided to rely almost entirely on the state to regenerate society, it had no use for his political programme either. Not surprisingly he was both personally and ideologically marginalised. Although deeply unhappy, he never felt bitter or resentful towards his quondam colleagues and read the runes aright. He knew that in every joint family a time came when it was *de regie* for its head to hand over the reins of power to his chosen heir and gracefully retire to the forests, only offering advice when sought. Having entrusted the custody of his beloved India to Nehru, he moved to distant trouble spots, came to Delhi when invited, offered the political *sannyāsin's* detached guidance only when asked, and spent his time soothing the feelings of his disappointed followers, resolving differences between his senior colleagues, healing the wounds of the Partition and in general holding together and sustaining the dented morale and self-confidence of the national family. He was never a wistful old man missing his youth and unable to resist a temptation to create an occasional mischief and chivvy a colleague, or reluctant to give up or share his power. Like most of his countrymen he knew how to grow old personally, but unlike them he also knew well how to grow old politically, with grace and dignity.

While it is easy to see why the new government should have sought to marginalise Gandhi and consign him to political oblivion, it is deeply puzzling why he ceased to be a distinct *intellectual* and *moral* presence almost immediately after his death. No distinct Gandhian voice was to be heard in the debate on India's economic, cultural and political development, no systematic attempt was made to provide a creative reinterpretation of his ideas, no Gandhian programme of moral and social regeneration suited to the new conditions was worked out, and his thought was allowed to become an esoteric dialect spoken only by a few and understood by even fewer.[9] It is true that the Congress had always stood in an ambiguous relationship to him and never fully accepted his ideas, that Nehru, his chosen political heir, enjoyed a unique moral and political authority unavailable to any of his followers whom he skilfully neutralised, and that once India embarked on the path of state-sponsored, large-scale industrialisation, Gandhi's thought appeared less and less relevant.

None of these and other explanations, however, resolves the puzzle. A sizeable number of Congressmen were genuinely committed to Gandhi's ideas and had been carrying on his great work in the villages and tribal areas. He had also created several organisations devoted to the specific items of his Constructive Programme and providing an influential ideological and political base for a Gandhian movement. Nehru was Gandhi's *political* heir and did not and would not have been allowed to claim his spiritual and ideological mantle. Even after India had embarked on the path of industrial development, there was ample room both for a distinct Gandhian voice and his tripartite strategy discussed earlier, especially as the path was rough and threw up many a social, economic and moral problem, to at least some of which his answers were relevant.

Without at all suggesting that it provides a complete or even an adequate explanation, it would seen that *some* light might be thrown on the puzzle by the internal structure of Gandhi's thought. It was based on a few general principles which each moral and political agent was expected sincerely to endeavour to realise in practice. The principles were indeterminate and abstract but the situations in which they were to be realised were unique and constantly changing. Gandhi therefore needed to provide either the intermediate principles to relate the two or at least some guidance on how to interpret, reconcile and relate the general principles to concrete situations. He did not offer either, and thought of moral and political life in the image of a lonely sailor charting his way through stormy and unfamiliar seas with nothing to guide him save the distant loadstars. This is how he organised his own life. He tried to live up to his principles and explore their full potential in ever new situations. As he ran into unexpected difficulties and dilemmas or acquired new insights, he redefined and revised them. Thus he introduced new distinctions and exceptions in his theory of *ahimsa*, reinterpreted and added new 'weapons' to his method of *satyāgraha*, and explored new ways of restructuring the institution of the state.

While all this was only to be expected and led to fascinating 'discoveries', it naturally left his colleagues and followers bewildered and even breathless. He did, no doubt, explain at length why he had sometimes changed his mind and arrived at apparently strange decisions. He argued that new circumstances required new interpretations of his unchanging Euclidean ideals. He did not, however, indicate how to decide when the circumstances had changed and, since they were always changing, when they could be said to have changed so significantly as to warrant reinterpretations of the ideals. Furthermore, his explanations were *ad hoc* and circumstantial and could not give his followers the interpretive tools needed to *project* his ideals, *anticipate* his future positions and, above all, decide for themselves how to act. Obviously they lacked the confidence and the capacity to act on their own and awaited his lead. On every major question, be it the Partition of India, fighting the 1946 elections, responding to the structure of the state proposed by the new Constitution or their role in independent India, they kept turning to him for guidance and showed a remarkable lack of initiative. It was hardly surprising that most of them felt lost after his death. They simply did not know what his ideals required them to do in a situation where not the foreigners but their own countrymen, some of them erstwhile Gandhians, ruled the country and the question was no longer one of political independence but of moral, cultural, economic and social development.

Surprising at it may seem in a man who led millions, Gandhi shared with the great Hindu sages and seers an intense horror of followers. He deeply cherished his freedom to live by his truth and, since his truth was necessarily subject to constant evolution, continually to rethink his views. This meant two things. First, he was deeply worried that unable to appreciate the nature of his quest and the inescapable fluidity of his thought, his followers might abstract and fossilise his specific ideas or schematise them into a formal and rigid system, and fight over the 'real' Gandhi, and even 'correct' his own 'inconsistencies'. Second, even as he cherished his freedom to live by his truth, he valued theirs and did not in the least wish to violate or abridge it either by foisting his truth on them or morally overpowering them into meekly accepting it. He therefore systematically discouraged followers and remarked, 'Let no one say that he is a follower of Gandhi. It is enough that I should be my own follower'. He kept insisting that he wanted 'fellow-scientists' and 'co-experimenters' inspired by his ideals and stimulated by his example into making their own discoveries, not disciples and followers lazily looking for a crisp message or a neat blueprint. He was intensely aware of what the Catholic church had done to Christ, the Communists to Marx, the Buddhists to the Buddha and the Muslims to Mohammed, and was determined to avoid their fate. He was aware too that by presenting their thoughts in a dogmatic manner and discouraging their revision, the great men were themselves partly responsible for encouraging their subsequent vulgarisation, and was anxious not to repeat their mistake.

In this respect Gandhi's cast of mind and structure of thought were profoundly Hindu. Taking his ideals as his unchanging loadstars he embarked on the voyage of life in the spirit of a great adventurer. His thought therefore could not be detached either from the concrete and constantly changing situations by which he found himself addressed or from his uniquely personal and creative interpretations and applications of his ideals. Not surprisingly his thought took on many of the basic qualities of life itself. It was fluid, open, restless, in constant motion and incapable of being arrested without distortion, so much so that to talk of Gandhi's 'thoughts' or 'ideas' is to misunderstand their true nature. His 'thoughts' were little more than temporary resting points to be left behind with the challenge of a new situation or a new insight. Gandhi the thinker was thus inseparable from his thoughts. They derived their energy and coherence not from within their own autonomous world but from him, a unique thinking subject, and their consistency was to be found not in their internal and unmediated relations but in his personal 'growth from truth to truth' in a constant endeavour to approximate his ideals. Gandhi's thoughts were 'his' not only in the biographical but the deeper epistemological sense of being grounded in and non-detachable from his personality. Their very character therefore militated against their being 'followed', 'put into practice' or turned into dogmas around which political parties could be formed. They demanded to be constantly and imaginatively reinterpreted and even revised in the light of new situations and the agent's own personality. Although a leader of millions he was not a leader of the masses. He required each of them to think and decide for himself how far he, a unique and self-determining agent, approved of Gandhi's actions and wished to join, not follow, him in his struggle. Gandhi's thought thus ruled out Gandhism. He himself put the point well:

> I do not know myself who is a Gandhian. Gandhism is a meaningless word for me. An ism follows the propounder of a system. I am not one, hence I cannot be the cause for an ism. If an ism is built up it will not endure, and if it does it will not be Gandhism. This deserves to be properly understood.[10]

A true Gandhian can never be a Gandhist, a meek exponent of an inherited dogma. He has to be a Gandhi himself, drawing inspiration from his ideals and his manner of interpreting and living up to them but also relating them to his own unique personal and existential situation, courageously making his own experiments, evolving his own programme of action and eventually going beyond him. That Gandhi's thought *leaves room* for another Gandhi is a great tribute to its rare openness and a source of its strength; that it constantly *needs* one to carry it forward and preserve its vitality is a measure of its subjectivity and a source of its subsequent decline. In its innermost core it remains elitist and purist. It depends on great and determined men to actualise it and is morally too finical and fastidious to permit a somewhat vulgarised but politically indispensable programme of action. Like his cosmic spirit Gandhi's spirit is helpless without the co-operation of men and women courageous enough to set sail with the heroic abandon of a lonely mariner. In their absence it helplessly hovers over the Indian sky, inspiring isolated individuals and groups sensitive enough to catch glimpses of it but unable to incarnate itself in a political body organised and committed enough to make it a worldly reality.

Notes

INTRODUCTION

1. See Introduction in Bhikhu Parekh and Thomas Pantham, (eds) *Political Discourse: Explorations in Indian and Western Political Thought* (Sage, 1987); and Bhikhu Parekh, *The Philosophy of Political Philosophy* (University of Hull, 1986).
2. For a detailed discussion, see ch. 7, pp. 191 ff.
3. Although he greatly admired the Zulus and attacked their brutal treatment by the whites, for several years Gandhi had difficulty accepting the blacks as his equals. His political activities in South Africa were largely confined to the Asians and there were no blacks on his communal farm.
4. Raghavan Iyer, *The Moral and Political Writings of Mahatma Gandhi* (Oxford: Clarendon Press, 1987) vol. 1, p. 28. This work is hereafter cited as Iyer.
5. 'Gandhi and His Translators', in *Gandhi Marg*, June 1986.
6. Maureen Swan, *Gandhi: and the South African Experience* (Johannesburg: 1985) is a most welcome addition to the exiguous literature on the subject.

1 CRITIQUE OF MODERN CIVILISATION

1. For good discussions, see Eric Stokes, *The English Utilitarians in India* (Cambridge: 1964); Ashis Nandy, *The Intimate Enemy* (Delhi: Oxford University Press 1983); Bipan Chandra, *Nationalism and Colonialism in Modern India* (Delhi: 1979).
2. For useful information and analysis, see Francis Hutchins, *The Illusion of Permanence; British Imperialism in India* (Princeton University Press, 1967); Northcote Parkinson, *East and West* (New York: Mentor 1965); Kenneth Ballhatchet, *Race, Sex and Class Under the Raj (London: Weidenfeld and Nicholson 1980)*; V. G. Kiernan, *The Lords of Human Kind* (London: 1972), and James Morris, *Farewell to Trumpets: An Imperial Retreat* (London: Faber and Faber 1978).
3. For a good discussion, see Nandy, op. cit., ch. 1.
4. For Gandhi's critique of modern civilisation and the sources of the quotations in the chapter, see *Hind Swaraj* and Iyer, vol. 1, part IV.

5. *Unto This Last* – a Paraphrase, p. IX
6. *Young India* (hereafter YI) 20 December 1928 and 21 November 1931.
7. *Hind Swaraj* (hereafter HS), p. 39.
8. HS, pp. 38 and 40.
9. Gandhi sometimes translated it as 'hypnotised'.
10. HS, pp. 43 and 46.
11. Ibid., p. 52. Translation amended.
12. Iyer, vol. 1, p. 293.
13. Ibid., p. 298.
14. Ibid., p. 328.
15. YI, 17 September 1925.
16. YI, 7 October 1926 and 12 November 1931; HS, pp. 93 f.
17. HS, p. 49.
18. HS, p. 37.
19. Ibid., pp. 58 f.
20. Ibid., pp. 55 f.
21. Ibid., p. 67.
22. YI, 3 September 1925.
23. HS, pp. 31 f.
24. Ibid., p. 33.
25. Ibid., p. 68.
26. Ibid., p. 33
27. *Collected Works* (hereafter CW), vol. 32, p. 219.

2 INDIAN CIVILISATION AND NATIONAL REGENERATION

1. For Gandhi's views on Indian civilisation, see YI (Young India), 22 June 1921; 3 April 1924; 7 October 1926; 5 February 1925; and H (Harijan), 5, 19 May 1946.
2. HS, p. 61; YI, 24 November 1927.
3. YI, 11 August 1927 and 7 November 1929; HS, pp. 64–6; H, 27 February 1937.
4. H, 9 May 1936.
5. YI, 17 November 1920 and H, 2 November 1947.
6. HS, p. 49; YI, 11 August 1927.
7. Gandhi thought that India was unique in having developed 'cultural democracy'.
8. Iyer, vol. 1, p. 474.
9. Ibid., p. 469.
10. HS, p. 49.
11. Iyer, vol. 1, p. 470.
12. YI, 21 March 1929.
13. Iyer, vol. 1, p. 473.
14. Ibid., p. 473.
15. CW, vol. 13, p. 524; vol. 14, pp. 362 and 513; vol. 16, p. 186; H, 28 January 1939.

16. H, 1 August 1936 and 30 March 1940.
17. Iyer, vol. 1, p. 305.
18. It is interesting that Gandhi repeats many of the criticisms made by the British.
19. HS, p. 103. Gandhi thought that India was in a 'fallen state', ibid.
20. CW, vol. 90, p. 215.
21. Ibid., vol. 15, p. 2
22. H, 29 August 1936. For Gandhi the Indians had become 'inert' and 'helpless'. The contrast between 'energy' and 'inertness' runs right through Gandhi's works.
23. YI, 20 December 1928.
24. CW, vol. 14, pp. 444, 469, 475 and 510.
25. YI, 6 August 1919.
26. YI, 2 June 1927.
27. YI, 6 August 1919.
28. YI, 19 March 1925.
29. CW, vol. 5, p. 293.
30. Ibid., pp. 313 f.
31. YI, 21 March 1929.
32. CW, vol. 24, p. 211.
33. CW, vol. 19, p. 225.
34. 'All then that can be said of India is that individuals have made serious attempts, with greater success than elsewhere, to popularise the doctrine. But there is no warrant for the belief that it has taken deep root among the people', ibid., vol. 14, p. 475.
35. Iyer, vol. II, p. 321.
36. Iyer, vol. 1, pp. 307 f.
37. YI, 21 March 1928.
38. CW, vol. 14, pp. 260 f.
39. Ibid., pp. 261.
40. YI, 8 January 1925; 26 January 1921; 7 October 1926 and 11 August 1927.
41. YI, 5 July 1928.
42. YI, 2 June 1927, and 11 August 1927.
43. YI, 7 October 1926.
44. YI, 26 January 1921, 1 September 1921 and 6 December 1928.
45. Quoted in Krishnadas, *Seven Months with Mahatma Gandhi* (abridged edn; Ahmedabad: Navajivan, 1961) p. 191.
46. Iyer, vol. 11, pp. 310 and 340 and vol. 1, pp. 199 f and 408 ff; YI, 2 August 1931 and 3 September 1925.
47. YI, 12 March 1925, and 17 June 1926; H, 23 July 1947. See also *From Yeravada Mandir* (Ahmedabad: Navajivan, 1932), ch. XIV.
48. YI, 30 April 1931. For Gandhi every man is a 'trustee' of his culture, ibid.
49. Iyer, vol. 11, p. 190.
50. YI, 12 June 1924 and 29 January 1925. For Gandhi the opposite of *swarāj* is 'pararāj, that is, foreign rule whether they be Indian or Englishmen', CW, vol. X, p. 205.
51. YI, 22 September 1920 and 1 June 1921.

52. Iyer, vol. II, pp. 440 f and 444 f; CW, vol. 14, p. 520.
53. Iyer, vol. II, pp. 440 f and 444 f; CW, vol. 14, pp. 444 and 515. Gandhi remarks: 'As a Hindu I do not believe in war, but if anything can even partially reconcile me to it, it was the rich experience we gained at the front. It was certainly not the thirst for blood that took thousands of men to the battlefield..; they went to the battlefield because it was their duty. And how many proud, rude, savage spirits has it not broken into gentle creatures of God?' CW, vol. 3, pp. 222 f. For a most sensitive and perceptive discussion, *see* Peter Brock, *The Mahatma and Mother India* (Ahmedabad: Navajivan, 1983), ch. 2.
54. CW, vol. 14, pp. 474, 477, 509 and 510. Erik Erikson in his *Gandhi's Truth* (New York: W. W. Norton 1969), pp. 371 f thinks that this may be the cause of his serious illness in August 1918.
55. H, 8 April 1939; YI, 3 November 1927 and 2 June 1920.
56. *See* Gandhi, *Constructive Programme: Its Meaning and Place* (Ahmedabad: Navajivan, 1945). See also H, 11 January 1936; YI, 18 March 1926 and Iyer, vol. 1, pp. 425 ff.
57. 'He is a true physician who probes the cause of disease and if you pose as a physician for the disease of India, you have to find out its true cause.' HS, p. 39.

3   PHILOSOPHY OF RELIGION

1. *Autobiography*, p. 113. Translation amended.
2. For good discussions, see M. Hiriyanna, *Outlines of Indian Philosophy* (London: Allen & Unwin, 1932); Paul Younger, *Introduction to Indian Religious Thought* (Philadelphia: Westminster Press.1972); Surendranath Dasgupta, *A History of Indian Philosophy* (Cambridge University Press, 1922) vols. I–V; Chandradhar Sharma, *A Critical Survey of Indian Philosophy* (Motilal Banarasidass, Delhi, 1976).
3. For useful references, see Rama Shanker Srivastava, *Contemporary Indian Philosophy* (Ranchi: Sharda, 1984); Ripusudan Prasad Srivastava, *Contemporary Indian Idealism* Delhi: Motilal Banarsidass, 1973); and V. S. Naravane, *Modern Indian Thought* (Bombay: Publishing House, Asia 1964).
4. *Autobiography*, Preface; YI, 11 October 1928; Harijan, 18 August 1946.
5. CW, vol. 48, p. 404; YI, 7 February 1929 and 31 December 1931 H, 15 April 1939.
6. CW, vol. 50, pp. 200 f.
7. H, 23 March, 1940 and 28 July 1946. For Gandhi the idea of a personal God encourages a 'false hope' for miracles, generates fear and can never satisfy the intellect.
8. Iyer, vol. 11, p. 174.
9. CW, vol. 50, p. 201.
10. H, 12 July 1947.
11. Iyer, vol. II, p. 172.
12. YI, 24 November 1927.

13. H, 23 March 1940 and 16 February 1934; YI, 11 October 1928; CW, vol. 77, p. 390.
14. YI, 21 January 1926.
15. YI, 14 October 1926 and 26 September 1929; H, 6 March 1937.
16. CW, vol. 82, p. 368; vol. 49, p. 268; vol. 71, p. 45; Mahadev Desai's Diary, vol. 1 p. 109. For Gandhi India's epistemological pluralism went hand-in-hand with its stress on the plurality of cognitive faculties and plural modes of cognition. The term *buddhi*, often mistranslated as reason, had for Gandhi and the Hindus a much broader meaning and included discernment, discrimination and wisdom.
17. Iyer, vol. II, p. 87.
18. YI, 24 September 1925 and 14 April 1927; H, 26 January 1934.
19. CW, vol. 41, p. 435.
20. YI, 11 October 1928 and 1 October 1931; H, 26 September 1936.
21. H, 8 July 1933.
22. CW, vol. 33, p. 232.
23. H, 25 April 1936.
24. CW, vol. 50 pp. 188 f.
25. YI, 11 August 1920; 12 August 1920 and 25 September 1924.
26. Iyer, vol. 1, pp. 542 f.
27. YI, 22 September 1927 and 16 February 1934.
28. Iyer, vol. II, p. 539.
29. YI, 19 January 1928; and H, 2 February 1934 and 28 July, 1946.
30. Iyer, vol. 1, p. 477.
31. H, 23 March 1940.
32. CW, vol. 25, p. 208.
33. Iyer, vol. 1, p. 27.
34. YI, 21 March 1929.
35. J. J. Doke, *M. K. Gandhi – An Indian Patriot* (Madras: Natesan 1909), p. 12. Margaret Chatterjee, *Gandhi's Religious Thought* (London: Macmillan, 1983) is an excellent guide to Gandhi's religious ideas.

4 SPIRITUALITY, POLITICS AND THE REINTERPRETATION OF HINDUISM

1. For Gandhi's discussion of moral life see *Discourses on the Gita* (Ahmedabad: Navajivan, 1960): *From Yeravada Mandir* (Ahmedabad: Navajivan, 1932); and Mahadev Desai, *The Gita According to Gandhi*, (Ahmedabad: Navajivan, 1935). *Discourses* has suffered much from a bad translation.
2. *From Yeravada Mandir* (Navajivan, 1932), ch.s 1–5.
3. CW, vol. 50, p. 218; Iyer, vol. 11, pp. 552 f.
4. YI, 4 December 1924.
5. CW, vol. 22, p. 108.
6. *Discourses on the Gita*, ch. 1. The original Gujarati, like the *Gita*'s Sanskrit, better captures the distinction between a life of action and an active or activist life than their English equivalents.

7. CW, vol. 50, p. 226.
8. H, 2 June 1946 and 7 April 1946; see also Preface to *Autobiography*.
9. Iyer, vol. 1, pp. 16 f, 140 f and 149; Iyer, vol. II, p. 77; H, 13 June 1936; and preface to *Autobiography*.
10. H, 22 August 1936, 29 August 1936 and 8 May 1937.
11. Iyer, vol. 1, p. 59, and H. 26 December 1936.
12. Iyer, vol. II, p. 286. For Gandhi an action is moral when 'there is not even the selfishness of loving behind it', ibid.
13. Ibid., p. 56. Promotion of another's well-being, when prompted by self-interest, is 'not worthless', but to call it moral 'would detract from the moral idea', ibid.
14. YI, 11 September 1924; 6 August 1925; 3 December 1925; and 4 August 1927. See also H, 29 August 1936; 11 March 1939; and 22 August 1936.
15. CW, vol. 50, p. 217.
16. Iyer, vol. II, p. 75.
17. Iyer, vol. 1, p. 88.
18. YI, 2 March 1922; 18 June 1925; and 1 October 1931.
19. H, 12 September 1936.
20. Iyer, vol. 1, pp. 137 f.
21. Preface to *Autobiography*. Translation amended.
22. Iyer, vol. 11, pp. 53 and 62; H, 29 March 1935.
23. YI, 23 February 1922.
24. Iyer, vol. 1, p. 420. 'It is in the outside world that we are tested', ibid.
25. Iyer, vol. 11, pp. 67 f.
26. H, 8 December 1946.
27. Iyer, vol. 11, pp. 134 f, 256 f and 262; and vol. 1, pp. 13 f.
28. Iyer, vol. 1, pp. 13 f, and H, 8 September 1940.
29. YI, 25 October 1928.
30. CW, vol. 50, p. 237.
31. H, 8 September 1940.
32. CW, vol. 50, p. 194; H, 29 August 1936; Preface to *Autobiography*.
33. YI, 8 April 1926.
34. CW, vol. 50, p. 204.
35. YI, 24 September 1925.
36. YI, 14 July 1920 and H, 9 June 1946.
37. *See* Iyer, vol. 1, p. 69 for a withering attack on 'mere pedants' who 'neither swim across themselves nor help others to do so', and only rely on 'debating or the gift of clever speech'. See also ibid., vol. 1, pp. 79 and 321. At CW vol. 27, p. 308 Gandhi remarks, 'It is good to swim in the waters of tradition, but to sink in them is suicide'.
38. Iyer, vol. 1, p. 321.
39. Gandhi was aware of the way leaders of the earlier generations had tried to reform Hinduism and thought that he was continuing their work a step further. As he put it, the 'Brahmo Samaj liberated Reason and left room enough for faith', and its contribution consisted in 'liberalising and rationalising Hinduism', Iyer, vol. 1, pp. 448 and 449. Gandhi hoped to do to Hinduism what Martin Luther had done to Christianity. It is hardly surprising that almost all his Christian friends were Protestants.

5 THEORY OF THE STATE

1. HS, pp. 31 f; CW, vol. 75, 220 f. Some of the central categories of Hindu political theory made it difficult for the Indian leaders to come to terms with the modern state. See the author's 'Some Reflections on the Hindu Tradition of Political Thought' in Thomas Pantham and Kenneth Deutsch (eds), *Political Thought in Modern India* (Delhi: Sage, 1986); and 'Hindu Political Thought' in David Miller (ed.) *Blackwell Encyclopaedia of Political Thought* (Blackwell, 1987).
2. See Interview with N. K. Bose in *Modern Review*, October 1935.
3. YI, 18 November 1928.
4. H, 26 July 1942 and 14 January 1939.
5. H, 2 March 1947 and 1 September 1940.
6. H, 11 March 1930. See also Sriman Narayan Agarwal, *Gandhian Constitution for Free India* (Allahabad, 1946), and Gandhi's Foreword to it. Agarwal does not always get Gandhi right. Gandhi wrote his *Foreword* on 30 November 1945. In H, 28 July 1946 he expressed views different from those attributed to him by Agarwal.
7. H, 28 July 1946.
8. H, 30 December 1939; 1 September 1940 and 25 January 1942.
9. H, 1 September 1940 and 12 May 1940. For a useful collection of Gandhi's views on democracy, see R. K. Prabhu (ed.) *Democracy: Real and Deceptive*, (Ahmedabad: Navajivan, 1961).
10. CW, vol. 32, pp. 150 f.
11. CW, vol. 90, pp. 218 and 220.
12. Iyer, vol. I, pp. 424 f.
13. Ibid., p. 427.
14. YI, 12 August 1920.
15. CW, vol. 17, p. 93; H, 21 July 1940 and 18 January 1948.
16. YI, 20 July 1926.
17. Iyer, vol. II, p. 355.
18. YI, 22 July 1920.
19. YI, 18 August 1920 and 1 June 1921.
20. YI, 1 December 1920, 1 June 1921 and 5 January 1922. It was 'contrary to manhood' and a 'mere superstition' to think that every law should be uncritically obeyed, HS, pp. 80 and 81.
21. YI, 24 March 1920 and 8 January 1925.
22. CW, vol. 8, p. 459; vol. 9, pp. 60, 76 f and 197 f; *Satyagraha in South Africa*, pp. 250 f.
23. YI, 27 March 1930.
24. H, 5 May 1946.
25. CW, vol. 24, p. 224.
26. H, 3 August 1947; 2 November 1947; and 27 April 1940.
27. Iyer, vol. II, pp. 332 f and CW, vol. 11, p. 125.
28. H, 23 October 1937.
29. YI, 1 May 1924 and 8 May 1920.
30. Iyer, vol. II, p. 265.
31. CW, vol. 3, p. 413; vol. 23, pp. 508 f; vol. 14, p. 1 f; H, 18 February 1939 and 1 February 1940.

32. CW, vol. 23, p. 508; vol. 28, p. 304; H, 3 August 1947 and 6 May 1936.
33. For Gandhi's critique of capitalism see Iyer, vol. III, Part V and the relevant entries in R. K. Prabhu and U. R. Rao, *The Mind of Mahatma Gandhi* (Ahmedabad: Navajivan, 1967).
34. YI, 11 December 1924 and 15 November 1928; H, 13 February 1937 and 13 March 1937.
35. H, 17 February 1946 and 4 August 1946.
36. YI, 13 October 1921; 27 October 1921 and 26 October 1924.
37. H, 1 September 1946.
38. YI, 26 March 1931 and 26 November 1931; H, 3 December 1938 and 3 June 1939.
39. H, 31 March 1946.
40. H, 16 December 1939.
41. YI, 16 April 1931 and 17 September 1931.
42. R. P. Dutt, *India Today* (Bombay, 1949), p. 329; Hiren Mukerjee, *Ghandi: A Study* (Delhi, 1979), p. 73; E. M. S. Namboodiripad, *The Mahatma and the Ism* (Delhi: People's Publishing House, 1985), pp. 28 ff.
43. G. D. Birla, *Bapu: A Unique Association* (Bombay: Bharatiya Vidya Bhavan, 1977), pp. 362, 364, 369 and 370.
44. Ibid., pp. 377 f.
45. Ibid., p. 380.
46. Ibid., pp. 381 f.
47. Louis Fischer, op. cit., p. 480.

6 *SATYĀGRAHA* AND A NON-RATIONALIST THEORY OF RATIONALITY

1. For good discussions see the books by Bondurant, Iyer and Gene Sharp listed in the bibliography.
2. YI, 19 March 1925.
3. CW, vol. 1V, p. 237.
4. Ibid., p. 149.
5. Ibid., pp. 146 ff and 256 ff.
6. *Satyagraha in South Africa* (Ahmedabad: Navajivan, 1928) p. 76.
7. YI, 5 November 1931.
8. For Gandhi's discussion of violence, see Iyer, vol. II, part VI. See also D. G. Tendulkar, *Mahatma* (Bombay, 1951–4) vol. III, pp. 318 f.
9. H, 10 December 1938 and 9 September 1933.
10. Iyer, vol. 1, 527 f.
11. YI, 15 May 1924.
12. YI, 2 February 1921.
13. H, 18 August 1940 and YI, 19 February 1925 and 4 August 1921.
14. Richard Gregg, *The Power of Non-Violence* (London: 1936).
15. Tendulkar, op. cit., vol. 111, pp. 318 f; YI, 19 February 1925, and H, 25 March 1939.
16. H, 9 September 1933 and 10 December 1938.

17. For a useful discussion see Maureen Swan, *Gandhi: The South African Experience* (Ravan Press, Johannesburg, 1985), chs IV, V and VI. He makes countless remarks later in life where he emphasises the need for economic boycott to exert 'pressure' on the government and 'bring it to its knees'. He says, 'when the textile trade is destroyed, the British will get straightened out', Desai, *Diary* vol. 6, p. 356. Translation amended.

18. CW, XXV111, p. 440; Iyer, vol. 1, p. 411. Many Christian pacifists who naively saw Gandhi in the image of Jesus complained that his non-violence was 'militant' and had many an element of the organised violence of the army. His use of such terms as the 'weapon' of *satyagraha*, 'non-violent warfare' and 'forcing' and 'compelling' the government alienated them.

19. CW, vol. 10, p. 397. 'It is my certain conviction that no man loses his freedom except through his own weakness'. Again, 'The moment the slave resolves that he will no longer be a slave, his fetters fall'; he must decide to refuse to 'accept the role of a slave'. In HS, p. 100 he asks the Indians not to 'play the part of the ruled'.

20. *See* the articles by Edward Thompson and Kingsley Martin in S. Radhakrishnan (ed.), *Mahatma Gandhi: Essays and Reflections on His Life and Work* (Bombay: Jaico, 1956), pp. 230 f and 342 f. The two articles offer perceptive analyses of Gandhi's unusual method of conducting negotiations. *See also* Louis Fischer, *The Life of Mahatma Gandhi* (Bombay: Bharatiya Vidya Bhavan 1983), pp. 532 f.

21. YI, 1 May 1924; H, 9 September 1933, 15 April 1933 and 11 March 1939. Gandhi even thought of an 'unbroken chain of fasts', H, 8 July 1933.

22. Amiya Chakravarty, *A Saint at Work: A View of Gandhi's Work and Message* (Philadelphia, 1950) pp. 23 f.

23. M. D. Lewis (ed.), *Gandhi* (London: D. C. Heath, 1966) p. 64.

24. Negley Farson in Eugene Lyons, *We Cover the World* (New York, 1937) pp. 141 f.

25. Quoted in Robert Payne, *The Life and Death of Mahatma Gandhi* (London, 1969) p. 397.

26. Ibid., p. 398.

27. *Autobiography* (London: Bodley Head 1958) p. 546.

28. For a further critical discussion see the author's 'Gandhi's Theory of Non-violence: His Reply to the Terrorists' in Noel O'Sullivan (ed.), *Terrorism, Ideology and Revolution*, (London: Harvester Press, 1986).

7 PARTITION AND THE NON-NATIONALIST DISCOURSE

1. *The Pioneer*, 5 October 1893. See also Syed Sudfiuddin Pirzada (ed.), *Foundations of Pakistan: All India Muslim League Documents: 1906–1947* (National Publishing House, Dacca) 1969, vol. 1, p. xxxvii.

2. For a full statement, see ibid., p. xx.

3. Quoted in Rama Nand Agarwala, *National Movement Constitutional Development* (Delhi: Metropolitan 1956) p. 63. See also Sir Reginald Coupland, *The Indian Problem* vol. 1 (London, 1942), pp. 29 f; and Sir

Maurice Gwyer and A. Appadorai (eds), *Speeches and Documents on the Indian Constitution, 1921–47* vol. 1 (Delhi: Oxford University Press, 1957) p. 260.

4. Quoted in T. Wallbank (ed.), *The Partition of India: Causes and Responsibilities* (New York, 1966) p. 40.
5. Ibid., pp. 31 f.
6. Harijan, 15 June 1940; Gwyer and Appadorai, op. cit., p. 422.
7. There is some confusion about the nature of the informal arrangement.
8. Since the idea of the nation had already been in the air for quite some time, it is difficult to give the exact date when it became part of the mainstream political debate. Jinnah gave considerable importance to it in one of his best speeches on 22 March 1940. It is worth noting that he did not mention it in his Deliverance Day statement of 24 December 1939 where one would have expected it. Instead he still talked of 'truly popular Ministries', 'patriotic' Muslims, Muslim 'minorities' and 'justice to minorities'. To be fair to Jinnah, it should be said that several Hindus shared his view and thought that the Muslims were so different from them that Partition was both unavoidable and desirable. Bhai Parmanand in his *Arya Samaj or Hindu Sangathan* (Delhi, 1923) argued that the only satisfactory way to secure peace was 'to effect complete severance between the two peoples'. Lala Lajpat Rai repeated the view in *Tribune* (Lahore), 14 December 1924). Raja Maheshwar Dayal Seth of Hindu Mahasabha carried on important negotiations with Jinnah in 1942. See *The Indian Annual Register*, vol. 11, 1944, p. 60.
9. Gwyer and Appadorai, p. 60.
10. These and other statements by Jinnah and Gandhi are taken from the correspondence between the two. The correspondence consists of 21 letters and took place in September 1944.
11. Jinnah's speech at the League's annual session in 1940.
12. See Ram Gopal, *Indian Muslims: A Political History* (Delhi: Asia Publishing House, 1964) p. 304.
13. See the statement by Jinnah on 27 June 1946 in Gwyer and Appadorai, pp. 5 and 6.
14. See Gandhi's reply to Jinnah's letter dated 16 September 1944.
15. YI, 30 April 1931.
16. Jinnah's later dated 15 August 1944.
17. Gwyer and Appadorai, p. 565. This was part of Jinnah's statement of 14 July 1945 on the Simla Conference.
18. Ibid., pp. 565 f.
19. This is part of Jinnah's telegraphic reply to Azad on 8 August 1940.
20. See Jinnah's extraordinary remark in his letter to the Congress President dated 2 August 1938: 'Muslims in the Congress do not and cannot represent the Mussulmans of India for the simple reason that . . . as members of the Congress they have disabled themselves from representing or speaking on behalf of the Muslim Community'. Gwyer and Appadorai, p. 432. In *The Discovery of India* (Delhi: Oxford University Press, 1946) and *Towards Freedom* (New York: 1941), Nehru

says that for the Congress to have conceded Jinnah's demand not to appoint a Muslim would have changed 'the fundamental character of the Congress' and 'was inconceivable for us'.

21. For a complete text of Jinnah's speech, see M. A. Karandikar, *Islam: India's Translation to Modernity* (Eastern Publishers, 1961), pp. 281 f.
22. *Harijan*, 6 April 1940.
23. In *Nationalism* (London: Hutchinson, 1962), Kedourie more or less equates it with the central European variety of it. In his *Nationalism in Asia and Africa* (New York: World Publishing, 1970) he analyses Asian and African independence movements almost entirely in European terms, and fails to appreciate that many a leader in these countries often used the terms nation and nationalism in almost wholly non-European senses. Both Peter Worsley, *The Third World* (London, 1964), and K. R. Minogue, *Nationalism* (London, 1967) suffer from similar limitations. None of these writers cites primary sources in the original and they almost ignore indigenous 'nationalist' discourse.

8   CRITICAL APPRECIATION

1. Iyer, vol. 1, p. 129.
2. See A. Coomaraswamy in S. Radhakrishnan (ed.), *Mahatma Gandhi*, op. cit., pp. 43 f.
3. Iyer, vol. 1, pp. 69 and 71.
4. Ibid., p. 69.
5. 'I have looked upon woman. . always with the veneration due to my own mother', H, 23 July 1938. Elsewhere he observed, 'the manner in which *Brahmacharya* came to me irresistibly drew me to woman as the mother of man. She became too sacred for sexual love'; H, 4 November 1939.
6. J. L. Nehru, *The Discovery of India* (Delhi, 1982), pp. 358 f.
7. For thoroughly well-researched accounts, see Judith Brown, *Gandhi's Rise to Power* (Cambridge, 1972) and *Gandhi and Civil Disobedience* (Cambridge, 1977). See also Gopal Krishna, 'The Development of the Indian National Congress as a Mass Organisation' in *Journal of Asian Studies*, vol. 25, May 1966 and R. Kumar (ed.) *Essays on Gandhian Politics* (Oxford, 1971).
8. 'I do not consider Congress as a party organisation, even as the British parliament, though it contains all parties and has one party or other dominating it from time to time, is not a party organisation', YI, 28 April 1920.
9. Vinoba Bhave was the obvious exception. I have argued elsewhere that he generally misunderstood Gandhi and gave his thought a wrong turn. See the author's *Mahatma Gandhi: Two Essays* (Hull Papers in Politics, 1986).
10. Iyer, vol. 1, p. 64. 'I love to hear the word, "Down with Gandhism". An "ism" deserves to be destroyed . . . I have never dreamt of establishing a sect'. Ibid., pp. 61 and 423.

GLOSSARY

āchārya	learned commentator, philosopher
adhikār	deserved right
advaita	non-duality, monism
ānanda	supreme joy, bliss
ahimsā	non-injury, non-violence, renunciation of the wish to kill; abstention from any hostile thought, word, or act; non-coercion
anāsakti	non-attachment
artha	material welfare, wealth
āshram	commune of spiritual aspirants centred on the person of a *guru*
ātman	soul
bhakti	devotion, faith
brahmacharyāshram	first of the four stages of life devoted to learning, and requiring celibacy
darshan	vision, glimpse
dayā	mercy, kindness
dharma	duty, righteousness, moral law
dharmayuddha	righteous war
dukha	sorrow, sadness
harijan	'people of the Lord', formerly untouchables
hartāl	cessation of work as an expression of protest against or disapproval of a government policy
himsā	injury, violence, wish to harm
jnāna	knowledge, wisdom
kāma	desire, pleasure
karma	law of ethical causation and moral retribution; action
karmayoga	spiritual realisation through the life of action

kshatriya	caste of warriors
kurukshetra	scene of the great war described in the Hindu epic *Mahabharata*
lokasangraha	preservation of the community
māyā	appearance or only relatively real; often wrongly translated as illusion or unreal
moksha	liberation, salvation
panchāyat	a small popularly elected body in charge of running the affairs of a village
pararāj	foreign rule
purushārthas	the basic goals of life
rāj	rule
rishi	seer
rta	natural or cosmic law or order
runa	debt; obligation
sākshātkar	vision of the divine
sangh	fellowship, association
sannyāsa	renunciation of the world
sannyāsi	monk or man of renunciation
sāstras	sacred texts
satya	truth; reality
satyāgraha	non-violent resistance
siddhis	spiritual powers
smriti	sacred code of laws; a definitive text
swadeshi	pertaining to one's region or country; traditional way of life
swarāj	self-rule; political and cultural independence
talukā	a small regional unit made up of villages
tapas	penance
varnāshramadharma	duties relevant to the four stages of life and the four castes
yajna	sacred sacrifice or offering in the spirit of surrender to God
yama	rules, spiritual self-discipline
yoga	spiritual discipline; union with the divine
yuga	historical epoch
yugadharma	duties appropriate to an historical epoch
yugapurusha	epochal man; a person representing the distinctive ethos of his age; one putting the stamp of his personality on his age.

Bibliography

PRIMARY SOURCES

The Collected Works of Mahatma Gandhi (Ahmedabad: Ministry of Information and Broadcasting, Government of India, Navajivan, 1958).

Constructive Programme: Its Meaning and Place (Ahmedabad: Navajivan, 1948).

Conversations of Gandhiji Chandrashankar Shukla (ed.), (Bombay: Vora, 1949).

Delhi Diary (Ahmedabad: Navajivan, 1958) vol. 1.

The Diary of Mahadev Desai, trans. V. G. Desai (Ahmedabad: Navajivan, 1953) vol. 1.

Discourses on the Gita (Ahmedabad: Navajivan, 1960).

Ethical Religion (Madras: Ganesan, 1922).

From Yeravada Mandir, trans. V. G. Desai, (Ahmedabad: Navajivan, 1932).

Hind Swaraj (Ahmedabad: Navajivan, 1938).

Key to Health, (Ahmedabad: Navijivan, 1948).

The Mind of Mahatma Gandhi, R. K. Prabhu and U. R. Rao (Ahmedabad: Navajivan, 1967).

The Moral and Political Writings of Mahatma Gandhi, Raghavan Iyer (ed.), 2 vols. (Oxford: Clarendon Press, 1986).

More Conversations of Gandhiji Chandrashankar Shukla (ed.), (Bombay: Vora, 1950).

Satyagraha in South Africa, trans. V. G. Desai (Ahmedabad: Navajivan, 1928).

The Story of My Experiments with Truth, trans. Mahadev Desai (Ahmedabad: Navajivan, 1956).

Unto This Last, A Paraphrase (Ahmedabad: Navajivan, 1956).

SECONDARY SOURCES

Bedekar, D. K., *Towards Understanding Gandhi* (Bombay: Popular Prakashann, 1975).

Biswas, S. C., *Gandhi: Theory and Practice, Social Impact and Contemporary Relevance* (Indian Institute of Advanced Study, 1969).

Bondurant, J. V., *Conquest of Violence* (New Jersey: Princeton University Press, 1965).

Brock, P., *The Mahatma and Mother India* (Ahmedabad: Navajivan, 1983).

Brown, J. M., *Gandhi's Rise to Power* (Cambridge University Press, 1972).

Brown, J. M., *Gandhi and Civil Disobedience* (Cambridge University Press, 1977).

Bose, N. K., *Studies in Gandhism* (Ahmedabad: Navajivan, 1972).

Chandra, B., *Nationalism and Colonialism in Modern India* (Delhi: Orient Longman, 1979).

Chatterjee, M., *Gandhi's Religious Thought* (London: Macmillan, 1983).

Dalton, D., *Indian Idea of Freedom* (Haryana: Academic Press, 1982).

Damle, P. R., *Glimpses of Gandhiji* (Pune: Shubhada Saraswat, 1982).

Das, B. and Mishra, G., *Gandhi in Today's India* (Ashish Publishing House, 1979).

Dasgupta, S., *Philosophical Assumptions for Training in Non-Violence* (Ahmedabad: Gujarat Vidyapith, 1984).

Desai, A. R., *Social Background of Indian Nationalism* (Bombay: Popular Prakashan, 1982).

Desai, M., *The Story of Bardoli* (Ahmedabad: Navajivan, 1957).

Dhawan, G., *The Political Philosophy of Mahatma Gandhi* (Ahmedabad Navajivan, 1962).

Erikson, E. H., *Gandhi's Truth* (New York: W. W. Norton, 1969).

Fischer, L., *The Life of Mahatma Gandhi* (Bombay: Bhartiya Vidya Bhavan, 1983).

Hegde, V. S., *Gandhi's Philosophy of Law* (Delhi: Naurang Rai Concept Publishing Co., 1976).

Hiriyanna, M. A., *Outlines of Indian Philosophy* (London: Allen & Unwin, 1973).

Horsburgh, H. J. N., *Non-Violence and Aggression* (Oxford University Press, 1968).

Hutchins, F. G., *India's Revolution* (Cambridge, Mass.: Harvard University Press, 1973).

Iyer, R., *Moral and Political Writings of Mahatma Gandhi*, vols. I, II and III, (Oxford: Clarendon Press, 1986).

Iyer, R., *The Moral and Political Thought of Mahatma Gandhi* (Oxford University Press, 1973).

Keer, D., *Mahatma Gandhi: Political Saint and Unarmed Prophet* (Bombay: Popular Prakashan, 1973).

Khanna, S., *Gandhi and the Good Life* (Delhi: Gandhi Peace Foundation, 1985).

Krishna, D., *Social Philosophy Past and Future* (Simla: Indian Institute of Advanced Study, 1969).

Krishnadas, *Seven Months with Mahatma Gandhi* (Bombay: Bhartiya Vidya Bhavan, 1983).

Kumar, R. (ed.), *Essays in Gandhian Politics* (Oxford: Clarendon Press, 1971).

Lahiry, A., *Gandhi in Indian Politics* (Calcutta: Firma KLM Pvt. Ltd., 1976).

Lewis, M. D., *Maker of Modern India?* (New York: D. C. Heath, 1965).

Mathur, J. S. and Sharma P. C., *Facets of Gandhian Thought* (Ahmedabad: Navajivan, 1975).

Mathur, J. S. and Sharma P. C., *Non-Violence and Social Change* (Ahmedabad: Navajivan, 1977).

Mehta, V., *Mahatma Gandhi and His Apostles* (London: André Deutsch, 1977).

Nanda, B. R., *Gokhale, Gandhi and the Nehrus* (London: Allen & Unwin, 1974).

Nandy A., *The Intimate Enemy* (Oxford University Press, 1983).

Narasimhaiah, C. D., *Gandhi and the West* (Mysore University Press, 1969).

Nehru, J., *The Discovery of India* (Oxford University Press, 1946).

Niebuhr, R., *Moral Man and Immoral Society* (New York: Charles Scribner's Sons, 1960).

O'Sullivan, N. (ed.), *Terrorism, Ideology and Revolution* (Harvester Press, 1986).

Patel, C. N., *Mahatma Gandhi in His Gujarati Writings* (Delhi: Sahitya Akademi, 1981).

Pyarelal, *Towards New Horizons* (Ahmedabad: Navajivan, 1959).

Pyarelal, *Mahatma Gandhi – The Early Phase*, vol. I (Ahmedabad: Navajivan, 1965).

Radhakrishnan, S., *Mahatma Gandhi – Essays and Reflections on His Life and Work* (Jaico Publishing House, 1956).

Rattan, R., *Gandhi's Concept of Political Obligation* (Delhi: Minerva Associates, 1972).

Roy, D. K., *Among the Great* (Pondicherry: All India Books, 1945).

Roy, R., *Self and Society, A Study in Gandhian Thought* (Delhi: Sage Publications, 1985).

Sharp, C., *Gandhi Wields the Weapon of Moral Power* (Ahmedabad: Navajivan, 1960).

Swan, M., *Gandhi – The South African Experience* (Johannesburg: Ravan Press, 1985).

Tähtinen, U., *Ahimsa: Non-violence in Indian Tradition* (Ahmedabad: Navajivan, 1976).

Tomlinson, P. R., *The Indian National Congress and the Raj, 1929–1942* (London: Macmillan Press, 1976).

Varma, V. P., *The Political Philosophy of Mahatma Gandhi and Sarvodya* (Delhi: Lakshmi Naraian Agarwal, 1959).

Watson, F. and Brown, M., *Talking of Gandhiji* (London: Orient Longman, 1957).

Woodcock, G., *Gandhi* (London: Fontana, 1972).

Yajnik, I. K., *Gandhi As I Know Him* (Delhi: Danish Mahal, 1943).

Younger, P., *Introduction to Indian Religious Thought* (London: Westminster Press, 1972).

Index

Action 3, 85, 86, 87, 196
Advaita 90, 92, 96
Agarwal, S. N. 232
Agarwala, R. N. 234
Ahimsā 60, 80, 104, 108, 120
Aiyar, Mutuswami 145
Akbar 41
Ali, Syed Amir 172, 175
Ambedkar, B. R. 211
Andrews, C. F. 48
Anthropocentric view 3, 85, 86, 87, 196
Appadorai, A. 235
Aristotle 85
Ātman 68, 70, 92, 93, 94
Atonement 160
Authority 121, 122, 123, 124, 220
Autonomy 3, 32, 34, 55, 59, 96, 195
Azad, M. 181

Bacon, F. 4
Bajaj, J. 138
Ballhatchet, K. 226
Banerjee, S. N. 18, 145
Bentham, J. 4, 13
Berkeley, Bishop 13
Bhaktiyoga 208
Bhave, V. 236
Bible 30, 66, 82
Birla, G. D. 140, 141, 233
Blackstone, W. 4
Bondurant, J. 233
Bose, N. K. 187, 232
Bose, S. 216
Boycott 153, 157, 158, 167
Brahma Sutras 68
Brahman 68, 69, 70, 71, 92, 93, 103, 105

Brahmos 81, 231
British Rule 6, 11, 15, 45, 155, 184, 211, 213
Brock, Peter 229
Broomfield, Judge 168
Brown, J. 236
Buber, M. 169, 202
Buddha 76, 78, 98, 209
Buddhism 40, 41, 48, 51, 67, 223

Cabinet Mission Plan 181
Capitalism 15, 16, 30, 35, 118, 134, 135, 136, 138, 139, 140, 203, 206, 216, 233
Carlyle, T. 4, 21, 33
Carnegie, A. 145
Carvaka 78
Caste 39, 42, 43, 46, 47, 48, 51, 57, 66, 105, 112, 118, 171, 180, 205, 206, 210, 216, 217
Chakravarty, A. 162, 234
Chandra, B. 226
Character 4, 6, 49, 51, 61, 76, 80, 82, 93, 101, 117, 124, 126, 127, 130, 134, 150, 205, 208
Chatterjee, M. 230
Christ, Jesus 41, 65, 66, 76, 151, 160, 161, 223
Christianity 7, 11, 14, 15, 20, 24, 34, 39, 40, 42, 43, 65, 67, 72, 79, 83, 84, 92, 160, 167
Citizen 28, 29, 30, 112, 113, 115, 117, 120, 123, 124, 125, 126, 127, 128, 130, 136, 171, 173, 201, 204, 205
Civil Disobedience 153, 159, 169
Civilisation 6, 7, 11, 12, 13, 14, 15, 16, 17, 18, 19, 20, 21, 23, 24, 25,

26, 27, 31, 32, 33, 35, 38, 39, 40,
41, 42, 43, 44, 48, 52, 53, 54, 62,
112, 113, 118, 130, 136, 137,
145, 146, 176, 177, 178, 179,
184, 188, 190, 191, 193, 194,
208, 209, 210, 211
Coercion 156, 157, 160, 161, 204
Colonialism 5, 11, 14, 15, 16, 17, 18,
19, 36, 90, 91, 117, 129, 173, 192
Communism 134, 136, 138, 139, 167
Community 29, 56, 57, 58, 89, 98,
184, 197, 199, 201, 205
Compassion 48, 66
Conflict 165, 185, 202, 215, 218
Congress, Indian National 117, 121,
155, 172, 173, 174, 177, 180,
181, 182, 211, 213, 214, 215,
216, 217, 218, 220, 221, 235, 236
Congress Culture 217, 218, 219
Conscience 47, 104, 108, 111, 123,
126, 127, 158, 160, 161, 186,
201, 209, 216
Consensual truth 215, 216
Consent 123, 197
Constructive Programme 56, 62, 63,
101, 116, 121, 220, 221
Conversion 41, 43, 83, 178
Coomarswamy, A. 236
Co-operation 5, 45, 91, 123, 124,
125, 154, 155, 158, 161, 167,
201, 202, 215, 216
Cosmic Spirit 70, 71, 72, 75, 76, 78,
79, 80, 86, 87, 91, 92, 95, 96,
102, 224
Cosmocentric Anthropology 85, 86,
196
Coupland, R. 234
Courage 5, 38, 46, 47, 49, 53, 60, 61,
77, 101, 113, 116, 203, 212, 213
Crime 130, 131, 132, 133
Critical Theory 164
Cultural Democracy 227
Culture 1, 15, 22, 28, 38, 39, 40, 44,
45, 46, 48, 57, 59, 62, 101, 113,
115, 170, 173, 176, 186, 189,
191, 195, 205, 207, 212, 215,
217, 218

Dantwala 139, 140

Dasgupta, S. 229
Degeneration 12, 36, 45, 46, 51, 52,
55, 58, 99, 188
Democracy 29, 30, 115, 116, 123,
124, 179
Desai, M. 8, 230
Desire 21, 96, 97
Detachment 96, 97, 98, 195
Deutsch, K. 232
Dharma 44, 45, 105, 106, 108, 160,
210
Dialogue 2, 39, 43, 54, 80, 82, 84,
150, 157, 166, 167, 196, 207
Dignity 5, 19, 22, 33, 46, 67, 72, 87,
99, 107, 125, 128, 129, 136, 157,
172, 200, 203, 221
Discourse 2, 145, 207, 211
Disobedience 28, 126, 127, 167
Dissent 112, 216
Diversity 39, 40, 80, 112, 177
Doke, J. J. 230
Domination 11, 26
Duty 125, 126, 129, 158, 160, 181,
182, 197, 229
Dyer, General 5, 49

East India Company 16, 47
Ecology 57, 58
Energy 5, 134, 136, 156, 166, 228,
241
Equality 14, 33, 34, 41, 62, 80, 175,
188, 199
Epistemology 203, 215, 216, 218,
224, 230
Erikson, Erik 229
Evil 32, 71, 75, 79, 129, 130, 146,
147, 150, 156, 161, 201, 202
Experiment 76, 77, 81, 95, 98, 132,
223, 224
Exploitation 5, 18, 19, 25, 28, 29, 33,
34, 45, 59, 85, 90, 127, 128, 130,
135, 137, 149, 155, 196

Faith 39, 44, 75, 76, 105, 165, 167,
178
Farson, N. 234
Fascism 29
Fast 159, 160, 161, 162, 163
Fischer, L. 234

Force 41, 112, 129, 133, 148, 151, 153
Freedom 93, 94, 106, 113, 196, 203, 223

Gandhi, Manu 8
Gandhi Seva Sangh 121
Gandhism 224, 236
Ghosh, Aurobindo 189, 190, 192, 194, 210
Gita 48, 53, 65, 68, 82, 88, 105, 208, 230
Global Political Theory 4
God 7, 15, 22, 39, 65, 67, 68, 69, 70, 72, 73, 77, 78, 79, 80, 82, 85, 92, 96, 100, 102, 107, 109, 229
Gokhale, B. G. 18, 100, 103, 186, 206
Gopal, Ram 235
Gregg, R. 151, 233
Gwyer, M. 235

Harm 49, 38
Hegel, G. 69
Hinduism 39, 41, 65, 67, 77, 78, 79, 80, 83, 109, 176, 179, 184, 188, 189, 190, 198, 206, 231
Hindus 5, 7, 39, 41, 42, 43, 45, 51, 52, 53, 55, 56, 66, 72, 73, 82, 83, 92, 93, 94, 95, 96, 100, 103, 104, 106, 108, 145, 155, 162, 163, 172, 174, 176, 177, 178, 186, 189, 190, 203, 206, 211
Hiriyanna, M. 229
History 17, 42, 43, 51, 55, 167, 176, 184, 188, 189, 190, 193
Hitler 169, 202
Human Nature, 3, 139
Humanity 33, 89, 90, 96, 99, 102, 104, 149, 150, 197, 198, 205
Human Unity 4, 34
Hume, D. 13
Hypocrisy 47, 49, 50, 51, 146

Identity 22, 95, 103, 113, 188, 190, 216, 217
Ideology 12, 14, 15, 16, 20, 21, 110, 131, 136, 140, 155, 166, 169
Illusion 6, 95, 112, 155, 156, 209
Impersonal Conception of God 68, 69, 70, 79, 80

Imperialism 18, 25, 35, 87, 196
Independence 1, 3, 18, 55, 59, 63, 101, 110, 113, 116, 118, 120, 121, 141, 174
Individual 3, 34, 37, 80, 92, 93, 94, 95, 96, 105, 106
Individuality 92, 93, 94, 95, 106
Injustice 99, 103, 104, 121, 106, 146, 149, 156, 158, 160, 165, 170
Integrity 7, 40, 43, 57, 58, 59, 80, 87, 94, 109, 110, 134, 145, 148, 161, 191, 199
Iqbal, M. 175
Islam 4, 40, 41, 43, 48, 65, 79, 80, 176
Iyer, R. 226, 233, 236

Jains 48, 66, 78
Jallianwalla Bagh 153
Jews 4, 7, 37, 84, 169
Jinnah 7, 167, 175, 176, 177, 178, 179, 180, 181, 183, 187, 235
Jnānayoga 208
Jones, S. 81
Judaism 79
Justice 14, 118, 119, 120, 128, 149, 217

Kabir 76
Karma 93, 94, 160
Karandikar, M. A. 236
Karmayoga 106, 208
Kasturbhai Lalbhai 191
Kedourie, E. 236
Khan, Syed Ahmad 171, 172, 175, 177
Kher, B. G. 174
Kiernan, V. G. 226
Koran 65, 66, 82, 188
Krishna 16, 48
Krishna, G. 236
Krishnadas 228
Kruger, P. 5
Kumar, R. 236

Law 27, 72, 28, 110, 111, 118, 119, 123, 125, 126, 138, 140, 150, 196, 200, 232
League, Muslim 175, 180, 181, 182
Lewis, M. D. 234

Liberal Democracy 29, 115, 116, 124, 173, 213, 214
Liberation 198, 209
Liberty 14, 33, 34, 113, 128, 130
Life of action 91, 92, 103, 105
Locke, John 13
Lok Sava Sangh 123
Lokayata Schools 78
Lord Olivier 172
Lord Willingdon 46
Love 42, 58, 80, 96, 97, 98, 99, 102, 103, 108, 119, 131, 132, 144, 147, 150, 151, 152, 153, 160, 167
Loyalty 57, 126, 129, 145, 208, 214
Luther, Martin 230
Lyons, E. 234

Mādhavācharya 68, 69
Mahābhārata 17, 48
Mahavira, Jain 78, 209
Maine, Henry 4, 145
Majmudar, R. C. 168
Malaviya, M. M. 53
Man 16, 17, 24, 25, 26, 39, 86, 88, 90
Manhood 126, 232
Manicheism 201
Manliness 60, 61
Manu 48
Martin, K. 234
Marx 3, 4, 5, 33, 34, 140, 198, 223
Materialism 6, 16, 17, 19, 21, 35, 37
Max Muller 145
Māyā 44, 55, 95, 155, 156, 201
Medical science 9, 26, 27, 28, 31, 63, 131
Mehta, Pherozeshah 145
Mill, J. S. 4, 13, 171
Miller, D. 232
Miller, W. 168
Minogue, K. R. 236
Miracles 72
Missionaries 42, 80, 83
Mohammed 76, 223
Moksha 8, 38, 66, 93, 95, 96, 99, 100, 102, 103, 104, 106, 109, 209
Monotheism 67, 68
Moral Inertia 167, 201
Moral theory 105, 204
Morality 3, 11, 15, 17, 18, 21, 24, 28, 29, 30, 32, 34, 38, 44, 65, 100, 101, 104, 109, 112, 142, 146, 147, 156, 158, 161, 165, 166, 197
Moses 76
Morris, J. 226
Mountbatten, Lord 194
Mukerjee, H. 233
Muslim 7, 39, 107, 129, 159, 162, 172, 173, 174, 175, 176, 177, 178, 181, 185, 186, 188, 189, 203, 236
Mysticism 9

Namboodiripad, E. M. S. 233
Nanak 76
Naoroji, D. 18
Naravane, V. S. 18
Natal 47, 152, 60, 127, 154
Nation 62, 176, 177, 178, 180, 186, 194, 196
Nationalisation 137, 138
Nationalism 3, 56, 57, 177, 182, 191, 192, 193, 194
National Character 45, 46, 52, 53, 60
National Physician 9, 63
Nationality 57, 113, 171, 172, 173, 175
National Regeneration 62, 63, 101, 119, 156, 205, 211
National Self-examination 36, 45
Natural Laws 72, 75, 85
Nehru, J. L. 8, 44, 120, 170, 187, 188, 206, 210, 212, 220, 221, 235
Nietzsche, F. W. 33
Nimbarka 68
Nirguna Brahman 69, 70, 71
Non-co-operation 51, 55, 129, 155, 159
Non-statal polity 113, 114, 115, 116, 118, 120, 122
Non-violence 3, 37, 48, 49, 51, 61, 110, 112, 113, 126, 130, 140, 168, 170, 220, 222

Objectivity 144, 145, 146
O'Dwyer, Michael 49
Oppression 5, 6, 7, 13, 18, 25, 33, 41, 87, 90, 138, 149, 154, 155
O'Sullivan, N. K. 234

Pakistan 183, 184, 187

Pal, B. C. 103, 192, 214
Pantham, T. 226, 232
Pararāj 228
Parkinson, N. 226
Parmanand, Bhai 235
Participation 28, 101
Partition of India 7, 43, 56, 161, 167, 183, 221, 189, 182
Patanjali 106
Patel, Vallabhbhai 120, 184
Patel, Vithhalbhai 120, 151, 184
Patriotism 29, 30, 57
Paul Christodas 145
Payne, R. 234
Penance 75, 160, 195
People's Movement 290
Persuasion 143, 164, 217
Philosophical Anthropology 3, 86, 197
Philosophical Hinduism 104, 105, 106, 107
Philosophy 17, 65, 68, 85, 204, 209, 211, 212
Pincott, F. 145
Plato 85
Pluralism 40, 41, 43, 94, 177, 184, 230
Pluralist Epistemology 39, 43
Polak, Mrs. 81
Political action 6, 61, 103, 156
Political Community 198, 199, 200
Political Culture 173, 213, 215, 218
Political Parties 29, 30, 216, 219
Political Philosophy 2, 4, 5, 6, 7, 197, 198, 200, 226
Political Praxis 156, 164, 166
Political Theory 3, 5, 146, 164, 185, 195, 220
Politics 100, 101, 104, 106, 156, 157, 158, 173, 183, 185, 194, 209
Popular Hinduism 104, 206
Power 1, 2, 60, 63, 73, 110, 115, 117, 123, 126, 130, 153, 154, 155, 156, 212, 220
Prabhu, R. K. 233
Pragmatism 80
Prasad, Rajendra 120
Prejudice 145, 165, 167, 204
Private Property 25, 62, 134, 139, 196

Protest 61, 79, 130
Public Opinion 29, 117, 120, 152
Punishment 123, 130, 131, 133, 150, 169
Pyarelal 8

Race 4, 33, 87, 193, 200
Racism 4, 5, 7, 144, 202, 203
Radhakrishnan, S. 236
Rai, Lala Lajpat 214, 235
Raichandbhai 66, 76
Raman Maharshi 210
Rāmānuja 68, 69
Rāmāyana 48
Ramkrishna Paramhansa 29, 76, 77
Rammohan Roy 15, 36, 45, 81
Ranade, M. G. 103
Rao, U. R. 233
Rational Discussion 9, 41, 143, 144, 148, 156, 159, 164, 165
Rationalism 34, 164, 166
Rationality 34, 72, 86, 87, 144, 146, 164, 165, 166
Reason 31, 71, 73, 74, 76, 108, 144, 146, 150, 156, 164, 166, 230, 231
Reform 42, 101, 104, 105, 108, 124, 132, 133, 136, 139, 161, 210
Regeneration 6, 17, 52, 54, 55, 56, 100, 121, 140, 220
Relative truth 8, 93, 147, 203, 204, 218
Religion 6, 12, 13, 31, 37, 39, 40, 42, 45, 48, 51, 52, 57, 66, 69, 75, 76, 77, 78, 79, 80, 81, 82, 95, 100, 101, 102, 104, 108, 128, 145, 156, 171, 173, 177, 178, 179, 180, 182, 183, 186, 193, 196, 204, 206, 208, 209
Representation 177, 172, 173, 177, 180
Responsibility 110, 111, 124, 125, 131, 133, 149, 160, 163, 194, 201
Revelation 39
Revolution 56, 136, 166
Rights 3, 14, 128, 129, 130, 158, 171, 177, 181, 182, 191, 196, 197
Rousseau, Jean Jacques 21, 33
Ruskin, J. 4, 20, 21, 33, 34
Rta 68, 72

Saguna Brahman 69, 70
Salvation 65, 82, 102, 104, 155
Saṁkara 48, 68, 69
Sannyāsa 106
Saraswati, D. 54
Satyāgraha 7, 56, 60, 61, 63, 94, 95, 106, 107, 117, 120, 121, 138, 140, 149, 150, 151, 152, 153, 157, 161, 166, 167, 168, 169, 183, 203, 210, 212, 218, 222
Savarkar, V. D. 54, 189, 194
Science 30, 35, 39, 54, 76, 79, 205, 209, 223
Science of the Spirit 37
Secular 109, 182, 183, 194
Self 70, 92, 93, 95, 96, 103
Selfishness 47, 49, 50, 59, 103, 104, 106, 135, 144, 231
Self-determination 34, 86, 179, 180, 191, 198, 199
Self-Interest 24, 59, 87, 88, 97, 144, 145, 146, 149, 158, 167, 199, 231
Self-realisation 93, 103
Self-respect 7, 22, 33, 60, 90, 101, 116, 125, 128, 129, 131, 133, 136, 150, 170, 181, 199, 211, 212
Self-sacrifice 50, 60, 167
Service 88, 98, 99, 101, 102, 103, 105, 106, 109, 138, 160, 208
Sexuality 8, 103, 210
Sharma, C 229
Sharp, G. 233
Shrivastava, R. P. 229
Shrivatava, R. S. 229
Sikhs 173, 179, 180
Sin 65, 129, 132, 141, 145
Slade, M. 81
Slavery 23, 126
Socialism 139, 140, 174, 216
Socrates 20
Soul 24, 30, 38, 44, 45, 52, 53, 54, 57, 66, 68, 92, 102, 103, 112, 118, 119, 129, 132, 148, 206
South Africa 4, 5, 7, 15, 44, 46, 61, 65, 90, 91, 110, 126, 128, 130, 144, 146, 154, 155, 165, 169, 186, 211, 226
Spencer, H. 13
Spinoza, B. 69
Spirituality 8, 19, 35, 37, 39, 44, 48, 76, 79, 80, 81, 83, 87, 89, 92, 93, 100, 101, 103, 104, 105, 107, 109, 112, 119, 130, 136, 152, 158, 160, 170, 189, 194, 200, 207, 210
Spiritual Energy 148, 151
Spiritual Law 72
Spiritual Scientist 39, 76
Spiritualisation of Politics 6, 102, 103, 104, 194, 200
State 3, 6, 14, 27, 28, 29, 57, 94, 100, 101, 110, 112, 115, 116, 117, 118, 119, 121, 124, 125, 129, 130, 133, 136, 138, 139, 140, 167, 171, 173, 175, 182, 184, 193, 194, 196, 200, 201, 204, 213, 220
Stokes, E. 226
Strike 152, 153, 157, 158, 159
Style of Negotiation 158, 159
Sub-nation 170
Suffering 80, 90, 99, 104, 105, 149, 150, 151, 152, 153, 156, 157, 158, 160, 162, 163, 164, 167, 168, 169, 170, 185, 209
Surgery of the Soul 9, 149
Swadeshi 56, 58, 59, 61, 63, 98, 116, 194
Swāminārayan 51
Swan, M. 226, 234
Swarāj 59, 115, 116, 228
Symbolic Discourse 63, 207, 211, 212
Synthesis 19, 37, 39, 40f, 54f, 189, 193

Tagore, R. 206
Tāntras 9
Tapas 99, 100
Tapasyā 52, 106
Tata, J. 141
Tendulkar, D. G. 233
Terrorists 19, 128, 129, 130, 211
Theology 81, 82
Theory of Man 3, 21, 32, 33, 38, 85f, 196, 198, 202, 209, 210
Thompson, E. 234
Thoreau, H. 4, 20, 21
Tilak, B. G. 19, 53, 103, 189, 190, 194, 200, 214

Tolerance 39, 40, 41, 131, 153, 177, 189, 193, 217
Tolstoy, L. 4, 20, 21, 33, 34, 65
Tradition 1, 2, 3, 4, 12, 31, 40, 41, 43, 57, 58, 59, 67, 70, 74, 75, 76, 79, 85, 92, 93, 95, 96, 103, 104, 106, 108, 134, 176, 190, 191, 195, 196, 231
Transvaal 5, 60, 152
Trevelyan, C. 145
Trusteeship 62, 138, 139, 140
Truth 39, 42, 52, 55, 59, 65, 67, 70, 71, 72, 75, 78, 83, 90, 93, 94, 96, 108, 142, 143, 147, 148, 150, 156
Two-Nation Theory 174, 184
Tyabji, B. 172

Unity of Creation 90
Unity of Life 90
Unity of Man 48, 90, 104, 107, 135, 167, 197
Upanishads 68
Untouchability 46, 62, 66, 97, 99, 100, 107, 108, 118, 144, 159, 161, 202, 203, 206, 209, 210

Vaishnavism 51, 65, 69
Vallabhācharya 51, 68, 69

Vedantic Philosophy 68, 69, 104, 106
Vedas 66, 68, 81, 108
Vicarious Atonement 195
Violence 3, 6, 19, 25, 26, 28, 29, 33, 40, 46, 61, 90, 94, 97, 112, 117, 118, 120, 127, 129, 132, 133, 136, 140, 146, 147, 148, 150, 151, 153, 160, 161, 165, 166, 168, 170
Vivekananda, Swami 19, 77, 95, 109, 208

Wallbank, T. 235
War 25, 61, 229
Western Philosophy 83, 85, 87
Western Political Philosophy 1, 2, 3, 196, 197, 199
Worship 39, 40, 80, 107
Worsley, P. 236

Yajna 52, 88, 89, 99, 107, 108, 119, 134, 136, 162, 197
Yajnavalkya 213
Yoga 38, 106
Yuga 109
Younger, P. 229

Zoroaster 76